Art and Spiritual Experience

Art and Spiritual Experience

Exploring the Romantic Period

David M. Greenwood

GRACEWING

First published in England in 2018
by
Gracewing
2 Southern Avenue
Leominster
Herefordshire HR6 0QF
United Kingdom
www.gracewing.co.uk

The right of David M. Greenwood
to be identified as the author of this work
has been asserted in accordance with
the Copyright, Designs and Patents Act 1988.

ISBN 978 085244 925 7

Typeset by Word and Page, Chester, UK

Cover design by Bernardita Peña Hurtado

CONTENTS

FOREWORD

The Alister Hardy Trust was established to build on the pioneering initiative of Sir Alister Hardy and to promote and to develop his legacy into the scientific investigation of religious and spiritual experience. When Sir Alister retired from his post as Linacre Professor of Zoology at the University of Oxford he established a research initiative and a research unit designed to collect accounts of religious experience. These accounts initiated an archive that now contains over 6,000 narrative responses to what has become known as the 'Hardy question': 'Have you ever been aware of or informed by a presence or power, whether you call it God or not, which is different from your everyday self?' Sir Alister's intention was that this repository of specimens of religious and spiritual experiences should furnish a laboratory to resource serious academic research and investigation.

David M. Greenwood has made an enormous contribution over many years to the Alister Hardy Trust and to the Alister Hardy Religious Experience Research Centre at the Lampeter Campus of the University of Wales Trinity Saint David. Formerly serving as administrator for the Research Centre, David was appointed as trustee in 2010 and has since then served as treasurer and vice-chair for the Trust. Like Sir Alister, David began his academic studies as a scientist, gaining both his B.Sc. and M.Sc. Later in life he turned his attention to theology, gaining his B.Th. It is this background of scientific method and theological understanding that David brought to his multidisciplinary doctoral research in the field of religious experience, together with aesthetics and art history.

The richness of the Alister Hardy Archive is that it stimulates reflection and scientific investigation into many aspects of religious and spiritual experience, including the nature of religious and spiritual experiences, the typologies of religious and spiritual experiences, the fruits of religious and spiritual experiences, and the diverse triggers of religious and spiritual experiences. In his work, David has been especially attracted to an investigation of the triggers for such experiences. Within the Archive there are accounts of how works of art have opened the eyes, the minds and the hearts of individuals to become aware of or be influenced by a presence or power, whether they call it God or not, which is different from their everyday self. Here, indeed, are artistic windows into God or into transcendence.

David's fellow trustees within the Alister Hardy Trust have every reason, therefore, to be grateful to David for the way in which he has so carefully and systematically responded to the specific challenge raised by accounts in the Archive to explore in greater depth the connection between 'art and spiritual experience'. In rising to this challenge, David has wisely decided to focus on a specific period (the Romantic period), and a specific aspect of that period (landscape art) and on two specific painters (Samuel Palmer and Casper David Friedrich). Such analysis provides not only new insights into the specified field, but also establishes foundations on which others can build.

Leslie J. Francis
Chair of the Alister Hardy Trust
Professor of Religions and Education,
University of Warwick

ACKNOWLEDGEMENTS

In writing this book I am particularly indebted to my original Ph.D. supervisors at Aberystwyth University, John Harvey and Colin Cruise, whose help and encouragement have been invaluable. In addition, I must mention the help and support received from the trustees and directors of the Alister Hardy Trust, a charitable organisation which exists to support research into religious experience and which has supported the writing of this book. I am also indebted to the Trust for permission to reproduce a number of accounts of religious experience which are held in the archive at Lampeter.

As with all academic research, I have been reliant on the work of my predecessors. In this connection, acknowledgements are owing to many writers, particularly Michael Podro, Robert Rosenblum and William Vaughan, as well as Dr Cordula Grewe, whose specialist writing on the Nazarenes (a grouping of German painters) has been particularly helpful. In addition, I would mention especially Werner Hofmann and Joseph Koener, whose extensive works on Friedrich have been influential, as well as Rachel Campbell-Johnson and William Vaughan, who have written very helpfully on Samuel Palmer. Finally, I must single out for special mention those who have written specifically on theology and art: Rowan Williams, John Drury and George Pattison, whose works have proved an inspiration in enabling me to complete this work. There are, of course, many other writers whose works have been helpful and influential and these have, I hope, been accorded full acknowledgement in the notes and bibliography.

Lastly, I must thank my wife Juliet, who has not only encouraged me throughout but exhibited great patience when I have had to retire to my study to continue yet more work on this book.

INTRODUCTION

This study explores the way in which the visible world (especially landscape) has been used by artists at a particular time to suggest an invisible, transcendent eternal world.[1] This investigation is a multidisciplinary study crossing the boundaries between visual culture, philosophy (especially aesthetics) and theology. This book identifies that elusive quality or technique that enables us to understand why a particular work of art can be said to point us towards the transcendent.

Why 1780–1880?

The analysis examines the way in which the visible world and especially landscape has been used by British and German artists during the period roughly between 1780 and 1880 to intimate the spiritual, transcendent world. This period, of course, embraces approximately the age of Romanticism.

There are three main reasons for limiting the study to this period. First, it covers the revival of the discipline of aesthetics and the development of Idealism in Germany. Secondly, this was the period in England when Dissenters (those who dissented from the beliefs of the Established Church) still had to travel abroad for a university education, often to Germany. Thirdly, it was during this time that landscape art, as distinct from portraiture, biblical illustration and historical painting, came to be recognised as of

---

[1] Words such as 'transcendent', 'eternal' and 'mystical' will be discussed later, but for the purposes of this introduction, transcendent means that which is beyond normal human cognition, eternal suggests a timelessness where past, present and future are merged and compressed, and mystical refers to an occasion when one experiences a sense of the transcendent and eternal.

equal status with other genres within the discipline of fine art. Furthermore, as will be demonstrated, the relationship between art and philosophy in Britain and in Germany at this time was so close as to be almost symbiotic and I have, therefore, confined this book almost exclusively to those two countries. I have drawn on the works of two art historians working in this area: I have been influenced by the late Robert Rosenblum (1927–2006), whose book *Modern Painting and the Northern Romantic Tradition* (1975) argued the importance of the German contribution, which in the past had been overshadowed by that of France; William Vaughan, who has written widely on Romantic art and the works of Caspar David Friedrich (1774–1840), has been another scholar of particular influence. Both of these writers have taken the perspective of the art historian, whereas this book is distinct in having been written from the perspective of a theologian whose background is in science, theology and art history.

Chapter content

The book is in three parts; while the logic is maintained by reading from Chapter 1 through to Chapter 12, each part could be read independently.

Part I

This part, consisting of the first three chapters, sets out the aesthetical and philosophical background to the study, examining the contributions made by Alexander Baumgarten (1714–62), William Blake (1757–1827), Immanuel Kant (1724–1804), Friedrich Schiller (1759–1805), Friedrich Schelling (1775–1854) and Philipp Runge (1777–1810). A number of theories of art are examined within this section, with that of Michael Podro (1931–2008) being selected as providing a most useful set of criteria when considering art which may point towards the Transcendent. These criteria may be expressed and interpreted as follows:[2]

---

[2] M. Podro, *The Manifold in Perception: Theories of Art from Kant to Hildebrand* (Oxford: Clarendon Press, 1972), pp. 1–6.

1. Art reveals through the skill of the artist some aspect of a subject that would not be immediately apparent.

2. The artist's depiction of an object makes a reference to the perceptual process of the viewer, which enables an understanding to be achieved through, for example, the use of analogy.

3. The artist engages with the state of mind of the viewer to achieve an elevated or heightened emotional response to the work of art which may suggest a transcendence that lies behind the objects depicted.

Chapter 1 describes the reawakening of the study of aesthetics, which was begun by Baumgarten and continued by Kant, who established precise criteria necessary to define the beautiful and the sublime. Kant set out in great detail a formal treatise on aesthetic judgement and established the subject as one worthy of consideration as a separate discipline. The major discrepancy in Kant's argument is that he proposed on the one hand that the appreciation of beauty and the sublime was ontologically subjective, whilst declaring on the other hand that beauty and the sublime have a quality of universality that ought to be recognised by everyone. This discrepancy, described in Chapter 2, was recognised by Schiller, who developed the concept of a 'play-drive' operating within the mind as a description of the interplay between the two natures of the rational and sensual parts of the mind, which could lead to greater integration of the personality, leading to his suggestion that contemplation could be said to have a moral influence. This reading of Schiller would suggest that in spite of the creation of the play-drive there is still too great a separation between art and reality, sensuality and reason, to enable art to fully describe truth; for a further development it is necessary to turn to Georg Wilhelm Friedrich Hegel (1770–1831) and Schelling. Hegel's comment that truth no longer found its expression in the visual arts determined this paradigm (coherent system of beliefs), leaving Schelling, Runge and Carl Gustav Carus (1789–1869) to begin a new paradigm.

Building on the work of his predecessors, Schelling developed further the concept of intellectual intuition, which referred to the sensing of knowledge rather than the achievement of knowledge by rational thought alone. He concluded that painting was very well suited to express this transcendental knowledge, the infinite within the finite, but was dependent on the skill (genius) of the artist and receptivity of the observer. As set out in Chapter 3, Schelling inspired Runge and Carus, whose work particularly stressed the thought that the divine could and should be expressed through landscape painting. To emphasise this, Carus renamed landscape painting 'earth-life painting'.

Part II

Chapter 4 is concerned with defining the meaning of transcendence and the numinous. It deals with the characteristics of the religious experience and possible trigger factors, highlighting the theology of Friedrich Schleiermacher (1768–1834), his influence on Rudolf Otto (1869–1937) and the definition of the numinous. The particular factors which Otto ascribes to the expression of the numinous in art—great spatial distance, emptiness and darkness—are identified, and the chapter includes consideration of mystical experience (including nature-mysticism and the work of F. C. Happold (1893–1971), as well as the concept of eternity).[3] The trigger factors involved in invoking religious experience are discussed and those occasioned by the exposure to either the sublime or the beautiful examples of the natural world are described in some detail. The chapter concludes by extracting a number of case histories from the archive of spiritual experiences held by the Alister Hardy Religious Experience Research Centre. These case histories all highlight the evocation of a religious experience by an encounter with a work of art.

Chapter 5 opens the section concerned with specific works of art by two of the great spiritual painters of the period, Samuel Palmer (1805–81) in Britain (Chapters 5 and 6) and Caspar David

[3] R. Otto, *The Idea of the Holy* (London: Oxford University Press, 1958 [1917]); F. C. Happold, *Mysticism: A Study and an Anthology* (London: Penguin Books, 1964).

Friedrich (1774–1840) in Germany (Chapters 7 and 8). The works of Palmer which could be considered as pointing towards the transcendent are analysed and the common characteristics of distant horizons, a strong contrast between light and dark and the effect of leading the viewer to stare at the horizon, looking for something beyond the veil of the canvas, are identified. There are other specific qualities identified in individual pictures which are suggestive of pointing towards the transcendent. In addition, the biblical symbolism in Palmer is recognised, with his evocations of Edenic spiritual paradise, emphasised by the juxtaposition of extracts from a Psalm with a specific painting. Palmer maintained the intention always to reflect the glory of God's creation in his composition and in so doing provide works of inspiration for contemplation.

Chapters 7 and 8 place Friedrich in the context of German Romanticism and analyse a number of his works which portray the numinous and hence signpost the transcendent. Friedrich's characteristic emphasising of the view of the back of a visitor to a scene is examined in detail; it is argued that this use of the *Rückenfigur* invites the viewer to share the experience of the traveller. As in the case of Palmer, all the Friedrich paintings analysed meet the two criteria defined by Otto, of the contrast between light and dark and the suggestion of a tremendous distance or huge empty space. In addition the use of the lonely visitor in some paintings emphasises the insignificance of the human in the face of the forces of the natural world unleashed by the Creator. The divine gift within Friedrich enabled him to express for the receptive viewer something of the transcendence of that divinity.

Part III

The third part of the book is concerned with practical theology. Chapters 9 to 11 consider art as an aid to devotion and meditation and postulate that certain works of art could indeed be regarded as sacred. The sacramental universe was described by John Macquarrie (1919–2007) as 'a world in which all manner of things may become signs of transcendence or means of grace.'[4] Expressed another way, the most important and over-riding criterion required of a work of art—a hieroglyph or image of the divine—to be regarded as a sacrament is that it should assist in mankind's contemplation of his or her relationship with the Ultimate Reality. From this starting point the criteria that certain works of art must possess in order to point to the transcendent are reiterated. Consideration is then given to whether or not such works can be regarded as sacraments, using as an example a work by Friedrich.

The final two chapters are mainly concerned with the question of whether or not a work of art can be used as an aid to devotion or contemplation; it examines a number of works, from traditional altarpieces to landscape paintings. These chapters are more discursive and wide-ranging than previous chapters, describing works of art that, whether in use as altarpieces or as small paintings in private chapels, help the viewer towards an appreciation of that higher power or Ultimate Reality. Covering a wider period than the rest of the inquiry, the analyses begin in the Renaissance with Albrecht Dürer (1471–1528) and Raphael (1483–1520) and conclude in the twentieth century with a discussion of the colour field paintings of the abstract expressionist Mark Rothko (1903–70). The book concludes by drawing a number of parallels between works of art and the other artefacts used in church services, and ends with the aphorism of Friedrich Schlegel (1772–1829): 'Every *true* painting ought to be a hieroglyph, a *divine symbol*'.

---

[4] J. Macquarrie, *A Guide to the Sacraments* (London: SCM Press, 1997), p. vii.

PART I

Reawakening the Study of Aesthetics: The English and German Romantic Paradigm

Introduction

This chapter begins by setting out the development of aesthetics or philosophy of art from its origin with Baumgarten through to Hegel. I summarise some of the basic theories of art, and then give a description of Kantian ideas on the use of the imagination, leading to a synthesis of his views on taste and judgement. I describe theories on the purpose of art, with particular attention to German Idealism and the theories of art historian Michael Podro. In the final section I suggest that Hegel closed a paradigm, leaving the opportunity for a new paradigm to be opened by Schelling, with which I begin the next chapter.

At the end of the eighteenth century, art was beginning to be free from some of the conventions of the past, such as those of Renaissance art and Classicism, with the break from the academic schools being led by William Blake, amongst others. Blake, whose influence on Samuel Palmer will be described in a later chapter, was a poet, engraver and painter, and could be said to be the forerunner of Romanticism in Britain. Some artists, such as Joseph Mallord William Turner (1775–1851) and John Constable (1776–1837), were using this freedom to produce work that was free from history and whose subjects ranged from the political and the moral to those required to produce records for the future. Artists such as Palmer, Runge and Friedrich during the age of Romanticism were followed by Stanley Spencer (1891–1951) and David Jones (1895–1974) in Britain, and Vasily Kandinsky (1866–1944) and Piet Mondrian

(1872–1944) in Paris and the abstract expressionist Mark Rothko in America during the early years of the twentieth century, all of whom endeavoured to produce works which revealed or at least gave a glimpse of that ultimate reality that we call the Absolute or God. The first part of this study sets out a framework examining the aesthetic and philosophical trains of thought that were being developed during the latter part of the eighteenth century and the first half of the nineteenth century. Two paradigms can be identified, the first from Baumgarten to Hegel being the subject of this chapter, and the second, which opened with Schelling's approach to the philosophy of art, being the subject of Chapter 2.[1]

This book is concerned with the way in which the visible world (especially landscape) has been used by artists at a particular time to suggest an invisible, transcendent eternal world. To re-iterate, it is my contention that a paradigm can be traced from its beginning with Baumgarten, through its development by Kant and others such as Schiller, to its end with Hegel, at which point Schelling began a new paradigm which continues to the present time. It should be noted that Kant's views were subject to interpretation, upon which unity could not be established—some of these variant analyses will be elucidated with the exposition of Henry Crabb Robinson (1775–1867), whose views were of considerable interest in Britain at that time, being given some priority. These ideas were developed further by later philosophers, and their work will be described with the views of Robinson, Hegel and Schelling being given particular prominence.

Before Kant, René Descartes (1596–1650) had set scientific endeavour free from the tyrannical control of the Church by presenting a clear foundation for the advancement of philosophical principles with separation between mind and

---

[1] The word 'paradigm' is used by Thomas Kuhn to mean 'an entire constellation of beliefs, values, techniques, which are shared by the members of a particular community'. In this book, I use the word to encompass a logical pattern of thought. See Hans Küng, *Christianity* (London: SCM Press 1994), end paper quoting Kuhn.

matter. Unfortunately Descartes died before he was able to fully develop his ideas on dualism but the general principles which he propounded were most influential in the foundation of the age of Enlightenment.[2] By the time of the Romantic period, the situation had become much more subtle, with the boundaries between mind and matter, theology and philosophy becoming somewhat blurred. As the twentieth-century philosopher Isaiah Berlin (1909–97) expressed this paradigm shift, 'At its simplest the idea of romanticism saw the destruction of the notion of truth and validity in ethics and politics, not merely objective or absolute truth, but subjective and relative truth also—truth and validity as such.'[3] To express this thought another way, I suggest that during the early period of Romanticism there was a burgeoning realisation that there may not be absolute solutions to problems of morality or indeed knowledge. It is the human mind or the imagination that creates or gives birth to reason, which in turn leads to knowledge, usually with a degree of provisionality or limitation. Taking Isaac Newton (1642–1727) as an example, out of his extraordinary mind came theories on optics, gravity, planetary motion and the beginnings of the calculus, the last being developed further by Gottfried Wilhelm von Leibnitz (1646–1716) and others. At the time Newton was propounding his hypotheses and theories, he did not realise the limits within which they could be applied, and sometimes today one hears the suggestion that Newton has been superseded. This is not so; it is merely that we now know that

2   I should explain that the Enlightenment age began in the seventeenth century (John Locke (1632–1704) is usually quoted as one of the originators) and there is debate about when, or even if, it ended— some would say with the French Revolution, others may argue that it ended with the advent of Post-modernism. The age of Romanticism is contained within the period of Enlightenment; Romanticism began with Jean-Jacques Rousseau (1712–78), Kant and Blake and ended with the advent of Abstraction, although some would argue that it died out at the beginning of the Victorian period. The Enlightenment (especially in England) was particularly concerned with rational thought whilst Romanticism gave priority to the imagination and experience.

3   P. Watson, *The German Genius* (London: Simon and Schuster, 2010), p. 193, quoting Berlin.

his system of mathematics and mechanics cannot be applied to the very small (the performance of elementary particles) or the extremely large. Thus there is a provisionality of knowledge which has limits within which it can be applied and which may or may not be known at the time of its discovery. This provisionality does not only apply to scientific endeavour but equally to the humanities, where I would give as an example biblical hermeneutics. It is this provisionality applied to the philosophy of art and to the possibility of the suggestion of transcendence through art that is examined in these first two chapters.

Theories on the purpose of art

At the end of the eighteenth century and at the beginning of the nineteenth, there were a number of theories of art from, for example, William Hogarth (1697–1764), Blake, Gotthold Ephraim Lessing (1729–81), Friedrich Hölderlin (1770–1843) and Novalis (1772–1801).[4] In addition more formal philosophies were developed by Hegel, Schelling and the Schlegel brothers (August, 1767–1845, and Karl, 1772–1829). Furthermore, in respect of landscape art, Carl Ludwig Fernow (1763–1808), who influenced Carl Gustav Carus (1789–1869) both produced theories specifically related to that genre.

There are a number of models of an approach to a theology of art; Bergmann notes four—the ontological, the historical, the correlational and the social anthropological.[5] The ontological method is based on the idea that one can have knowledge about 'being' that can be expressed through art. The historical method is an approach based particularly on an examination of art which is related to the historical and philosophical context of the time. The correlational model developed by Paul Tillich (1886–1965) is a method by which, in the words of Bergmann: 'Art provides

---

[4] Novalis is the pseudonym of Georg Philipp Friedrich Freiherr von Hardenberg.
[5] S. Bergmann, *In the Beginning is the Icon: A Liberative Theology of Images, Visual Arts and Culture* (London: Equinox Publishing, 2009), pp. 66–70.

forms of expression for what is culturally salient in the situation, (with) the task of the theologian to relate these expressions to the Christian tradition.'[6] The social anthropological method is concerned with cross-cultural comparisons between the attitudes to the relationship between art and religion. As this study develops, I shall be concerned with utilising a synthesis of the ontological, historical and correlational models, although, in the main, it will be the ontological method which will be generally applicable. However, these theories of art and models of approaches to art are extensive and detailed, and while some will be examined in this chapter, a more succinct theory of direct relevance to this study has been developed by Michael Podro.

As highlighted in *The Manifold in Perception* (1972), Podro suggests there are three basic criteria when examining the relationship between reality and art from which can be derived a concept of the usefulness or value of art.[7] These criteria, which fit with the ontological method described above, may be expressed and interpreted as follows:

1. Art reveals through the skill of the artist some aspect of a subject that would not be immediately apparent.

2. The artist's depiction of an object makes a reference to the perceptual process of the viewer which enables an understanding to be achieved through, for example, the use of analogy.

3. The artist engages with the state of mind of the viewer to achieve an elevated or heightened emotional response to the work of art which may suggest a transcendence that lies behind the objects depicted.

The first of these criteria suggests something beyond copying or even mimesis—a word first used by Plato and, subsequently, by Aristotle to suggest representation or imitation.[8] The thought

---

[6] *Ibid.*, p. 74. See also P. Tillich, *On Art and Architecture*, ed. J. and J. Dillenberger (New York: Crossroad, 1989), p. 183.

[7] Podro, *The Manifold in Perception*, pp. 1–6.

[8] Plato used the term 'mimesis' in a rather derogatory way, suggesting that if the thing or person being imitated were bad then that characteristic could influence the actor or artist.

behind this first criterion, however, is that the artist reveals something which would not be immediately apparent on first looking at the subject itself; the artist has to view the subject with such intensity that it adduces an inner subtlety which can then be conveyed to the viewer. Unless the artist achieves this, then the work could only be regarded, as Hegel suggests, as a mere copy where the main judgemental criterion becomes an assessment of the accuracy of the copy.[9]

The second of these will most often convey a meaning by analogy. A good example of this is Raphael's *School of Athens* (1509). In this painting concerning knowledge, there is a synthesis of the divine and the worldly with, amongst others, Aristotle and Plato portrayed centrally under the main archway, Plato pointing to the sky (the divine) and Aristotle to the world around; and in the centre foreground is located one of the leading artists of the age, Michelangelo, writing on, but not carving, a block of marble. While the painting is entirely imaginary, the meaning which it is intended to convey is the unity of divine and worldly knowledge—uniting the spiritual and earthly. This was, of course, before Descartes argued for the separation of the two. Another example of this category and one which is more relevant to the period of this thesis is Palmer's portrayal of the *Repose on the Flight to Egypt* (c. 1824–8), where trees and shrubs represent the people concerned (see further Chapter 5). A particular characteristic of these drawings or paintings is that a response is required from the viewer, where individuals will each have their own reaction or interpretation, leading to an understanding personal to that individual. The ideal response will be exegesis (the objective taking of meaning out of the text or image) but could also be eisegesis (the subjective putting of meaning into a text or image).[10]

---

[9] G. W. F. Hegel, *Introductory Lectures on Aesthetics*, trans. B. Bosanquet, ed. M. Inwood (Harmondsworth: Penguin, 1993), p. 49. This translation was first published in 1886. The reasons for retaining this particular translation are set out in a foreword by Inwood, pp. xli–xliii.

[10] For a detailed discussion of the interpretation of text and image see J. Harvey, *The Bible as Visual Culture* (Sheffield: Sheffield Phoenix Press, 2013), pp. 11–13.

The third criterion derives from the second inasmuch as the work of art is intended to evoke an emotional response from the viewer, or as Podro expresses it 'through our absorption with a work of art, we achieve an emotional equilibrium, a purging or poise or inward harmony, which we do not normally possess.'[11] This response may be initiated by consideration of a work depicting the sublime, such as the apocalyptic designs of John Martin (1789–1854), or the spiritual, as in Palmer's *The Lonely Tower* (1879).

The boundaries between Podro's three categories, outlined above, are often blurred or overlap, but it is the second and third of these three types that are of particular concern for the examination of transcendence in art; the following paragraphs will expand on the approach to art and aesthetics adopted by the German and British artists and philosophers of the late eighteenth and early nineteenth centuries, beginning with Baumgarten.

The re-introduction of the word 'aesthetics' by Baumgarten

During the nineteenth century there was a burgeoning interest in a philosophy which could be said to have begun with the publication by Baumgarten of *Meditationes philosophicae de nonnullis ad poema pertinentibus* in 1735.[12] This work re-introduced the concept of aesthetics to philosophy, a subject which was further developed by Kant, whose theories were then interpreted and expanded by other philosophers, including Schiller, Schelling, Arthur Schopenhauer (1788–1860) and Hegel.[13]

---

[11] Podro, *The Manifold in Perception*, p. 5.
[12] 'Philosophical meditations on some requirements of the poem' mentioned in K. Hammermeister, *The German Aesthetic Tradition* (Cambridge: Cambridge University Press, 2002), p. 4.
[13] The word aesthetics is derived from Greek usage of the word, which meant perception and occurs in Plato (*Republic*) and Aristotle (*Poetics*). Although used also by Plotinus, Augustine and Aquinas it was Baumgarten who established the philosophy of aesthetics concerned with the 'science of the conditions of sensuous perception' or the 'philosophy of taste or of the perception of the beautiful'.

The essence of this philosophy, which was fashionable at the time of Palmer but would be questionable today, is that:

> The work of art [...] represents not the empirical object but its idea [...] every object is presented as the epitome of its existence, a state where it has reached its *telos*. Art captures the perfect moment and lifts the object out of the flow of time, allowing it to become eternal in its preservation through art.[14]

Two words here require particular elucidation—idea and *telos*. In this context, the 'idea' could be said to represent the interface between the experiencing mind, the subject, and something in this world, the object. Alternatively, the idea is a spiritual concept of reality and is expressed, in Baumgarten's philosophy, in the work of art. Turning now to *telos*, this is usually related to theology, where teleology may be regarded as the study of divine design. *Telos* is closely related in meaning to the anthropic principle, whereby it is considered that within the mathematical space-time singularity, that is referred to in the 'big bang theory' of creation, was everything that was necessary for the subsequent development of the cosmos as we know it today.[15] In *The German Genius*, Watson expressed the concept of teleology in simple terms as 'there is a continual process of creation, and its various levels are related to one another in a purposive manner.'[16]

Following Descartes's pronouncements, there were two primary ways of looking at the world during the Enlightenment— by the use of the mind and pure logic or reason, as promoted by

---

[14] Hammermeister, *The German Aesthetic Tradition*, p. 79.

[15] 'The anthropic principle begins by considering the fundamental constants of nature (e.g., the speed of light, Planck's constant) and the specific forms of the fundamental physical laws, such as relativity and quantum mechanics [...] What is surprising is that these constants and laws are precisely what are needed for the possibility that life will evolve in the universe, whether on earth as it has, or perhaps on many other planets in the universe.' T. Peters and G. Bennett (eds), *Bridging Science and Religion* (London: SCM Press, 2002), p. 57.

[16] Watson, *The German Genius*, p. 240.

Kant and other philosophers, and by the use of the imagination, as for example espoused by William Blake.[17] As Watson puts it: 'The rival ways of looking at the world—the cool detached light of disinterested scientific reason, and the red-blooded, passionate creations of the artist—constitute the modern incoherence. Both appear equally true, equally valid at times, but are fundamentally incompatible.'[18] This is rather overstating the case to make the point—this is only true of a very reductionist approach to science, adopted by some but rejected by other scientists. This was no doubt the situation at the end of the eighteenth century as it is still in the twenty-first century. However, it should perhaps be added at this juncture that Blake was very anxious to ensure the separation between the arts and science, not because he took a particularly reductionist approach to science but because he wished to ensure that art did not become 'an inferior category of science.'[19]

Kant too, from a very different perspective, also disagreed with Baumgarten (with his emphasis on the use of the senses rather than the intellect) and would argue that:

> For art to have any real meaning or insight, then the link between art and cognition must be broken—if this does not happen then artistic insight will always be seen as 'inferior' when its potential for cognition is compared with that of reason.[20]

As I mentioned above using the example of Newton, it is the mind that created reason. It is the artist who creates (into existence) and gives value, whilst the scientist examines that which already exists physically and uses this deductive knowledge to forecast

---

[17] Descartes really established this duality in the seventeenth century; it enabled religion and science to be treated as two separate disciplines and to progress with their separate lines of enquiry. This enabled the age of reason to develop rapidly without the scientists getting into the difficulties that befell Galileo and his predecessors.

[18] Watson, *The German Genius*, p. 195.

[19] M. Eaves, *William Blake's Theory of Art* (Princeton: Princeton University Press, 1982), p. 26.

[20] Hammermeister quoting Kant, *The German Aesthetic Tradition*, p. 23.

future patterns of the behaviour of systems. In other words, by the use of his or her imagination the artist creates, say, a picture, which evokes an emotional experiential response in the viewer, which in turn could perhaps enhance the viewer's appreciation of his or her psychological situation. In contrast the scientist, through observation and a specific experiment, may discover a basic principle which could then be applied more generally in furthering scientific knowledge. For example, Robert Hooke (1635–1703) established rules relating to the extension and compression of elastic materials which have continuing application in, for example, motor-vehicle design.[21]

This approach to knowledge—with the somewhat artificial separation between rationality and imagination—existed at the time of Blake during the early part of the nineteenth century. This needs to be kept at the forefront of our thought as works of art of that period are interpreted, even though a more modern interpretation may well give greater recognition to Baumgarten's and Hölderlin's rather more inclusive approach to the relationship between art and reality.

The sections which follow will examine briefly some of the theories of art being propounded by artists and philosophers of the time, beginning with Blake.

Blake and the supremacy of the imagination

Blake's theory, falling initially into the first of the Podro categories outlined above concerned with mimesis, followed the classical theory, which gives prominence to line over form or colour. In other words, he belonged to the 'two-dimensional linearists in the old esthetic battle between linear and painterly schools.'[22]

---

[21] Robert Hooke is particularly renowned for his law which states that the tension in a lightly stretched spring is proportional to its extension from its natural length.

[22] Eaves, *William Blake's Theory of Art*, p. 19. (Eaves quotes many sources in support of this statement.)

Flexible form and the emphasis on line develops, Blake suggests, from the evolution of the temple—the buildings which, for the Greeks, had considerable religious significance. The Greeks were also concerned with the ideal—that, in the words of Aristotle, 'Art completes what nature cannot bring to a finish.'[23] In discussing this statement Kenneth Clark (1903–83), in *The Nude—A Study of Ideal Art*, highlights Blake's comment that 'All Forms are Perfect in the Poet's Mind but these are not Abstracted or compounded from Nature, but are from Imagination.'[24] Summarising, Clark writes:

> What both Reynolds and Blake meant by ideal beauty was really the diffused memory of that particular physical type which was developed in Greece between the years of 480 and 440 BC and which in varying degrees of intensity and consciousness, furnished the mind of Western man with a pattern of perfection from the Renaissance until the present century.[25]

Whereas Clark was content to accept Blake's theory about art perfecting form and accepted that Blake had 'an exceptional power of secreting retinal images' he felt that Blake was unable to achieve that 'long and painful interaction between ideal form remembered and natural appearances observed, which is the foundation of all great drawing from Michelangelo to Degas.'[26] At this stage in the development of Blake's theory, there is little to suggest that he would later break away from the views of the prominent art historian of the time, Johann Winckelmann (1717–68), but whereas the latter was keen to ensure that rational thought would underlie his views on the Greek Ideal, Blake would depart from this attention to the rational, by giving much greater prominence to the use of the imagination.[27]

[23] K. Clark, *The Nude: A Study of Ideal Art* (London: The Reprint Society, 1958), p. 9, quoting Aristotle.
[24] *Ibid.*, p. 11, quoting Blake. To Blake form and outline were synonymous.
[25] *Ibid.*, p. 11.
[26] *Ibid.*, p. 207.
[27] A full discussion of the relationship between beauty and proportion, which was so important to ancient Greek philosophy, is beyond the scope

Setting aside the question of Blake's practical ability and continuing to think in terms of Podro's categories, Blake highlighted three different types of copying which take us from mimesis towards the spiritual. First there are the 'direct "servile" copies "both of Nature and Art" that are the musical scales of the visual artist, learning the "language of Art" by copying.'[28] The second form of copying is the imitation of nature. The third is the copying of 'imaginative forms from the artist's own mind, which is the copying every artist should be trying to do.'[29] In Blake's own words:

> The great and golden rule of art, as well as of life is this:
>   That the more distinct, sharp and wiery the bounding line, the more perfect the work of art; and the less keen and sharp, the greater is the evidence of weak imitation, plagiarism and bungling. Great inventors, in all ages, knew this: Protogenes and Apelles knew each other by this line. Rafael [*sic*] and Michael Angelo, and Durer, are known by this and this alone. The want of this determinate and bounding form evidences the want of idea in the artist's mind, and the pretence of the plagiary in all its branches.[30]

Although line, form and the approach to the ideal in art proposed by Aristotle were very important to Blake, the imagination, as mentioned above, was all-important.

At this juncture, it is worth highlighting the work of the art historian Ernst Gombrich (1909–2001), who suggests that in examining an image, there are three components to the analysis— representation, symbolism and expression.[31] I would propose that in Blake's philosophy of art, symbolism and expression are merged into one and are given precedence over representation by

of this book, but I would refer the reader to Clark's *The Nude*, where a full disquisition can be found on pp. 13–25 and indeed in the chapters beyond.
[28] Eaves, *William Blake's Theory of Art*, p. 28.
[29] *Ibid.*, p. 29.
[30] M. Myrone (ed.), *Seen in My Visions: A Descriptive Catalogue of Pictures by William Blake* (London: Tate Publishing, 2009), pp. 84–5.
[31] E. Gombrich, *Symbolic Images Studies in the Art of the Renaissance* (London: Phaidon Press, 1972), p. 124.

the artist. From this it follows that the personality and character of the artist attains an importance that would not apply to an artist working only in the area of copying that which he or she sees. The fine judgement that needs to be made by the viewer is to consider the extent to which transcendence has been revealed in a work of art; that is, in the interaction between the viewer and the artist there will follow an emotional response, the value of which can only be judged by the viewer.

Before returning to the paradigm that began with Baumgarten, it is essential to include a short discussion on the work of Edmund Burke (1730–97), whose *Philosophical Enquiry into the Origin of our Ideas of the Sublime and Beautiful* (second edition 1759) had considerable influence in both Britain and Germany.[32] Whilst the enquiry had great influence, it was not received with general acclamation—although Thomas Hardy (1840–1928) found in it 'a source of imaginative stimulus', Blake, who read the work when he was young, re-read it feeling 'the same Contempt and Abhorrence then that I do now.'[33] Blake continued 'They [Bacon, Locke, Burke and Reynolds] mock Inspiration and Vision.'[34]

Burke was a man of the Enlightenment—always concerned to express his view in a language that is as precise and logical as possible. In essence, Burke defines the beautiful as that which induces the feeling of love, whilst the sublime induces the feeling of astonishment or even terror. The beautiful is to be found in small things, in things which are smooth (for example leaves which are smooth rather than jagged), in things in which shape varies gradually such that one part of a body flows into another without any sort of discontinuity. In addition beautiful objects have delicacy rather than robustness and soft pastel colours which

---

[32] Whilst it is clearly beyond the scope of this chapter to deal in great detail with the theories of Burke with regard to the beautiful and the sublime, a full commentary and reprint of the Enquiry itself will be found in the following: E. Burke, *A Philosophical Enquiry into the Origin of our Ideas of the Sublime and Beautiful*, edited with an introduction and notes by James R. Boulton (London: Routledge and Kegan Paul, 1958).

[33] Burke, *A Philosophical Enquiry*, p. lxxxii.

[34] *Ibid.*, p. lxxxii, quoting Blake.

merge gradually from one into another rather than violent colours juxtaposed in a way that clashes. As an example of an object exhibiting these characteristics Burke highlights the peacock.

With regard to the sublime, Burke lists the characteristics which can give rise to feelings of terror—obscurity (for example in darkness or in night), where an object may appear more terrible because it cannot be appreciated clearly, or suggestions of great power (as in a tsunami), vastness and infinity. In addition, he accepts that things which exhibit magnificence, for example the night sky, and give rise to the idea of grandeur also fall into the category of the sublime. In comparing 'Beauty' with the 'Sublime', Burke wrote:

> For sublime objects are vast in their dimensions, beautiful ones comparatively small; beauty should be smooth, and polished; the great, rugged and negligent; [...] beauty should not be obscure; the great ought to be dark and gloomy; beauty should be light and delicate; the great ought to be solid and even massive. They are indeed ideas of a very different nature, one being founded on pain, the other on pleasure; and however they may vary afterwards from the direct nature of their causes, yet these causes keep up an eternal distinction between them, a distinction never to be forgotten by any whose business it is to affect the passions.[35]

Burke, having set out these distinctions, then sets out to try to define in rational terms the causes of inducement of feelings of the sublime and the beautiful by, for example, analysing the physical cause of love, in a way some, including Blake, would find too reductionist, leaving the working of the imagination out of the equation. It should however be remembered that Burke's essay was the first major work on the subject since Longinus (213–73 CE) and even if it lacked a certain sophistication, with a number of aphorisms no more than simply stated, it was of considerable influence at the time, particularly for Kant, who introduced a greater subtlety, with transcendence being established as a very significant parameter.

---

[35] *Ibid.*

Idealism and Kant

Kant, in his *Critique of Pure Reason* (1781) and *Critique of Practical Reason* (1788), began the period of German Idealism 'which constitutes a cultural phenomenon whose stature and influence has frequently been compared to nothing less than the golden age of Athens.'[36] Essentially, Kant argued that the human intellect is limited to the receipt of knowledge which can be derived using the logic of mathematics and reason on the one hand and which can be derived from empirical observation on the other. There is, however, a third branch of knowledge—the noumenal or transcendental—which may possibly be available through intellectual intuition.[37] This third type of knowledge has a nature which is more 'ideal' than the others—a designation that gave rise to Idealism. As Watson points out, Kant established his philosophy by considering the key concepts of Truth, Goodness and Beauty.[38] However, in order to keep this chapter within bounds, I will concentrate on aesthetics and consider first 'Beauty'.

The beautiful

The Critique of Judgement (1790) consists of a first part concerned with aesthetic judgement, which is subdivided into two sections dealing respectively with the analysis and

---

[36] Watson, *The German Genius*, p. 138, quoting K. Americks.
[37] The Kantian approach to a distinction between the noumenal and the phenomenal is very succinctly expressed by L. W. Beck, who writes in the *Oxford Companion to Philosophy*: 'Kant called the determination of noumena and phenomena the "noblest enterprise of antiquity" but in the *Critique of Pure Reason* he denied that noumenal as objects of pure reason are objects of knowledge, since reason gives knowledge only of objects of sensible intuition (phenomena). Noumena "in the negative sense" are objects of which we have no sensible intuition and hence no knowledge at all; these are things-in-themselves. Noumena "in the positive sense" (e.g. soul and God) are conceived of as objects of intellectual intuition.'
[38] Watson, *The German Genius*, p. 139.

the dialectic of aesthetic judgement. The first section is then divided into two books analysing the beautiful and the sublime. The second part is divided into two sections concerned with the analysis and dialectic of teleological judgement. The paragraphs which follow concentrate on the first part. It should be noted that the work of Kant, and indeed of Hegel and Schelling, is theoretical and cannot necessarily be considered in the light of the Podro categories outlined above, although it could perhaps be said that it applies more particularly to categories two and three. Beginning with an examination of the beautiful, Kant divided the first book into chapters or, to use his term, moments (*Das Moment*),[39] at the end of which he gave definitions of the beautiful:

> Definition of the beautiful derived from the first moment: *Taste* is the faculty of estimating an object or mode of representation by means of a delight or aversion *apart from any interest*. The object of such delight is called *beautiful*. (§5)[40]

> Definition of the beautiful drawn from the second moment: The *beautiful* is that which, apart from a concept, pleases universally. (§9)[41]

> Definition of the beautiful derived from this third moment: *Beauty* is the form of finality in an object, so far as perceived in it *apart from the representation of an end*. (§17)[42]

> Definition of the beautiful drawn from the fourth moment: The beautiful is that which, apart from a concept, is cognised as object of a necessary delight. (§22)[43]

---

[39] *Das Moment* = (deciding) factor, consideration, element, aspect.
[40] These definitions are taken from the translation by J. Meredith of Immanuel Kant, *The Critique of Judgement* (Oxford: Clarendon Press, 1952) (reissue of the first editions of the two parts issued as two books), part one, p. 50.
[41] *Ibid.*, p. 60.
[42] *Ibid.*, p. 80.
[43] *Ibid.*, p. 84.

In considering these definitions, it is important to remember that
Kant's view of perceptual knowledge was that it consists of three
components: sensibility (passive reception of sensory stimuli),
imagination (ordering of sensory manifold into a unity) and
understanding (provision of a concept under which to subsume
the results of imagination's activity).[44] It is also important to
remember the question that Kant endeavours to answer—Can
the synthesis of imagination, thought and feeling of pleasure be
regarded as of universal applicability in the case of a beautiful
object? Suggesting an alternative view of the character of
judgement, James Sallis writes:

> In the case of a beautiful object, the apprehended form
> is referred to the cognitive faculties in such a way that a
> harmony is displayed and a feeling of pleasure produced
> [...] the harmony is pre-eminently one between the
> operations of imagination and of understanding.[45]

In other words, a viewed object is not of itself or inherently
beautiful—but can only be described as beautiful if it engenders
in the viewer the sensation of pleasure that comes from the
interaction of imagination and feeling. Aesthetic pleasure
is derived, then, from the interplay between imagination
and comprehension, even though one may only strive for
understanding never actually attaining it, a thought which links
through to Kant's definition of the aesthetic idea:

> By an aesthetic idea I mean the representation of imagina-
> tion that incites much thought, yet without the possibility
> of any definite thought whatever, i.e. *concept*, being ad-
> equate to it, and which language, consequently can
> never get quite on level terms with or render completely
> intelligible.—It is easily seen, that an aesthetic idea is the
> counterpart (pendant) of a *rational idea*, which, conversely,
> is a concept, to which no *intuition* (representation of the
> imagination) can be adequate. (§49)[46]

---

[44] Hammermeister, *The German Aesthetic Tradition*, p. 29.
[45] J. Sallis, *Spacings of Reason and Imagination in Texts of Kant, Fichte, Hegel*
(Chicago: University of Chicago Press, 1987), p. 93.
[46] Meredith, *Immanuel Kant*, p. 174.

Kant makes an important distinction between aesthetic pleasure and rational pleasure. Rational pleasure may, for example, be expressed in terms of one's preference for a particular food or drink over another, whereas aesthetic pleasure does not take an interest in the existence of the object itself.

In this first moment definition, Kant is saying that whilst pleasure resulting from one preference over another is personal and subjective, aesthetic pleasure has a universal applicability but is still ontologically subjective. Whilst normally in the exercise of judgement the process of looking at an object is followed by the use of intellect and imagination leading to understanding, Kant argues that in aesthetic judgement the latter stage of understanding is never reached; there may be a 'free-play' of the faculties which try to achieve but never reach a stage of understanding—he is here expressing in another way the aesthetic idea referred to above.

Kant, in my view, struggles to demonstrate this universality, ending in a circular argument, and coming to define the beautiful, as he does in the definition of the second moment, as that which, without any concept, pleases universally. However, as Elizabeth Prettejohn has pointed out, if a judgement is purely personal then it does not meet one of Kant's other important criteria— that the judgement must be disinterested or unbiased—which is expressed clearly in the definition of the first moment.[47] But the question remains: is it ever possible for a judgement to be so free of all personal prejudices, likes and dislikes? In the third moment there is the suggestion that beauty in itself has no purpose—no end in itself, apart from the representation itself. If it is remembered that Kant is almost certainly referring to natural objects, rather than man-made art, then indeed beauty in itself probably serves no purpose. Whilst one could perhaps suggest that the beauty in a male bird serves the purpose of attracting the female, the beauty in a flower (which Kant does cite) would seem to be purposeless except possibly in attracting pollinating

[47] E. Prettejohn, *Beauty and Art 1750–2000* (Oxford: Oxford University Press, 2005), pp. 46–7.

insects. Regarding the definition of the fourth moment, which is very similar to the second, Kant exhibits a weakness in the development of his argument inasmuch as he writes: 'The assertion is not that everyone will fall in with (my) judgement but rather that everyone *ought* to agree with it.'[48]

Kant then relies on an appeal to common sense and 'attributes to it on that account *exemplary* validity.'[49] This is then followed by a further weakness, where Kant admits to not endeavouring to answer the question, which remains open, as to whether taste is a 'natural and original faculty' and the question as to whether the 'ought', the objective necessity of the coincidence of the feeling of all with the particular feeling of each, only betokens the possibility of arriving at some sort of unanimity in these matters (§22).[50]

This difficulty of achieving pure objectivity was identified by Robinson, whose influence on Palmer and others was considerable, and who wrote, endeavouring to explain the difficulty:

> Tho' it is the essence of beauty to be in itself complete and absolute; there are still many objects, whose acknowledged beauty is still dependent on their fitness to an end beyond themselves. Hence Kant distinguished between free beauty which is beauty *par excellence* and, dependent beauty. The former alone is the object of pure taste; And in the complication of human feelings perhaps rarely exists: But it nevertheless remains apart for the spectator. In judging of a building for instance, it is difficult if not impossible to form a purely aesthetical judgement of its form, without all reference whatever to the purpose of the structure.[51]

I digress here by mentioning my own reaction to two situations. Considering the two great piano concertos of Johannes Brahms (1833–97), I find the first much more emotionally engaging than

---

[48] Meredith, *Immanuel Kant*, p. 84.
[49] *Ibid.*
[50] *Ibid.*, p. 85.
[51] J. Vigus, *Essays on Kant, Schelling and German Aesthetics by Henry Crabb Robinson* (London: Modern Humanities Research Association, 2010), p. 53.

the second—perhaps because the first was written after the death in 1856 of Brahms's friend Robert Schumann (1810–56) and expresses his own and Clara Schumann's (1819–96) grief (particularly in the first two movements) and then in the third there is almost what could be regarded as a joyful celebration or resurrection, whereas the second concerto, equally large and difficult to play, may perhaps be regarded as pure music but leaves me uninvolved. Is it the programme element in the first concerto that is necessary for my complete involvement or is it that the first work is subtly transcendental whereas the second is not? This question is unanswerable, but it illustrates the difficulty of trying to apply Kant's objective approach to those areas of artistic endeavour where the senses and emotions are involved.

Considering now the visual arts, I find a transcendental quality in Palmer's sepia drawings whereas I am unmoved by Rothko's colour field paintings. Other viewers, I know, will express the opposite point of view, sometimes to the extent of having a religious experience when viewing a colour field, where the subtle variation in wavelength between the two colours gives rise to an apparent vibration along the line of colour change. This again illustrates the personal nature of artistic appreciation and I must therefore disagree with Kant that there ought to be a universal recognition of quality in art, be it transcendence, or beauty.

Acknowledging the impossibility of truly summarising Kant's views on the beautiful as part of a chapter, I will conclude this section on beauty by suggesting that whilst much of the deliberation around the subject is of value in helping us to understand the process of judgement, Kant's constant striving to demonstrate universality is a distracting weakness. I therefore much prefer his concept of beauty (as expressed in the definitions of the first and third moments), that it is the form of 'purposiveness in an object, insofar as it is perceived without representation of a purpose' (Hammermeister's translation) as well as being an object giving rise to aesthetic (but not necessarily rational) pleasure.[52]

---

[52] Hammermeister, *The German Aesthetic Tradition*, p. 32.

I shall be returning to a consideration of the beautiful in the section below on fine art, but let us now analyse Kant's approach to the sublime.

The sublime

Kant divides the sublime into two types. First, the mathematically sublime or absolutely great: we can, of course, always think of a number larger than any particular integer, and it is necessary, therefore, to have a term which expresses a quantity greater than any number that could be thought of, leading to the concept of infinity, which is essential in the mathematical discipline of the calculus. Without going into detail, an integer divided by zero would be fairly meaningless whereas an integer divided by a number which tends towards zero becomes meaningful and would have a result that tends toward infinity. In graphical form such a relationship (x = 1/y) could be plotted, with the resultant graph becoming asymptotic to, but never quite reaching—until infinity, the x axis as y reduces and the y axis as y increases.

Secondly, there is the dynamically sublime in nature: an experience of nature with fear attached—e.g. thunderstorms, earthquakes or majestic snow-covered heights with the possibility of avalanche. In Kant's words 'nature considered in an aesthetic judgement as might that has no dominion over us, is dynamically sublime'.[53]

The mathematical view of the sublime is concerned with magnitude. Kant highlights the impossibility of defining objectively any particular number—the concept of number is purely intuitive, enabling only a comparative magnitude to be measured. As magnitude is increased, there is a tendency towards the infinite or the sublime, where the limit of the imagination is reached, for example in contemplation of the outer reaches of the cosmos. There is a correspondence here with mathematics, where, in order to deal with matters beyond normal physical representation, abstraction into symbolism is employed, as

---

[53] *Ibid.*, p. 109, quoting Kant.

exemplified in the simple (x = 1/y) example quoted above. A more detailed exposition will be found, for example, in the works of Blaise Pascal (1623–62), Leibnitz and Pierre-Simon Laplace (1749–1827), and their interpreters.[54]

Makkreel emphasises that for Kant, whilst mathematical apprehension can go on towards infinity, for aesthetic comprehension there is a maximum beyond which that comprehension cannot go. 'When the imagination's capacity to intuit simultaneously a series of units reaches a limit, aesthetic comprehension encounters the immeasurable and the feeling of the sublime.'[55] In other words, in contemplation of the sublime both apprehension and comprehension are at work, with the sublime itself being achieved when aesthetic comprehension reaches its limit. Kant expresses this quite succinctly in his final paragraph of §25 when he writes: 'The sublime is that, the mere capacity of thinking which evidences a faculty of mind transcending every standard of sense.'[56]

It is generally the second form of the sublime with which the artist is more obviously concerned—the dynamical. Instead of magnitude being the defining element, it is power (usually of nature) which is the object of contemplation. However, there is also a link to the mathematical concept of the extremely large— it being a characteristic of many works of art endeavouring to depict the sublime, such as *Gordale Scar* (1811–15) by James Ward (1769–1859), that one cannot absorb the whole of that work from one single standpoint unless one is considering the work from such a distance that no detail may be discerned.

While (natural) power is the object of contemplation, power alone is insufficient as an indication of the sublime, as the use of the imagination may lead only to anxiety and not necessarily transcending all senses. But there is always a separation of the

---

[54] For example, H. T. H. Piaggio, *An Elementary Treatise on Differential Equations and their Applications* (London: G. Bell & Sons, 1952).

[55] R. Makkreel, *Imagination and Interpretation in Kant* (Chicago: University of Chicago Press, 1994), p. 70.

[56] Meredith, *Immanuel Kant*, p. 98.

human from the power of nature—an independence from nature which gives rise to the sublime experience which Kant sets out as follows:

> The irresistibility of (nature) forces us on the one side to acknowledge our physical helplessness, but on the other side reveals a faculty of estimating ourselves independent of it. On this faculty rests a self-preservation of a very different kind as that which can be challenged and endangered by nature, so that humanity remains unhumiliated in our person, even though man would be defeated by that force.[57]

Robinson expresses this sense of the sublime rather differently, describing a

> mixed feeling: in which painful emotions may be detected, tho' outweighed by a preponderance of pleasure. This arises from the double Nature of Man, who as a *sensible* being is oppressed by the might & greatness of nature, to which he is still superior as a *rational and moral being*. When we behold the sublime objects of Nature, such as Torrents, Mountains, Tempests, we are made sensible of our weakness, & feel too that we cannot even measure or comprehend these objects, but this Sensation is accompanied by another, which outweighs the first & converts the insipient pain into delight. We are led to feel more or less obscurely the higher worth & dignity of our moral and intellectual nature.[58]

This view of the sublime rings a chord with Samuel Taylor Coleridge (1772–1834); as David Vallins writes, 'even in these relatively early writings [of Coleridge] there is often an explicit sense that the sublimity associated with landscapes is due (as Kant most famously suggested) to the intuition of something that lies beyond or behind them and which the mind can never know or comprehend so clearly or directly as any part of the physical world.'[59] For example, one might think of Glen Coe

[57] Hammermeister, *The German Aesthetic Tradition*, p. 34, quoting Kant.
[58] Vigus, *Essays on Kant*, p. 131.
[59] D. Vallins (ed.), *Coleridge's Writings*, vol. 5, *On the Sublime* (Basingstoke:

(Scotland) in mid-winter during a period of deep snow when one would be aware of both the beauty of the scene and the danger from avalanche. These thoughts of the grandeur and danger of the creative power of nature (and God) may lead the viewer to contemplate death and eternity.

Relating this reaction to the sublime to art history, Caspar David Friedrich in his series of *Rückenfigur* paintings provides examples in which the viewer of the painting is invited to share in the sublime feelings being experienced by the viewer in the picture.[60] There are a number of such paintings, but in particular I would highlight *Woman in Morning Light* (*c.* 1809), *Two Men by the Sea* (*c.* 1817) and *Wanderer above a Sea of Mists* (*c.* 1818). In the first of these two examples, there is contemplation of the wonder of nature's light as the sun rises and sets respectively and in all the *Rückenfigur* paintings the viewer is invited to join the figure(s) in contemplation of the sublime scene. In *Wanderer above a Sea of Mists* the mystery of the sublime is emphasised by both the aerial perspective, where the view of the mountain tops seems to go on for ever, and by the fog below the viewing figure, which obscures the extent of the depths of the valleys below.

The difficulty of creating works of art without purpose—Kant on fine art

Kant endeavours to solve this problem in §43 and the following paragraphs, with the introduction of the concept of genius. He explains:

> *Genius* is the talent (natural endowment) which gives the rule to art. Since talent, as an innate productive faculty of the artist, belongs itself to nature, we may put it this way:

Palgrave Macmillan, 2003), p. 36. Coleridge, who with William Wordsworth (1770–1850), spent time studying in Germany, was influential, along with Robinson, in bringing the German Idealist philosophy to Britain.

[60] Figure seen from the rear: Rücken—back, Figur—figure.

Genius is the innate mental aptitude (*ingenium*) *through which* nature gives the rule to art.[61]

Fine art is a product which must be art and not nature, but 'nevertheless must be clothed, *with the aspect* of nature',[62] and which must appear to be 'uncontrived, natural and effortless' and to be totally original; it must therefore be the product of genius.[63] The artist of genius must therefore be 'an outstandingly talented person brought forth by nature so that he or she can in turn produce works of art'.[64] As Prettejohn emphasises in respect of the *Wanderer above a Sea of Mists*:

> [The painting] goes above and beyond merely realising its intention (to produce a representation of a landscape). It is a work of genius in Kant's sense, for it stimulates the observer's mind to range freely over the widest variety of further musings—above pictorial space, human perceptions of space, or natural space; about the relationship of human beings to nature, the spiritual dimensions of a sublime experience, or the presence of the divine in nature.

Kant then explains that the innate talent or faculty within the artist (genius) is such as to enable him or her to present, through this talent, the aesthetic idea. In other words, the imagination is used to create 'a second nature out of the material supplied to it by actual nature'.[65] As Hammermeister points out, for Kant 'Fine art [...] is a mode of representation that is purposeful in itself, and [...] advances the culture of the mental powers in the interest of social communication'.[66] Art can therefore be regarded as good for a community or society and hence to symbolise a moral quality—a principle that Kant outlines in the concluding paragraphs of the 'Dialectic of Aesthetic Judgement' (the second section of the *Critique of Aesthetic Judgement*) §59—'Beauty as a

---

[61] Meredith, *Immanuel Kant*, p. 168.
[62] *Ibid.*, pp. 166–7.
[63] Hammermeister, *The German Aesthetic Tradition*, p. 35.
[64] *Ibid.*, p. 35.
[65] Meredith, *Immanuel Kant*, p. 176.
[66] Hammermeister, *The German Aesthetic Tradition*, p. 37.

symbol of morality.'[67] This is a very complex part of the *Critique* but his argument is that all representation is either symbolic, where the concept is the engagement of reason, or schematic, where the engagement is intuition involving the imagination. The imagination, Kant intimates, is a uniquely human faculty, and, as Hammermeister suggests, Kant also argues that there is a hierarchy of beautiful forms at 'the top of which we can find the human figure as the ideal of beauty.'[68]

This detailed argument is far from clear but I would suggest that Kant could be interpreted as saying that art has a purpose or function in the establishment of community and consequently has a moral function. In his concluding remarks, Kant refers to the fact that we call buildings 'majestic and stately, or plains laughing and gay; even colours are called innocent, modest, soft, because they excite sensations containing something analogous to the consciousness of the state of mind produced by moral judgements.'[69]

To conclude this section on Kant, it is appropriate to recapitulate his definitions of the beautiful with which I began, but using my own words:

1. *Taste* is the ability to estimate an object or its representation by means of a delight. The object of such delight is called *beautiful*.

2. The *beautiful* is that which, viewed disinterestedly (i.e. without prejudice), pleases universally.

3. *Beauty* is the form of completion in an object but without any aim or purpose.

4. The *beautiful* is that which is recognised as an object of a necessary delight.

5. In consideration of the sublime, the *imagination* is involved to an extent that approaches its limit and is not grounded, as in the contemplation of beauty, by externality, but by an internal attitude of mind.

[67] Meredith, *Immanuel Kant*, p. 221.
[68] Hammermeister, *The German Aesthetic Tradition*, p. 38.
[69] Meredith, *Immanuel Kant*, p. 225.

Kant was the first philosopher to set out in great detail a formal treatise on aesthetic judgement, and he established the subject as one worthy of consideration as a separate discipline. As will be apparent from the above, there are a number of aspects of this disquisition which are open to question, to further consideration and indeed to amendment, but he did establish the agenda with which successive philosophers and artists have been able to engage. It is with the first of these philosophers to follow him, Schiller, that the next chapter continues.

2

The Influence of Schiller, Hegel and Schelling

The system of drives

The major discrepancy in Kant's argument is that he proposes that on the one hand the appreciation of beauty and the sublime is ontologically subjective, whilst on the other beauty and the sublime have a quality of universality that ought to be recognised by everyone. J. C. Friedrich von Schiller (1759–1805) identified these two faults in Kant's argument as: 1. its subjectivism, and 2. the rigid split between sensibility (or use of the imagination) and rationality. In addition Schiller saw the philosophy of aesthetics as a stepping stone on the route towards the achievement of a moral state.

Schiller's starting point, set out in *The Aesthetic Education of Mankind*, is personality, where his view is that man is both part of nature and also has freedom.[1] Extending the model of man's impulses propounded by Johann Gottlieb Fichte (1762–1814), Schiller promulgates a system of drives. The first is the sense drive, determined by 'sensuality, perception and the primacy of the matter of the world over the ego.'[2] The second is the form drive, which arises from 'the unchangeable part of man' (*compare facto*: Fichte's argument for pure ego, source for the direct intellectual intuition of things).[3] These two drives, the first passive and concerned with reception, the second rational

---

[1]   J. C. Friedrich von Schiller, *Letters upon the Aesthetic Education of Man*, 1794, now available at http://www.fordham.edu/halsall/mod/schiller-education.asp

[2]   Hammermeister, *The German Aesthetic Tradition*, p. 51.

[3]   *Ibid.*, p. 52.

and active, are independent and 'the dependence of satisfactory experience upon their balance has no special relation to aesthetic perception or to art'.[4] Schiller saw the solution here to be the postulation of a third drive—a unifying force which he called the *Spieltrieb* or play-drive—and which I would regard as equivalent to the free play of the imagination referred to by Kant. Schiller writes:

> Reason demands, on transcendental grounds, that a partnership between the sense drive and the form drive should exist, namely a play-drive, because only the union of reality with form, of contingency with necessity, of suffering with freedom fulfils the conception of humanity.[5]

This is not easy to understand but Podro explains that 'the active, rational part of the human mind, and its passive receptive aspect are thought of not simply as grounds or conditions of experience, but as two forces, the equilibrium of which is always likely to be disturbed'.[6] The *Spieltrieb* is the free play acting within the imagination or mind which is 'searching for a coincidence of the two demands of the mind'.[7]

Hammermeister further defines the play-drive as the aesthetic principle, with the term 'play' referring to the contemplation of the 'beautiful that frees man both from the atemporality of the law and sensual desire by situating him in between both'.[8] This concept is further explained by Podro, who writes:

> The harmony of the mind which is the object of the play-drive thus has three conditions: first, that we do not simply impose our mental schemata on our observations without also remaining sensitive as to whether the material really fits our projection, secondly that we do try to project and thirdly that the material does correspond to expectations that are initially set up.[9]

---

[4] Podro, *The Manifold in Perception*, p. 49.
[5] Hammermeister, *The German Aesthetic Tradition*, p. 53, quoting Schiller.
[6] Podro, *The Manifold in Perception*, p. 48.
[7] *Ibid.*, p. 50.
[8] Hammermeister, *The German Aesthetic Tradition*, p. 53.
[9] *Ibid.*, p. 50.

Perhaps another way of looking at this is to think in terms of being involved in reading a novel, listening to a symphony or looking at a painting, but also remaining outside or independent of that work of art. Another, and perhaps more appropriate, example from the art form of music would be one of the 'Great' fugues for the organ by Johann Sebastian Bach (1685–1750), perhaps the one in C major. There are several ways of listening to this—one could adopt the technical approach and listen to the way in which Bach introduces the theme and then weaves it through the various voices to the climax on full organ (form drive), or alternatively one could allow the magnificence of the music as a whole to involve the emotions, enabling one to become almost lost in the atmosphere of sound (sense drive). A third approach, engaging the play-drive, would be to permit the emotions to be involved but not to the exclusion of an awareness of the interweaving of the theme between the voices. But even while engaging the play-drive one still remains outside the music and independent of it. Thus, for Schiller, the aesthetic and the real domains have to remain separate.

Whilst this is so, it can also be argued that when contemplating a work of art, this interplay between the two natures of the rational and sensual parts of the mind can lead to greater integration of the personality and thus the contemplation could be said to have a moral influence.[10] On the other hand the separation between the aesthetic and the real will always leave open the possibility of the attainment of a better reality, which, expressed in political terms, suggests that art can provide an alternative way of changing an unsatisfactory regime into a satisfactory system without actual revolutionary action.

Although it could be said that Schiller has suggested a method which, with development, could point a way to uniting sensibility and rationality, his argument fails to be wholly convincing. Similarly his answer to the question of universality is incomplete, but, again, he makes a useful contribution. The fundamental question, however, which must still be asked (and indeed is

---

[10] See comments above on §59 (p. 27).

implicit in Schiller's objectives) is whether Schiller helps to point to a way in which art could be said to define truth. A reading of Schiller would suggest that in spite of the creation of the play-drive there is still too great a separation between art and reality, sensuality and reason, to enable art fully to describe truth; for a further development it is necessary to turn to Schelling and Hegel.

Schelling and Hegel were exact contemporaries and influenced each other. Hegel was the philosopher whose views completed the paradigm which began with Baumgarten. There would therefore be logic in dealing with Schelling before Hegel; however, as Schelling has written a specific philosophy of art, dealing with both theory and practice, and his ideas flow more naturally into the work of Runge, Carus and, indeed, the theme of this study, I will deal briefly with Hegel before examining the work of Schelling.

Hegel concludes the paradigm

Hegel's main claim to fame is probably concerned with social philosophy. His view of human nature led him to believe that communities would eventually come together in a benign symbiosis. One of his pupils was Karl Marx (1818–83), and it is unsurprising that the Hegelian approach eventually found favour in the foundation of communism. However, he also dealt quite fully with the subject of aesthetics in a series of lectures. The essence of his theory is set out in *Introductory Lectures on Aesthetics*.[11]

Hegel was influenced strongly by Johann Joachim Winckelmann (1717–68), of whom he wrote:

> by contemplation of the ideal works of the ancients, [Winckelmann] received a sort of inspiration, through which he opened a new sense for the study of art. He is to be regarded as one of those who, in the sphere of art, have known how to initiate a new organ for the human spirit.[12]

---

[11] Originally given as lectures, 1818–29.
[12] D. Irwin, *Winckelmann Writings on Art* (London: Phaidon Press, 1972), p. 50, quoting Hegel.

Winckelmann endeavoured to write a history of classical art, and whilst he had available Pliny's list of artists of the time and would have been aware from written histories of the contemporary social and political problems, his originality was in interpreting an ancient work of art purely from the work itself, without any accurate knowledge of the context within which the work had been produced.[13] In essence Winckelmann identified two modes in the analysis of the Greek ideal—the beautiful mode and the high mode. The beautiful mode was concerned with sensuality whereas the high mode was concerned with austerity. Winckelmann inspired Hegel and others 'because he succeeded in vividly presenting classic Greek sculpture as the visual embodiment of the larger values thought to be inherent in Greek culture as a whole'.[14]

Perhaps because of this influence, Hegel is from the outset concerned with created fine art; as he states:

> Fine art only achieves its highest task when it has taken its place in the same sphere with religion and philosophy, and has become simply a mode of revealing to consciousness and bringing to utterance the Divine Nature, the deepest interests of humanity, and the most comprehensive truths of the mind.[15]

(This definition would conform to categories two and three of Podro's theory outlined above.) Hegel's approach is both scientific and historical—intimating that in ancient Greek civilisation art was the only discipline sufficiently developed to aspire to the qualities set out above. Thereafter philosophy and theology gradually became better established and able to express views about the divine without the need for visual artistic representation—a position achieved, in his view, at the time of his writing. But it was important, Hegel emphasised, to remember

[13] For a succinct summary of Winckelmann's achievements see Prettejohn, *Beauty and Art*, pp. 15–22.

[14] A. Potts, *Flesh and the Ideal: Winckelmann and the Origin of Art History* (New Haven and London: Yale University Press, 1994), p. 20.

[15] *Ibid.*, p. 9.

that the 'truth of art remains in the senses; hence "appearance" does by no means signify a deception but, instead, the luminous emanation of the truth of essence [...] This is indeed the only function of art: to be one stage of the development of absolute spirit and to be the truth of this stage.'[16] In developing his ideas, Hegel refers to the work of Plato and his theoretical approach to the philosophic conception of the beautiful, and indicates that its true nature must contain 'reconciled within it, the two extremes [...] by combining metaphysical universality with the determinateness of real particularity.'[17] He then proposes his own system, which is very well described by Inwood: 'the philosophical system is concerned with logic, dealing with thought about the world; nature, dealing with thought about the natural world; and the philosophy of the mind or spirit.'[18] The philosophy of the mind is concerned with 'individual psychology; objective spirit, i.e. morality, social and economic institutions, the state and political history; and art, absolute spirit, religion and philosophy.'[19]

From the period of Greek civilisation onwards the last three have operated in parallel, with art, as mentioned above, originally in the ascendency. In developing his thought, Hegel adopts a teleological approach, where the artist, in continuing the creative force of the Absolute, is able, through his or her involvement with that force, to portray the development of that force. As Inwood suggests, 'art does not simply reveal God: it is one of the ways in which God reveals, and then actualizes, himself.'[20] Hegel's concept of God is worthy of note, as it impinges very much on the role of the artist:

> The solid unity which the God has in sculpture breaks up into the multitudinous inner lives of individuals, whose unity is not sensuous, but purely ideal. It is only in this stage that God Himself comes to be really and truly spirit in His (God's) community; for He here begins to be a to-

[16] Hammermeister, *The German Aesthetic Tradition*, p. 94.
[17] Hegel, *Introductory Lectures on Aesthetics*, p. 27.
[18] *Ibid.*, p. xiii.
[19] *Ibid.*, p. xiii.
[20] *Ibid.*, p. xviii.

and-fro, an alternation between His unity within himself and his realisation in the individual's knowledge and in its separate being, as also in the common nature and union of the multitude. In the community, God is released from the abstractness of unexpanded self-identity, as well as from the simple absorption in a bodily medium, by which sculpture represents Him. And He is thus exalted into spiritual existence and into knowledge, into the reflected appearance which essentially displays itself as inward and as subjectivity. Therefore the higher content is now the spiritual nature, and that in its absolute shape.[21]

In this line of thought Hegel seems to be presaging the work of twentieth-century existentialists, such as Rudolf Bultmann (1884–1976), Tillich and Macquarrie, and of the concept of God developed by Karl Rahner (1904–84), who devotes many pages to the self-realisation of God.[22] To describe the existential approach in any detail is beyond the scope of this work, but essentially, in existentialist metaphysics, God is realised through grace in the individual human being. Applying this to the visual arts, there is an ontologically dynamic relationship between the artist and God; as Martin Heidegger (1889–1976) expresses it—'The artist is the origin of the work. The work is the origin of the artist. Neither *is* without the other.'[23]

Continuing this line of thought and returning to Hegel, the work of art embraces the Idea, which he describes as both concept and the reality of the concept, and which can be applied to man in his totality—body and mind, and to the unified universe itself. The Idea, rather like the sublime, is very difficult to grasp at once, with its separate aspects emerging over time. As Inwood explains, 'each of the art forms (symbolism, classicism and romanticism) [...] corresponds to a different way of conceiving

---

[21] *Ibid.*, p. 92.
[22] Sallis, *Spacings of Reason and Imagination in Texts of Kant, Fichte, Hegel*; see particularly ch. 2, 'Man in the Presence of Absolute Mystery', which deals with man's relationship to his Transcendent Ground, pp. 24–43.
[23] J. Macquarrie, *Existentialism* (London: Penguin Books, 1972), p. 267, quoting Heidegger.

the Idea and, therefore the form in which the Idea appears'.[24] In order to clarify this, Hegel indicates that first the Idea gives rise to the beginning of Art (symbolic form); then Art in classical form fully embodies the Ideal—'is the first to afford the production and intuition of the completed Ideal, and to establish it as a realised fact', whilst the Romantic form dissolves this unity but in turn leads to 'concrete intellectual being which has the function of revealing itself as spiritual existence for the inward world of spirit'.[25] In summarising this, the essence of his philosophy of aesthetics, Hegel writes:

> We may take in the abstract the character of the symbolic, classical, and romantic forms of art, which represent the three relations of the Idea to its embodiment in the sphere of art. They consist in the aspiration after, and the attainment and transcendence of, the Ideal as the true Idea of beauty.[26]

I cannot complete this short section on Hegel without reference to his expostulation that, at the time of his writing, truth no longer found its expression in the visual arts; 'thought and reflection have overtaken beautiful art'.[27] Perhaps this should be regarded as setting art free from the particular philosophical constraints placed upon it by Hegel—thus art could be used as a means of expressing any of the categories described by Podro, including mimesis. While theology and philosophy had achieved greater sophistication at the time of Hegel and continued to do so after his death, there is no reason why art should not continue to strive towards spiritual truths, evolving new modes of expression— eventually to include abstract expressionism.

However, it can be seen that Hegel has closed a paradigm concerned with an analysis of art which began with Baumgarten. A new paradigm was then opened up by Schelling, Runge and Carus, descriptions of whose work will follow.

[24] Hegel, *Introductory Lectures on Aesthetics*, p. 177.
[25] *Ibid.*, pp. 84–7.
[26] *Ibid.*, p. 88.
[27] Hammermeister, *The German Aesthetic Tradition*, p. 102, quoting Hegel.

A new paradigm is opened by Schelling—Transcendental knowledge

The German Idealists, as we have seen, referred to a third type of knowledge—transcendental knowledge—and it is this type of knowledge to which Schelling paid particular attention. In so doing he was following in the footsteps of Fichte, a student of Kant. In addition, he considered the work of Baruch Spinoza (1632–77), a Dutch philosopher who set out his thesis, 'the rational science of the absolute', which developed the thought of Descartes, in a work entitled *Ethics* (1677).[28] Schelling developed his own ideas over a long period of correspondence with Hegel, Hölderlin, Schlegel and others. In deliberating how one may approach this transcendent branch of knowledge, Schelling considered the role of the mystic—who seeks 'annihilation in an absolute [which] is beyond all individuality and subjectivity'.[29] But he rejected this approach as somewhat limited; he saw a consideration of aesthetics and art as potentially more fruitful: 'The complete solution to transcendental idealism's highest problem is to be found, not in observation of nature, but only in observation of the work of art'.[30]

Schelling, one of the most influential philosophers of the Romantic period, produced few books and papers in his lifetime. His son eventually produced *Sämmtliche Werke (Collected Works* in 14 volumes) in 1856–61, and *Die Philosophie der Kunst (The Philosophy of Art)* in 1859, and it is to this latter work and to Schelling's elevation of the work of art that my attention is turned. In the discourse which follows, the works of art to which reference is made would comply particularly with Podro's category 3 as outlined in Chapter 1, but first I must say more about the concept of intellectual intuition—the term used rather negatively by Kant but developed in a positive sense by Fichte

---

[28] A. White, *Schelling: An Introduction to the System of Freedom* (New Haven: Yale University Press, 1983), p. 8.

[29] *Ibid.*, p. 34.

[30] *Ibid.*, p. 69, quoting Schelling.

and by Schelling. Essentially, intellectual intuition refers to the sensing, rather than the achievement, of knowledge by rational thought alone. The term is a difficult one to understand fully, but Robinson, writing in 1804, assists in its explanation.

Robinson was an enthusiastic follower of Schelling, recording, almost verbatim, aphorisms of that philosopher, and he was influential within the literary and artistic scene in Britain at that time. One important source of this influence can be found in Robinson's lectures prepared for the author of *D'Allemagne* (1810–13), Madame Germaine de Staël (1766–1817), a writer who, initially, had difficulty in relating to Schelling, thinking him obscure and mystical, lacking the clarity she expected of all philosophers. Robinson refers to the negativity of the philosophy of Kant with its insistence that 'all our knowledge is confined to that of things as they appear to us, not as they are in themselves'; he then explains that Schelling reverses the system in which Kant becomes 'entangled in the snares of speculative reason, has recourse to practical reason and throws himself into the arms of faith.'[31] I quote in full Robinson's explanation of the term 'intellectual intuition'—a concept of which both Palmer in Britain and Friedrich in Germany would have been aware:

> The Thing *as it is in itself* which Kant placed *before* him as the unattainable End of our Enquires, Schelling puts *behind* him as the starting post from which he sets out; pretending to *know* what Kant asserts can only be *believed.* Schelling calls it *the absolute* and *assumes* it, not as an abstract or general thought, but as a substance whose reality is immediately felt by the Mind. And he calls the consciousness of this being *intellectual intuition.* Schelling honestly declares I cannot prove this *absolute being*; it must be immediately felt [...] All Notions (Ideas generales) are grounded *on* Sensations, tho' not, as erroneously thought by Locke and his disciples, arising *out* of them. The *conception* of the relations of things is accompanied by a *sense* of the Things in which the relation exists. Without the intuition or sense of space, the mathematician would

---

[31] Vigus, *Essays on Kant*, p. 125, quoting Robinson.

be unable to think a single proposition: without an original organical Susceptibility of colour and sound, there could be no taste for painting and musick. Love is pure Sense [...] There lies in the mind an infinity of sensations and notions undeveloped, and all education and all instruction instead of being as—commonly conceived communication *from without* is but the awakening that which is *within*.[32]

Relating this theoretical approach to the more practical application, Schelling suggests that the universe is one coherent whole and that one great unifying law governs the process that maintains the continuance of creation.[33] This leads to one of the most important aphorisms of Schelling: 'The first of the two unities, that which constitutes the informing of the infinite into the finite, expresses itself within the work of art primarily as sublimity; the other, that which constitutes the informing of the finite into the infinite, as beauty'.[34] The genius of the artist is thus required to discern, through his or her intellectual intuition, the immensity of nature and to express that immensity in the work of art.

Hammermeister writes:

the work of art [...] represents not the empirical object but its idea [...] every object is presented as the epitome of its existence, a state where it has reached its *telos*. Art captures the perfect moment and lifts the object out of the flow of time, allowing it to become eternal in its preservation through art.[35]

This concept of art as expressing the idea or essence of a subject is set out by Schelling at the end of his introduction

[32] *Ibid.*, pp. 125–6. Robinson's italics and capitals.
[33] Whilst this is my own interpretation of both Schelling and Robinson, it also reflects the modern idea that there is a 'Unifying Theory of Everything'—a theory which scientists have sought throughout the past century.
[34] F. W. J. Schelling, *The Philosophy of Art*, ed. and trans. Douglas W. Scott (Minneapolis: University of Minneapolis Press, 1989), p. 85. (This work was published after Schelling's death by his son.)
[35] Hammermeister, *The German Aesthetic Tradition*, p. 79.

to *The Philosophy of Art*, where he writes: 'According to my entire understanding here, art is itself an emanation of the absolute.'[36] In Schelling's philosophy the absolute is equated with God and the artist has a revelatory role, as set out in the *System of Transcendental Idealism* (1804), whereby he or she is required to unite in a work of art, through inspired intellectual intuition, the objective and the idea underlining its existence. Alone amongst the philosophers of the period Schelling elevated art to its high point, suggesting that its takes precedence over all other disciplines:

> Art is therefore the Highest to the philosopher, because as it were it opens the most holy where in eternal and primary union burns as if in one flame what is separated in nature and history and what must flee each other in life and act as well in thought.[37]

This is similar to the idea that the artist can be regarded as co-creator or, as B. M. G. Reardon summarises very succinctly in an endnote in his *Religion in an Age of Romanticism*, emphasising Schlegel's influence on Schelling, 'he [Schelling] treats of the metaphysical significance of art as the finite manifestation of the Absolute, for art, he maintains, is the eternal Idea pictorialized by the imagination.'[38]

In other words truth in nature (science) and philosophy can only be found through the unifying influence of art—a synthesis of the real and the ideal. Here, there is a clear distinction (similar to that drawn by Robinson above) between Kant and Schelling inasmuch as Kant believed that the transcendental faculties of the mind are 'not to be confused with the objects through which they become conscious of themselves' whereas for Schelling the 'ideal of absolute can and does appear within things in the

[36] Schelling, *The Philosophy of Art*, p. 19.
[37] Hammermeister, *The German Aesthetic Tradition*, quoting Schelling, *System of Transcendental Idealism* (Hamburg: Meiner, 1992), p. 475.
[38] B. M. G. Reardon, *Religion in an Age of Romanticism* (Cambridge: Cambridge University Press, 1985), p. 276, note 58.

world.'[39] In this way Schelling is very clear that there should be no distinction between Kant's noumenal (things that are thought) and the phenomenal (things that appear). In this sense of the action of two forces which Hegel referred to as dialectic there is a link back to the philosophy of Plotinus (204–70 CE), a philosophy which the German Idealists called Neoplatonism—the action of all things coming out of nature and of all things returning to nature.[40] As Hammermeister emphasises:

> Schelling's Neo-platonic aesthetics define art and truth as two different perspectives on the absolute. An object is beautiful when it is so adequate to its idea that the infinite (the concept) enters the real. In fewer words, in beauty the real becomes ideal [...] The work of art is not identical with the idea, but is the reflection of the idea. Its beauty is not an achievement of the artist; rather, it is due to the reflecting quality of the infinite that is characterised by truth and beauty.[41]

In this context beauty may be considered as the splendour of God. Examining that which is actually happening in this process, the artist's sensual perception is encountering an emanation of the absolute and is then using his or her intellectual intuition to interpret in a work of art that transcendent force. Then the work of art in interacting with the receptive imagination of the listener (in the case of music) or the viewer (in the case of visual art) endeavours to reveal that transcendence. Whereas Schiller creates the concept of drives to endeavour to bring out the transcendent, Schelling insists that it is only the genius artist who is able to elucidate the eternal truths, and in a passage that has existentialist overtones he writes:

> *This eternal concept of the human being in God as the immediate cause of his productions is that which one calls*

---

[39] Schelling, *The Philosophy of Art*, p. xi.
[40] For a summary of the meaning and origin of Neoplatonism see T. Honderich, *The Oxford Companion to Philosophy* (Oxford: Oxford University Press, 2005), p. 648b.
[41] Hammermeister, *The German Aesthetic Tradition*, p. 81.

genius, as it were the daemon, the in-dwelling element of
divinity in human beings. It is so to speak, a piece of the
absoluteness of God. Each artist can thus produce only
as much as is united or allied with the eternal concept of
his own essence in God. The more within that essence in
and for itself the universe is intuited, the more organic
he is; the more he links finitude to infinitude, the more
productive will he be.[42]

Endeavouring to ground this philosophical language in the
practice of art, Schelling devotes the second part of his *Philosophy
of Art* to describing the 'construction of the forms of art.'[43]
It is beyond the scope of this chapter to summarise the whole
of this major work, but essentially it is concerned with the way
in which the infinite may be expressed within the finite. He
deals first of all with music, with harmony, melody and rhythm
expressing the harmony of the whole cosmos, suggesting that
'the forms of music as the forms of ideas viewed concretely are
also the forms of the being and life of the cosmic bodies as such;
hence, music is nothing other than the perceived rhythm and
harmony of the visible universe itself.'[44] This concept, originating
with Pythagoras (571–495 BCE), who was concerned to identify
a link between music, mathematics and the cosmos, has been
much used by composers over the ages—the *Ode to St Cecilia*
(1739) by George Frederick Handel (1685–1759), the oratorio
The Creation (1796–8) by Joseph Haydn (1732–1809) and the
suite *The Planets* (1914–16) by Gustav Holst (1874–1934) come
immediately to mind, as well as some of the more modern pieces
of music inspired by the prospect of space travel.[45]
    Beginning his section on visual art, Schelling's starting point is
the nature of light and the effect that it may have on the body. He
then makes the link between gravity and light: 'It is gravity that
reappears here in the higher potence, the absolute identity that,

[42] Schelling, *The Philosophy of Art*, p. 84. Schelling's italics.
[43] *Ibid.*, pp. 107 ff.
[44] *Ibid.*, p. 116.
[45] For a detailed article on this theme see Gillian More, writing in the *Guardian*, 3 July 2010.

be it in reflection or in refraction unites light and corporeality.'[46] (This may seem to be a linkage that is somewhat forced, but, of course, current thinking would see the link between the four fundamental forces of electromagnetism, weak and strong nuclear forces and gravity, so perhaps Schelling was ahead of his time.)[47] Schelling's next stage is to assert that light synthesised with corporeality is obscured light, or colour, which leads to his statement that: 'Light can appear as light only in opposition or contrast to non-light, and hence only as colour.'[48] Then, dismissing Newton's theory of colour as largely irrelevant so far as the artist is concerned, Schelling highlights the dependence of painting on the demonstration of contrast and of space. The artist can 'portray nothing without simultaneously portraying in the painting itself the space in which the object is found.'[49] He compares the two arts of music and painting to arithmetic and geometry, with the latter requiring space external to the particular figure under consideration. He then develops the thought that in painting all the forms of unity—the real, the ideal and the indifference

---

[46] Schelling, *The Philosophy of Art*, p. 121. It should be noted that 'potence' is Douglas Scott's translation of the German *Potenz*, which, as Vigus notes, preserves but does not choose between its connotations of 'potential, exponential and power'. Vigus continues 'According to Schelling, the absolute is an indivisible essence. All specific, distinct phenomena are thus to be conceived not as component parts, but as potential manifestations of the one absolute. Schelling sometimes employs the image of emanation, developed by the Neoplatonist philosopher Plotinus, to conceive this emergence of particularity from the one, undifferentiated absolute. Viewed in relation to the absolute, then, any particular phenomenon is something that is posited as a potence.' Vigus, *Essays on Kant*, pp. 64–5.

[47] The link with light here is that as an electron moves from one energy level to another, light in the form of a photon is emitted or absorbed. For a detailed discussion of this see any book on modern quantum mechanics or, for an approach designed for the general reader, see G. Miles, *Science and Religious Experience* (Eastbourne: Sussex Academic Press, 2007), pp. 84 ff.

[48] Schelling, *The Philosophy of Art*, p. 121.

[49] *Ibid.*, p. 127.

of the two—occur and are represented in drawing, chiaroscuro and colouring. He emphasises the importance of drawing in elevating beauty above all sensuality—'only through drawing is painting actually art, just as only through colour is painting actually painting'.[50] Schelling highlights Raphael and Antonio da Correggio (1489–1534) as two of the greatest masters in drawing, in chiaroscuro and in their treatment of colour. In particular he draws attention to *La Notte* (1529–30) by Correggio, where, arising from the magical use of chiaroscuro, 'an immortal light, emanating from a child, mystically and mysteriously illuminates the dark night'.[51] The fusing of light and dark is such that they become '*one* body and *one* soul'.[52] In this painting, by the skilled use of light the artist is surely endeavouring to demonstrate both the immanence (through the mother and child) and transcendence (through the angels above) of the absolute—or, as Schelling would put it, expressing the infinite within the finite.

Schelling emphasises that art has a number of stages concerning the relationship of light to the objects portrayed—the stages are either 'external, inflexible or inorganic or internal, flexible and organic'.[53] The first stage might be an inorganic still life where we may have insight into the mind or spirit of the person who decided upon the particular arrangement. The second stage, where the colours are external and organic, might be a flower painting, where 'to the extent that it were possible to express enough significance through the positioning of flowers such that an inner condition or disposition really were recognisable there, this kind of picture would be suitable for allegory'.[54] The third stage, flexible, organic and external, may well be animal painting, where the artist can bring out 'the symbolic significance of the figures themselves through energetic, strong portrayal, or through higher associations'.[55]

[50] *Ibid.*, p. 109.
[51] *Ibid.*, p. 137.
[52] *Ibid.*, p. 138.
[53] *Ibid.*, p. 143.
[54] *Ibid.*, p. 144.
[55] *Ibid.*

Regarding his approach to landscape painting, where light is externally inorganic yet flexible and living, Schelling writes:

> Landscape painting necessarily concerns itself with empirical truth, and the ultimate of which it is capable is to use precisely *this* empirical truth itself as a covering through which it allows a higher kind of truth to manifest itself [...] The true object, the idea, remains formless, and it is up to the observer to discover it from within the fragrant, formless essence before him [...] It can awaken ideas, or rather spirits of ideas, and, often, before our very eyes, it lifts the *veil* that conceals the invisible world from us [...] Everything in it depends on (light and) the arts of aerial perspective and thus on the completely empirical character of chiaroscuro.[56]

Schelling then discusses modes of representation—to represent the absolute or infinite there are only two options: either allegorical or symbolic. An allegorical representation would be a depiction of something under the guise of something else which is nonetheless appropriate as a means of conveying a message. By this means the artist can depict such sins as sloth or virtues such as generosity. An example Schelling cites is *Slander by Apelles* (1494)—a theme depicted by Sandro Botticelli (1445–1510) in which Fraud, Conspiracy, Repentance etc. are all shown by representative people exhibiting traits from which can be deduced their names.[57] Another example from Friedrich would be *Morning in the Riesengebirge* (1810–11), where the woman representing faith is drawing the traveller up the mountain 'along the narrow and difficult path which leadeth unto life'.[58]

A symbolic painting 'not only signifies or means the idea, *but is itself the idea*'.[59] The object portrayed can be either 'something

---

[56] *Ibid.*, pp. 144–5.
[57] See Calumny of Apelles (Botticelli) in Google images, and various web-based articles including a reprint of the description of the original painting.
[58] W. Hofmann, *Caspar David Friedrich* (London: Thames and Hudson, 2000), pp. 101–2 and p. 286 (the quotation is to be found on p. 286).
[59] Schelling, *The Philosophy of Art*, p. 151.

universally human that perpetually recurs and renews itself in life, or refer to a completely spiritual and intellectual idea [...] [such as] Raphael's *The School of Athens*, a painting to which reference has already been made.[60] Any image of Christ would be regarded as symbolic since it represents the 'completely unique identity of divine and human nature'.[61] Schelling concludes his section on painting with a list of aphorisms which arise from his consideration of the subject. Essentially, his argument is that painting is very well suited to express the infinite within the finite but is dependent on the skill (genius) of the artist and receptivity of the observer.

He then turns his attention to the plastic arts—sculpture and architecture. I will give only the briefest summary of this aspect of Schelling's analysis, as this book is concerned in essence with the way in which the numinous (the absolute) may be depicted in drawing and painting. Sculptors express their ideas through real bodily objects and within the real three-dimensional form portray the 'essence and the ideal of things, and accordingly the highest indifference of essence and form'.[62] Sculptures are nearly always symbolic as they possess both form and essence (idea) and are therefore very well placed to express the unity of the absolute. Sculptures of the human figure have a particular symbolic significance—and are 'a mediating agent insofar as he [the human being] originally was placed between fluid and hard elements'.[63] For example, Schelling suggests the head represents the heavens and particularly the sun, the breast the transition from heaven to earth and the cavity of the body the vault that heaven forms over the earth and so on. From this analysis he derives an argument that the human figure is an image of the universe, and hence

> a perfect conducting medium of the expressions of the soul, and since art as such, and sculpture in particular,

---

[60] *Ibid.*, p. 151.
[61] *Ibid.*
[62] *Ibid.*, p. 162.
[63] *Ibid.*, p. 185.

must portray ideas that are in fact elevated above matter, and yet must do so through external appearance, there is no object better suited to the formative arts than the human figure, the direct impression or copy of the soul and of reason.[64]

This exultation of the human form is echoed in a later century by Kenneth Clark, who refers to the nude 'as a means of expression [...] of universal and eternal value'.[65] In fact in *The Nude* Clark examines in some detail the way in which the human form has been used to express many of the conditions, such as pathos, to which Schelling refers.

To summarise, then, in Schelling's approach to the importance and significance of art we have the opening up of a new paradigm compared with the position of Hegel, whose work could be said to have closed the paradigm which began with Baumgarten. Far from the history of art coming to an end, in Schelling we have the importance of art, as a means of gaining insight into the role and purpose of existence, raised to new heights.

[64] *Ibid.*, p. 187.
[65] K. Clark, *The Nude: A Study of Ideal Art* (London: The Reprint Society, 1958), p. 7.

3

The Art Theories of
Philipp Runge and Carl Gustav Carus

Philipp Runge, a contemporary of Caspar David Friedrich, was a significant figure in German Romanticism. He wrote extensively on art theory as well as producing a significant body of drawings and paintings. In this chapter I am concerned only with his theory—the iconography of Runge and Friedrich will be examined in a subsequent chapter. For Runge, his Protestant Christianity was of the utmost importance and he endeavoured to integrate in his work both mysticism and Christian thought. He was also very aware of the influence of Classicism in paintings of his time and endeavoured to effect a change towards 'non-homocentric or Christian landscape art, as he called it.'[1] This art 'would formulate a new animistic symbolism, one based on nature's own and universally known elements and standing in close analogy to the artist's personal, deeply felt, intuited wonder at God's creation.'[2] In other words Runge wished to replace anthropomorphic Christian art with an art based on nature and landscape.[3]

He was enthusiastic about the integration of the traditionally separate disciplines of science, philosophy and art, and his art theory was designed for art students (not philosophers) as a pedagogical set of principles which embraced those disciplines. He summarised his ten-point programme (or, as Bisanz described it, manifesto) as follows:

[1] R. M. Bisanz, *German Romanticism and Philipp Otto Runge* (DeKalb: Northern Illinois Press, 1970), p. 126.
[2] *Ibid.*, p. 126.
[3] In his practice Runge only partially achieved this change, as will be discussed in a later chapter.

1. Our presentiment of God,
2. the perception of ourselves in connection with the whole,
3. religion and art; that is to express our highest feelings through words, tones or pictures; and here then visual art seeks first:
4. the subject; then 5. the composition, 6. the drawing,
7. the disposition of local colour, 8. aerial perspective,
9. colour value, and 10. tone.[4]

As Vaughan makes clear, this theory was not entirely original, being influenced by both Johann Jakob Heinse (1749–1803) and Johann Ludwig Tieck (1773–1853), who wrote on the burgeoning importance of landscape painting, and by the pantheistic writings of his teacher Ludwig Gotthard Kosegarten (1758–1818).[5] The originality came from the way in which he expressed his theory and his particular approach to the concept of God. In addition, parallels can be seen with the Podro theory set out at the beginning of Chapter 1, and especially criterion 1, the revealing of an aspect of a subject that would not be obvious. Examining first Runge's presentiment of God or 'consciousness of ourselves and our eternity', we have what would, I believe, later come to be identified as an existentialist viewpoint. As Runge expresses it:

> This deepest divination that God is above us, this living soul within us which derives from Him and returns to Him, this is the surest and most distinct consciousness of ourselves and our eternity.[6]

The parallel here with the viewpoint of Schelling is quite marked; it is unsurprising to learn that Runge maintained correspondence with that philosopher. In one such letter Runge writes, after referring to the study of the ancients and development of all the stages of art, that 'it cannot help the artist at all if he does not arrive at, or is not brought to view the present moment of

---

[4] Bisanz, *German Romanticism*, pp. 52–3, quoting Runge.
[5] W. Vaughan, *German Romanticism and English Art* (London: Yale University Press, 1979), pp. 41–3.
[6] Bisanz, *German Romanticism*, p. 49, quoting Runge.

his existence with all its pains and pleasures.'[7] This existentialist approach leads readily into point 2 of the Runge programme, which shows the influence of the sixteenth-century physician and mystic Paracelsus (Philippus Aureolus Theophrastus Bombastus von Hohenheim, 1493–1541), who developed a Neoplatonic holistic system of mysticism which suggested that 'as we know nature since we are nature, we know God since we are God.'[8] Endeavouring to cut through the complexity and to a certain extent irrelevant writings of Jakob Boehme (1575–1624), who was influenced by Paracelsus, Bisanz emphasises that it is the spirit of Boehme 'which makes all things possible to the imagination'. Runge, in explaining his point 2, writes:

> We feel that something relentlessly strict and terribly eternal is locked in the most violent battle with a sweet and infinite love, as something hard and soft, as rocks and water. The rougher this opposition becomes the farther away each thing departs from perfection and the more they unite the closer each thing comes to its perfection.[9]

Runge is suggesting that the artist, when experiencing this moment of transcendence or ecstasy, should endeavour to capture and communicate that transcendence using the 'universal common mould of meaningful symbols.'[10]

In point 3 of the programme we have a uniting of points 1 and 2—linking through to the practice of art as expressed in the remaining seven points, which are all fairly clear, with the possible exception of point 4, the choice of subject. Runge is emphatic that the choice of subject must be that of the artist; this is all part of the communication of the transcendence of God.

Whilst it is acknowledged that much of the above has been expressed previously, for example by Schelling, the significance is that Runge has summarised the theory for students of art, combining an existential approach to the transcendent with

---

[7] *Ibid.*, p. 48, quoting Runge.
[8] J. Bowden, *Who's Who in Theology* (London: SCM Press, 1992), p. 96.
[9] Bisanz, *German Romanticism*, p. 49, quoting Runge.
[10] *Ibid.*

some practical suggestions for its achievement. Point 3 marks the transition from theory to practice and is, perhaps, the most difficult to elucidate, but if combined with Kant's concept of the genius artist and the thought that the artist could be regarded as co-creator, the process towards which Runge is leading us becomes somewhat clearer. It is not known whether or not Runge was read widely during the nineteenth century, but his programme could possibly have influenced Kandinsky and Mondrian, who both wrote their own theories on the spiritual in art at the time of another significant change, when art entered the world of abstraction.

This following quotation demonstrates not only Runge's view of the eternal God but also illustrates his poetic use of language; it makes a fitting end to this section on Runge:

> When the sky above me abounds with countless stars [...] and I fling myself upon the grass under the glittering drops of dew, each leaf and each blade of grass teems with life, the earth lives and stirs beneath me, all resounds together in a single chord, then the soul jubilates aloud and soars into the boundless space around me, and there is no below and no above, no time, no beginning and no end, I hear and feel the living breath of God who holds and carries the world, in whom all lives and works: here is the highest that we divine—God![11]

Carus and the Nine Letters

Carl Gustav Carus was a philosopher, scientist and amateur artist, who, as a friend of Friedrich, became very interested in the use of landscape painting to express the numinous, eventually writing *Nine Letters on Landscape Painting* between 1815 and 1824. Schelling, Carl Fernow and Johann Wolfgang von Goethe (1749–1832) were major influences (as they were for Robinson and Coleridge), leading to Carus writing on philosophy and on Goethe himself. Most of Carus's extensive writings on Nature and

---

[11] *Ibid.*, p. 48, quoting Runge.

Idea, Symbolism of the Human Form and a biography of Goethe, to mention but a few, are only available in German. Fortunately, *Nine Letters on Landscape Painting* has been translated by David Britt (*c*. 1940–2002) and published with a major introduction by Oskar Bätschmann.[12]

Evidence of the influence of Schelling is immediately confirmed by Bätschmann, who, quoting from Carus's memoirs, writes:

> There appeared in these letters a curious blend of science and art, and it is this, if anything, that will give them a lasting place in literature. What Schelling was trying to express at that time through the concept of the *world soul* was precisely the cardinal point around which these thoughts revolved.[13]

Carus studied medicine at Leipzig University, where he became captivated by nature philosophy and its concern with the 'ineluctable connection of the cosmic edifice into a single, endless, organic whole—in a word, the idea of world soul.'[14] From his school-days, Carus was interested in painting, and on submitting four paintings to the Dresden Kunstakademie in 1816 he met Friedrich for the first time. Friedrich became and remained a close friend. Carus was particularly struck by Friedrich's approach to landscape, being especially impressed by how its 'mordant melancholy' raised landscape painting to a new level to embrace a 'radiant poetic tendency.'[15] The other significant, though not greatly acknowledged, influence on Carus was Fernow, who wrote on landscape painting during the years 1803–6. Fernow's approach to landscape painting suggested that at its best it had poetic qualities and was even akin to music, and was not limited in the manner of history painting. Referring to this limitation of history painting

---

[12] C. G. Carus, *Nine Letters on Landscape Painting*, with introduction by Oskar Bätschmann (Los Angeles: Getty Publications, 2002).

[13] *Ibid.*, p. 1. Bätschmann, quoting from *Lebenserinnerungen und Denkwürdigkeiten* (Leipzig: Brockhaus, 1865–6).

[14] *Ibid.*, p. 1.

[15] *Ibid.*, p. 3.

or 'dramatic painting' that is of value for the onlooker only, Bätschmann writes that in landscape painting:

> No such limitation exists; viewers find themselves inside the natural scene depicted, because the painting puts them into an 'aesthetic mood'. Fernow ascribed this effect not to the content or the specific objects in the picture but entirely to the total 'impression on the mind'. Herein lies the affinity between landscape painting and music: 'a beautiful landscape is steeped in a harmony of colours that affects the mind in much the same way as melody and harmony in music'. The term 'total impression' was taken up by Humboldt and used by Carus, who also referred to the affinity between landscape painting and music without mentioning Fernow's name.[16]

The remainder of this section will be concerned with the Nine Letters themselves; for a short summary of Carus's life, the reader is referred to Bätschmann's introduction to the *Nine Letters on Landscape Painting*.[17]

The Nine Letters fall into three parts, categorised in 1995 by Jutta Müller-Tamm; the first three letters are characterised as 'early Romantic' (a term with which I have sympathy, particularly in view of the flowery mode of expression, but with which Bätschmann disagreed), the next two are about style and the history of landscape painting, with the final four being concerned with landscape painting of the future based on science, under the new name of *Erdleben-Bildkunst* (earth-life painting).[18] It should be remembered that within the scientific world at this time there was an interest in classification—of plants (begun in *c.* 1730 and completed in 1758) by Carl Linnaeus (1707–78) and of clouds (1802) by Luke Howard (1772–1864), and throughout the

---

[16] *Ibid.*, p. 23. Alexander von Humboldt (1769–1859) was a geographer and explorer, who following his expedition to South America published *Ansichten der Natur* (Views of Nature) (1808), which influenced Carus. The two eventually met in Dresden in 1826 (see Carus, *Nine Letters on Landscape Painting*, p. 11).

[17] *Ibid.*, pp. 1–47.

[18] *Ibid.*, p. 36

nineteenth century with the establishment of the periodic table of the chemical elements.[19] Carus entered into this methodological way of thinking when writing his letters, and whilst this *Zeitgeist* permeates the letters generally, the particular interest in cloud classification comes to the fore in letter 6, where Carus refers to Goethe's papers on natural science and the anonymous poem *Howard's Ehrengedächtnis.*[20]

Taking the letters in the order in which they were written and highlighting those elements that are particularly relevant to this study, letter 1 evokes the winter-time atmosphere in which it was written; it is a Romantic Odyssean essay on the relationship between nature and science, painting and poetry, architecture and the harmony of sounds. Carus summarises this letter as indicating that he traces the 'free, poetic impulse at the point where it begins to assume a form and enter life as a work of art' through to the point where it 'expresses itself through the proportional relationships of speech music and solid mass' (architecture).[21]

In the second letter he examines in some detail the purpose and significance of landscape painting. He emphasises that landscape art can affect the viewer in two ways:

> *First, through the nature of the object depicted,* which will affect us in an image very much as it does in reality; and *second, insofar as the work of art is a creation of the human mind, which, by truthfully manifesting its thoughts* (just as in a higher sense, the universe may be called a manifestation of divine thoughts), elevates a kindred spirit above the common ground.[22]

By the use of the expression 'kindred spirit' Carus is here expressing a viewpoint which is very similar to Podro's third criterion.

---

[19] The development of the periodic table was begun by Antoine Lavoisier (1743–94) in 1789 and 'completed' with the known elements of that time by Dmitri Mendeleev (1834–1907) in 1869. See Royal Society of Chemists website: http://www.rsc.org/periodic-table/history/about

[20] *Ibid.*, p. 113.

[21] *Ibid.*, p. 85.

[22] *Ibid.*, p. 86. Carus's italics.

The third and final 'Romantic' letter endeavours to summarise the first two and, engaging with his interest and expertise in psychology, provides an overall conclusion regarding the reception of a work of art by the viewer—the kindred spirit.

This third letter is supplemented by three short essays on beauty. First, he defines beauty as that which makes us feel the divine essence in nature and the 'perfect interpenetration of reason and nature.'[23] Second, he writes on the inducing of particular moods. Third, he deals with the relationship between mental moods and natural states. Developing the ideas of the first two letters, he emphasises that the work of art is a product of the human creative mind, which, translated to landscape painting, means that the natural landscape must be 'apprehended and depicted from an aspect that coincides exactly with the inner mood in question', and as this meaning 'is conveyed solely through the depiction of objects, its articulation depends on the right choice of subject.'[24] Carus then concludes that the task of landscape painting is to represent 'a certain mood of mental life (meaning)' through the reproduction of a 'corresponding mood of natural life (truth).'[25] This is very similar to the approach of Schelling—the idea of the artist's sensual perception encountering an emanation of the Absolute and then using his or her intellectual intuition to interpret in a work of art that transcendent force. Then, through the work, the artist, in interacting with the receptive imagination of the viewer, endeavours to reveal that transcendence. In these first three letters, I do not sense that Carus is extending the philosophy of Schelling but is expressing the Schellingian concepts in an alternative way, which provides a useful perspective on that philosopher's approach to landscape art, and may well have been helpful to other artists of the time, although I have not come across any evidence of this influence other than the known discussions with Friedrich.

[23] *Ibid.*, p. 92.
[24] *Ibid.*, pp. 92–8.
[25] *Ibid.*, p. 95.

Letters 4 and 5 are concerned with style and history; they are largely factual and hence scarcely need summarising in this book.

Letter 6 waxes loquacious about the beauty and majesty of clouds, and emphasises the advantage to the artist of being steeped in scientific knowledge of that which he or she is depicting:

> Surely an artist steeped in the knowledge of the wonderful reciprocities of earth and fire and sea and air will speak more powerfully to us through his work; he will more purely and more freely unlock the viewer's soul [...] [that the viewer] may understand that the motions of clouds and the form of mountains, the outlines of trees and the waves of the sea are not random, chance events, but that all this has a higher, indwelling purpose and eternal meaning. For these things are the handiwork of that spirit who says of himself:
> I ply the whirring loom of Time And weave the living robe of God.[26]

This is a very interesting statement as it prompts the question: is the artist who has no scientific knowledge less able to depict landscape in a way that suggests transcendence than one who has scientific knowledge? My own view is that the artist needs to have a feeling for, and love of, nature, but that a detailed knowledge is not nearly so necessary as the ability to convey that inner feeling or sense of the divine through the skill of his or her artistry. Furthermore, scientific knowledge, as mentioned earlier, always has a certain provisionality, as I might suggest through the example of the atmosphere and cloud formation. Over recent years the Meteorological Office staff have developed computer modelling of the atmosphere to a level beyond that which might have been conceived even ten years ago, let alone at the time of Carus. But even with the knowledge gained from this sophisticated equipment capable of undertaking millions of calculations a second, the behaviour of the atmosphere is still only partially understood, with accurate

---

[26] *Ibid.*, pp. 114–15.

forecasting limited to approximately one week. So, to rephrase the question, would an artist-meteorologist be able better to portray the divine intelligence behind all creation than the non-scientist artist who nonetheless has an intuitive understanding of that creative force? I think the answer to this question can only be: probably not. Certainly, we know that Friedrich was opposed to the thought, put to him by both Goethe and Carus, that he should study Luke Howard's classification of the clouds. His reply was that to 'allow himself to be coerced into such categorizations would entirely undermine the art of landscape painting.'[27] I believe that Friedrich was exaggerating here to emphasise his disagreement with the proposition—I fail to see how the acquisition of such knowledge would diminish the landscape artist's ability to depict the encounter of his sensual perception with an emanation of the Absolute. No doubt Blake, who felt that the artist only had need of his imagination, would have been in full agreement with Friedrich.

The theme of letter 7 is to enhance the views expressed in letter 6, emphasising that Carus is not insisting that landscape should have a didactic purpose but that such works should have 'a new and distinctive effect on the mind of the viewer.'[28] After quoting a number of poetic descriptions of landscape, Carus then reveals his dislike of the word 'landscape', suggesting that *Erdleben-Bild* or *Erdleben-Bildkunst* (earth-life painting or earth-life art) would be more appropriate. He feels that this expression gives a much better sense that such paintings should suggest a living world, a world populated by people, and even suggests that these paintings should always include 'human figures expressive of life in the midst of nature.'[29] Whether or not landscape paintings should always include human figures is debatable—Schelling states that such figures must be portrayed as visitors or autochthonous (indigenous) people in a landscape, combined in such a way that the 'unique feelings attendant on

[27] *Ibid.*, p. 36.
[28] *Ibid.*, p. 117.
[29] *Ibid.*, p. 119.

our conceptions of such juxtaposition can be elicited'.[30] To take an example, Friedrich's *Monk by the Sea* (1809) would lose most of its meaning without the lonely isolated person on the seashore, but on the other hand the empty *Landscape in the Riesengebirge with Mist Rising* (1820–1) is effective in endeavouring to suggest that which lies beyond the veil of mist.

Before leaving letter 7, one further stricture needs comment. Carus suggests that to avoid 'an inner contradiction, earth-life paintings should not contain newly built, sharp-edged or freshly painted buildings'.[31] Friedrich seems to follow this suggestion, with the exception of *Landscape with Pavilion* (1797), but in Carus's favour I would say that the suggestion of transcendence is (rarely for Friedrich) not a strong feature of this painting.

In letter 8, Carus begins with a diatribe against the poor rendering of landscape by the amateur, exacerbated by the lack of attention given to the subject by the Academy. He emphasises the need for the training of both the eye and the hand; the eye 'must be opened to the true and wondrous life of nature, and the hand must be trained to do the soul's bidding, quickly, easily, and beautifully'.[32] He sees these qualities as being attained through the careful observance of shape and form on the one hand and of diversity on the other, and this observance, he argues, is rendered easier by a scientific knowledge of the laws on nature. He justifies this approach by comparing favourably a mountain formation drawn by a geologist with that drawn by an experienced artist and then emphasises that a drawing of any plant or animal will be better when produced by someone who really knows that animal or plant. The validity of this stricture depends on the meaning ascribed to the word 'know'. If we take the example of a horse, then one who looks after and rides that horse will develop and attain a natural affinity with that animal and will certainly know that animal. The question is whether or not a skilled artist can attain that same knowledge by observation

[30] Schelling, *The Philosophy of Art*, p. 146.
[31] Carus, *Nine Letters on Landscape Painting*, p. 119.
[32] *Ibid.*, p. 125.

alone; in answering that question I would say that if the resulting painting is going to convey some inner spiritual quality possessed by that animal then the owner/rider will have the advantage. But that owner/rider will also have to be a very competent painter to render the result meaningful. So, my argument would be that whilst scientific knowledge of the subject of a painting can be a great advantage, the attainment of a high level of competency in the artist is essential if a landscape painting is to exhibit those qualities of showing the divine essence in natural phenomena.

The remainder of this long letter consists of practical instruction that is necessary for the budding landscape artist in order that he or she may eventually achieve the desired result. Carus concludes:

> When the soul is saturated with the inner meaning of all these different forms; when it has clear intimations of the mysterious, divine life of nature; when the hand has taught itself to represent securely, and the eye to see purely and acutely; and when the artist's heart is purely and entirely a consecrated, joyous vessel in which to receive the light from above: then there will infallibly be earth-life paintings, of a new and higher kind, which will uplift the viewer into a higher contemplation of nature. These works will truly deserve to be named mystic and orphic; and earth-life painting will have attained its culmination.[33]

In the ninth and final letter, written nine years after the first, and returning in style to the rather flowery Romantic mode of expression of the first three letters, Carus refers again to his strong suggestion that the artist needs a scientific knowledge of the laws of nature. However, in this letter he expresses the view that the artist who expresses the numinous through his work is likely to be misunderstood and, as he writes, 'self-abnegation is the lot of any artist whose heart is in landscape painting, in the higher sense of the term.'[34] Such an artist would be unable to derive a living from art alone and Carus recommends the

---

[33] *Ibid.*, p. 131.
[34] *Ibid.*, p. 134.

development of another activity that could bring in an income, quoting Rousseau, who copied music for just that purpose.

To conclude this section on Carus, the most important and original contribution to the philosophy of art is his emphasis on the view that the artist really needs a scientific knowledge of the laws of nature if he or she is to produce earth-life paintings that depict the encounter of his or her sensual perception with an emanation of the absolute. My view, as argued above, is that while this knowledge may well help the artist, for most this is an unattainable level of perfection—it is even more important that the artist has a sensitivity or feeling for nature that enables the suggestion of the divine essence to be intimated within the earth-life painting. Apart from this scientific emphasis, the other themes of Carus's letters reflect the philosophy of Schelling but expressed in his own language, which was, in itself, a valuable contribution to scholarship at that time.

At the time of their publication (1831) the *Nine Letters on Landscape Painting* were not particularly well received, or, perhaps, understood. Bätschmann refers to the favourable reception by the theologian and art critic Karl Grüneisen (1802–78), but even he felt that Carus had been unduly dismissive of the great historical landscapes.[35] I believe that if Carus had not felt the need to introduce the alternative (more scientific) name for landscape he would have been better received, because it is the use of this term which seems to detract from the important message of the Letters. The final ignominy came with the publication in 1848 of a caricature by Moritz von Schwind (1804–71), showing anthropomorphic trees and vegetation; thereafter earth-life as a concept seems to have been buried.[36] Carus's other publications on psychology and Goethe seem to have been viewed positively, so perhaps it is because Carus was an amateur painter that his letters on the philosophy of landscape art were not well received. Bätschmann points out that *Psyche*

---

[35] *Ibid.*, p. 45.
[36] *Ibid.*, p. 47; von Schwind was later to become professor at the Munich Academy.

(1846) which mediates between 'Schelling's world soul theory and the psychoanalysis of Freud' enabled Carus to be one of the precursors of depth psychology.[37]

Summary

These first three chapters represent a very short summary of the currency of thoughts on aesthetics just before and during the period when Samuel Palmer and Caspar David Friedrich were practising their art. Art at this time was beginning to be free from some of the conventions of the past, with the break with the Academy being led, among others, by William Blake, whose influence on Palmer will be described later. Some artists were using this freedom to produce work that was free from history, ranging from the political, the moral, and the spiritual to memorials for the future (e.g. portraits). Artists considered in this book, such as Palmer, Runge and Friedrich, endeavoured to produce works which in the words of Schelling were 'united or allied with the eternal concept of his own essence in God'.

Following the acceptance of Descartes's expostulation that philosophy should be separated from theology, Baumgarten established the discipline of aesthetics and a role for art. Blake (in England) and Kant (in Germany) then developed this discipline, with Kant's views being the historically more influential. Blake was emphatic that for the artist imagination was of supreme importance—he did not decry scientific endeavour but it was not for the artist. Kant separated an approach to the beautiful from that to be adopted to the two types of the sublime. Essentially, he was concerned with the beautiful and sublime in nature rather than in created art, but concluded that fine art is a product which must be art and not nature, but 'nevertheless must be clothed, *with the aspect* of nature', and which must appear to be 'uncontrived, natural and effortless' and to be totally original; it must therefore be the product of genius.

[37] *Ibid.*, p. 51.

Schiller identified two problems with the Kantian approach: its subjectivism and the rigid split between sensibility and rationality. He endeavoured to solve these problems by formulating a play-drive, which represented the free interplay between the rational mind and the sensual mind. However, whilst this was a helpful concept, it was not totally convincing, with still too great a separation between art and reality, sensuality and reason, to enable art to describe truth fully, and further developments were left to Hegel and to Schelling. Both of these had an existentialist approach and elevated the role of the artist to include the expression of the transcendental. For Hegel, this was the artist continuing the creative force of the Absolute and, through his or her involvement with that force, portraying the development of that force—in other words part of the self-revelation of God. Whereas Hegel saw the role of art at that time as changing, owing to the ability to express theology in words, Schelling saw a continuing role for art, which would express the infinite through the finite. Finally, in the art theory of Runge and the letters of Carus, there is almost a reiteration of the existentialist philosophy of Schelling, but expressed in terms that were designed for the art student, with an emphasis away from figuration towards non-homocentric Christian landscape art, or, as Carus expressed it, earth-life painting.

With Hegel, Schelling, Runge and Carus the art with which they were concerned would fit almost exclusively into category 3 of Podro's theory of art (the artist engages with the state of mind of the viewer to achieve an elevated or heightened emotional response to the work of art which may suggest a transcendence that lies behind the objects depicted), and in tracing the thought of these philosophers and artists there has been a tendency to move from category 1 (art reveals through the skill of the artist some aspect of a subject that would not be immediately apparent) through to category 3.

But the fundamental question that remains to be answered is whether or not the genius artist is able to express the truth about the Ultimate Reality. A concept of the Absolute will always involve an element of faith, but I think it can be said that an artist who achieves the goals set out by Schelling, Runge and Carus will enable the receptive viewer to glimpse a revelation of that Ultimate Reality.

My concluding view is that Carus deserved (and still deserves) recognition of his opinions on the expression of the divine through landscape art; it is to be regretted that the only known influence that he had on art of the time is on that of Caspar David Friedrich's landscapes. Through the latter's friendship with Runge, it is possible that Runge was also aware of the work of Carus, but if so, then Runge was not sufficiently influenced to include appropriate references in his own works.

PART II

PART II

→ 4 ←

The Transcendent and the Numinous

The numinous

Friedrich Schleiermacher was a major influence on Rudolf Otto (1869–1937), who is the focus of this chapter on religious experience and the non-rational part of any description of God.[1] In discussing God there is a tendency to intuit or express in words the rational part of the ultimate Being; to discuss God in terms of the ineffable or non-rational part is difficult. This is because we do not have the words or the language to write easily about that which is beyond—the non-rational. There have been over many years a number of attempts to prove the existence of God; they have all failed because the nature of God is indefinable in its totality. We can suggest definitions such as Ground of all Being or 'something than which nothing greater can be conceived', but they all fail in their endeavour to define or even prove the existence of God because of the use solely of rational argument without reference to the non-rational component of the Ultimate Being.[2]

---

[1] Schleiermacher was promoted in the twentieth century by Otto, with references scattered throughout *The Idea of the Holy* (see note 4 below) and, by the editor, in the introduction to F. Schleiermacher, *On Religion: Speeches to its Cultured Despisers* (Cambridge: Cambridge University Press, 1966), p. xxxii and note 58. The editor, Richard Crouter, refers to the fact that Otto himself published an edition of *On Religion* and wrote a supplement to *The Idea of the Holy* which includes a chapter entitled 'How Schleiermacher Re-discovered the Sensus Numinis'.

[2] P. Tillich, *Systematic Theology*, vol. 1 (London: SCM Press, 1978), p. 156. This book was first published in 1951 by the University of Chicago. B. Davies, *An Introduction to the Philosophy of Religion* (Oxford: Oxford

Otto endeavoured to overcome this limitation by developing the thoughts of Schleiermacher, acknowledging the role of 'feeling' in the perception of the transcendent. This approach is fully developed in *The Idea of the Holy* (1923), where he introduces the word 'numinous' to describe the holy (or sacred), ignoring the latter's normal attributes of moral goodness and rationality. The missing mysterious component in the idea of the holy is that which expresses the 'living force' or 'unique original feeling-response'.[3] Otto then introduces the numinous as a category of value and as a state of mind found wherever the category is applied. In order to explain further, he then writes:

> This mental state (the numinous) is [...] irreducible to any other; and therefore, like every absolutely primary and elementary datum, while it admits of being discussed, it cannot be strictly defined. There is only one way to help another to an understanding of it. He must be guided and led on by discussion of the matter through the ways of his own mind, until he reaches the point at which the numinous in him perforce begins to stir, to start into life and into consciousness [...] In other words our X cannot, strictly speaking, be taught, it can only be evoked, awakened in the mind; as everything that comes of the spirit must be awakened.[4]

This numinous experience is capable of further analysis, which suggests elements of awe-fulness (compare with the sublime) and mysteriousness or inapproachability (compare with mysticism/ devotional contemplation), to which can also be added a sense of fascination—where, in spite of the fear of the awe-fulness and the inapproachability, one is nonetheless drawn almost inexorably towards something which is fascinating. This then leads into one of Otto's most important statements:

> The daunting and the fascinating now combine in a strange harmony of contrasts, and the resultant dual character of

University Press, 2nd edn, 1993), pp. 55 and 239, quoting Anselm, who writes in the *Proslogion*: *aliquid quo nihil maius cogitari possit.*
[3] Otto, *The Idea of the Holy*, p. 6.
[4] *Ibid.*, p. 7.

the numinous consciousness, to which the entire religious development bears witness, at any rate from the level of the 'daemonic dread' onwards, is at once the strangest and most noteworthy phenomenon in the whole history of religion [...] the mystery is for him (or her) not merely something to be wondered at but something that entrances him (or her); and beside that in it which bewilders and confounds, he (or she) feels something that captivates and transports him (or her) with a strange ravishment, rising often enough to the pitch of dizzy intoxication; it is the Dionysiac-element in the numen.[5]

If this language seems a little overblown for the twenty-first century, Otto is describing what I would consider to be the ultimate in religious experience as seen today in such phenomena as the Toronto Blessing and in the twentieth century by a number of revivalist meetings, where religious fervour has been achieved through the oratory of a gifted preacher. In addition, Otto's thoughts are quite close to those of Sir Alister Hardy (1896–1985), who described religious experience as 'a deep awareness of a benevolent non-physical power which appears to be wholly or partly beyond, and far greater than the individual self'.[6]

Variations within descriptions of religious experience

It is interesting at this juncture to consider the views of William James, whose Gifford Lectures of 1901–2 were published in book form as *The Varieties of Religious Experience*.[7] The approach adopted by James was that of the psychologist who proposed as a hypothesis that the external power to which the theologian refers is validated or felt in the controlling of the higher faculties

---

[5] *Ibid.*, p. 31.
[6] M. Rankin, *An Introduction to Religious and Spiritual Experience* (London: Continuum, 2008), p. 5, quoting Hardy, taken from *Spiritual Nature of Man* (1979) by Alister Hardy (Lampeter, Ceredigion: Religious Experience Research Centre, reprinted 1997).
[7] W. James, *The Varieties of Religious Experience* (London: Collins, 1971).

of the hidden mind—leading to a 'sense of union with the power beyond us (which) is a sense of something, not merely apparently, but literally true'. This view of religious experience, although expressed from the point of view of the psychologist, is not inconsistent with the position adopted by the theologian Otto. One can even see consistency with the description of religious experience by Hardy, who expressed much the same idea in the language of some seventy years later, the main difference being this emphasis on the benevolence of that power beyond.

The mystic experience

Having considered the approaches to religious experience of three authorities, all of whom were invited to give the Gifford Lectures on Natural Religion, and established some common ground, the next question to be considered concerns the inducement or triggering of such experience. In my discussion with Marianne Rankin (the author of *An Introduction to Religious and Spiritual Experience*, 2008), Rankin emphasises that from her researches she has established that religious experience can rarely be self-induced. Even if one places oneself in the same situation in which such an experience had previously been encountered it would be most unlikely for that experience to be repeated. This is consistent with Otto's view that the nature of numinous consciousness is such that it cannot be taught or transmitted. It must be 'awakened from the spirit [...] which can only be induced, incited and aroused'.[8] He cites the only direct means of experiencing the numinous as possibly being through reading, suggesting, for example, that unless one feels a sense of the numinous when reading of Isaiah's call vision then one is very unlikely to be made aware of the numinous by instruction.[9]

At this stage in the development of the concept of religious experience, two other authorities could be cited—Frederick C.

[8] Otto, *The Idea of the Holy*, p. 60.
[9] Isaiah's 'call vision' is to be found in Isaiah 6:1–8.

Happold (who is quoted by the specialist in social science and theology, Leslie Francis) and John Macquarrie (an established existentialist theologian, 1919–2007).

Happold lists a number of features which are characteristic of the mystical state which include the quality of ineffability, defined, in terms with which Otto would be in entire agreement, as defying 'expressing in terms which are fully intelligible to one who has not known some analogous experience'.[10] Whilst acknowledging that the mystical state is one of feeling, there is also a suggestion of the appreciation of some inner knowledge to which Happold (and William James) give the name 'noetic' (from the Greek *noesis*—intellectual comprehension).[11] Such experiential states very rarely last long; this reflects another essential characteristic of religious experience, that of transience.[12] Another two features highlighted by Happold are passivity, where the one receiving the experience is unaware of any activity on his or her own part to achieve that experience, and a sense of oneness or wholeness.

The two final characteristics that Happold identifies are a sense of timelessness and the loss of the sense of ego. Expressed differently, in a mystical state one may experience that which has been described as the ground of the spirit or spark of the soul; for this experience Happold quotes Meister Eckhart (1260–1327):

> For the power of the Holy Ghost seizes the very highest and purest, the spark of the soul, and carries it up the flame of love [...] The soul-spark is conveyed aloft into its source and is absorbed into God and is identified with God and is the spiritual light of God.[13]

A number of these features are picked up by Macquarrie—direct relation to God, cognition, self-knowledge, passivity and a sense of wholeness.[14] With regard to the characteristic of ineffability,

---

[10] Happold, *Mysticism*, p. 45.
[11] *Ibid.*
[12] *Ibid.*, p. 46.
[13] *Ibid.*, p. 49, quoting Eckhart.
[14] J. Macquarrie, *Two Worlds are One* (London: SCM Press, 2004), pp. 1–34.

Macquarrie discusses apophaticism—which, expressed simply, means that we can only speak of God in terms of what God is not; it is sometimes referred to as negative theology. In discussing passivity, the existentialist approach is much to the fore in Macquarrie's writings, where we are thrown into existence, able to think and to be aware of and wonder at the fact of our own existence.

Trigger factors

The most likely way of experiencing the numinous is through some external trigger factor, for example music or a religious service. Rankin in her *Introduction to Religious and Spiritual Experience* devotes some forty pages to describing trigger factors, dividing them into religious and non-religious categories. The religious factors range from worship and prayer through contemplation and meditation to pilgrimages and the effects upon us of sacred places.[15] The non-religious triggers range from medical conditions, for example depression, to experiences elicited in the outdoors by particular scenery, by music, by paintings or by sounds.[16] It is on these latter factors that I will now concentrate.

Relevant to this study are mystical states or religious experiences which have been induced by external factors—music, literature or the visual arts, or indeed directly by nature itself. Considering first music, prior to the composing of programme music such as the *Pastoral Symphony* (1808) of Beethoven (1770–1827), we had that which we might describe as pure music and which complied with the rules of harmony. A typical work of this nature is the *Well-Tempered Clavier* (1742) of J. S. Bach (1685–1750), which consists of forty-eight Preludes and Fugues utilising all the major and minor keys. These rules which usually led to any dissonance being resolved into consonance gave to music a form which provided stimuli to the listener. Depending upon

[15] Rankin, *An Introduction to Religious and Spiritual Experience*, pp. 53–77.
[16] *Ibid.*, pp. 78–92.

the susceptibility of the listener at that time, such music could have the effect of changing his or her mood or even inducing a mystical state. A multi-part setting of a Psalm, or more likely a part of a setting of a mass or, for example, Bach's setting of the *Passion according to St John* (1724) may have this effect.

If we now think of the music of the Romantic period and later, the situation is slightly different. Here, for example, one may be triggered into some form of transcendental state by thinking of the same place or activity that had inspired the composer to write the piece of music. Music such as the *Alpine Symphony* (1915) of Richard Strauss (1864–1949) or the *Fingal's Cave* overture (1830) of Felix Mendelssohn (1809–47) might be appropriate candidates.

Macquarrie highlights the Romantic period as one when feeling, imagination and personal experiences were beginning to have some priority over impersonal rationality, and when nature-mysticism began to be recognised. He quotes a defining moment as 1798, when the *Lyrical Ballads* of Wordsworth and Coleridge were published and when Wordsworth wrote *Lines Composed a Few Miles above Tintern Abbey*, 'in which he traces the development from a youthful sympathy with nature to a more mature mystical sense of divine Presence'.[17] Macquarrie emphasises that this nature-mysticism is not some higher form of pantheism:

> But in true mystical fashion [Wordsworth] is looking for a deeper reality in or behind or beyond these physical phenomena, and apparently finding that deeper reality, […] as in the way that all together they constitute a unity so harmonious that it strikes us with awe. This is what permits him to speak of a Presence in Nature.[18]

This statement, of course, accords not only with the 'awe-fulness' component of Otto's numinous but also with the idea of the sublime discussed in Chapter 1. Indeed, Otto suggests

---

[17] Macquarrie, *Two Worlds are One*, p. 216. See also the website: http://www.poetryfoundation.org/poem/174796.

[18] *Ibid.*, p. 217.

that the sublime is the most effective means of representing the numinous—citing in particular the giant megaliths that were erected in the past as well as the more recent architectural efforts at representing the sublime. Otto advocates furthermore that the numinous can be evoked especially by the Gothic, where the impressiveness lies not only in its expression of the sublime but also in its suggestion of something beyond.

It is a short step from the natural world inducing a state of mystical feeling to such a response being induced by the representation of that world.[19] Rankin quotes William Rothenstein (1872–1945), who, writing in *Men and Memories* (1931–2), records that 'one's very being seems to be absorbed in the fields, trees and the walls one is striving to paint [...] At rare moments while painting, I have felt myself caught, as it were, in a kind of cosmic rhythm; but such experiences are usually all too brief', an example of the mystical state being achieved whilst contemplating the natural world.[20] The exact qualities in a work of art that give rise to the evocation of the numinous will be examined in a later chapter; suffice it to say at this stage that Otto particularly suggests darkness, perhaps emphasised by the showing of the last vestige of light, as in the final moments of a sunset.

The other particular feature to which Otto draws attention is emptiness, which he describes as horizontal sublimity, and as evidence for which he cites oriental art—'the wide stretching desert, the boundless uniformity of the steppe, have real sublimity [...] they set vibrating chords of the numinous'.[21] All these features will be examined in detail in later chapters, when a number of particular paintings will be analysed in terms of those qualities which point to the transcendent, but in a chapter devoted to Otto and the numinous it would be a justifiable criticism had they not been mentioned here.

[19] In my first chapter, Kant's appreciation of the beautiful in nature is indirectly compared with Schelling's appreciation of the beautiful through contemplation of the representation of that beauty.

[20] Rankin, *An Introduction to Religious and Spiritual Experience*, quoting Alister Hardy, quoting W. Rothenstein, *Men and Memories*, p. 87.

[21] Otto, *The Idea of the Holy*, p. 69.

The third of these non-religious trigger factors is sound or its counterpart silence. Rankin highlights the effect of shamanic drumming as used to induce a spiritual journey as well as citing the effect of the sounds from large gongs, gradually building up to become louder and louder and eventually causing the listener to have a sensation which may eventually lead to a near-death experience.[22] However, most sounds are related to music and the relationship between the notes of the music and the spaces or silences between. Examples of music from the Classical and Romantic repertoire have been quoted above, to which I could add music from the modern twelve-tone repertoire (originated by the Austrian composer Arnold Schoenberg (1874–1951) and his acolyte Anton Webern (1885–1943)). I suggest that the location of the performance is all-important and that it is the environment chosen that acts as the decisive factor in the resulting experience— numinous or otherwise.

The archive of the Religious Experience Research Centre

An alternative source of material relating to experiences which are outside the norm is housed by the Alister Hardy Religious Experience Research Centre (RERC) at the Lampeter Campus of the University of Wales Trinity Saint David. This centre was originally set up in Oxford by Sir Alister Hardy when he retired from his post as Linacre Professor of Zoology at the University of Oxford. He had had a life-long interest in spirituality, having had such experiences in his youth. Hardy describes religious experience as 'a deep awareness of a benevolent non-physical power which appears to be partly or wholly beyond, and far greater than, the individual self'.[23] He collected many accounts of such experiences; the archive now encompasses over 6000 accounts. It is continuing to develop as a result of answers to

---

[22] Rankin, *An Introduction to Religious and Spiritual Experience*, pp. 89–90.

[23] *Ibid.*, p. 5, quoting Hardy.

his question: 'Have you ever been aware of or influenced by a presence or power, whether you call it God or not, which is different from your everyday self?'[24] A number of these accounts contain references to the ability of art to inspire such awareness; selected below is a small collection of such accounts from the archive which are relevant to the subject of art and experience.[25]

The first extract was sent in to the centre in 2005 by a female artist, aged 49, who found that the act of creating a work of art is akin to meditation, which is consistent with the thoughts of William Rothenstein and Ben Nicholson. For this respondent there is a sense of oneness between her creative self and the material world around, referring to an experience of unity with the forces of both the material world and the spiritual world within. In writing that she feels 'continuously a part of the material and spiritual world' she is surely expressing a sentiment that is very similar to that description of the mystical state described by Happold and Nicholas of Cusa (1400–64)—'unifying vision of the One in All and the All in One'. This is an experience which has resulted from the act of creating a work of art and, from her description, would appear to be a rare example of an experience that can be induced and repeated. She does not make it explicit that the experience is the same each time she sets out to work but the suggestion of repeatability is implicit. She writes:

> What is Creativity and what is the Creative Process like? My route into this subject is through art. Or more precisely the experience of producing art. A Buddhist colleague at work recently said, 'Art is like meditation; it's a change of awareness'. I agree with that. The experience starts with the drive towards the natural concentration you have as an artist to represent the natural world as you see it. So you start off this way with the concentration and focus. I

[24] *Ibid.*, p. 3.
[25] The archive has recently been digitised and is available on-line to authorised members of the Alister Hardy Trust. The search process at present is a fairly elementary single-word search on subject and text; it is anticipated that a more sophisticated search process will be introduced in the future.

always work outdoors, just wherever you are. I don't believe in the 'studio picture'. You sit in one position and you try to get on with it. Then your concentration builds as you are trying to see what is out there in the natural world, adopt the best artistic conventions and techniques, and then reconcile all the aesthetic issues in order to complete the finished result. And it ends with an intense awareness of the unity of all material and spiritual things. Also your awareness is that all is continuous. And that there is an extreme continuity between you and the material world around you. You have an extremely heightened awareness of your material surroundings, the ground around your feet, the grass just next to you, the shells on the beach, the interaction of earth, air, ground, sky and water, and the sea rolling in miniature tidal waves onto the beach. Not only are your senses heightened. But also it seems to be beyond that, also an experience of unity with the forces of both the material world and the spiritual world within that. It is not a precise, illuminating sort of experience. It is rather more generalised. You could not say from this experience that life had a special meaning and purpose. You could only say: 'Life has a meaning, and it is this: We are continuously a part of this material and spiritual world.' It is not that, 'There is a transcendent world. And I have discovered and know about that which will come in the future.' I don't think we need to go so far as to say this is a vision of a new world, nor of a new heaven and earth. In fact, as an artist, I would not worry about that aspect. We don't have to look at future aspects nor where we will be after personal death. What is important is the enhancement of creativity and awareness in the moment. The reason we don't have to do that 'transcendent-for-evermore' bit, is because, by this means, we can have great, great eternity in one great, great, moment. 'Eternity in the palm of your hand [...] Heaven in a wild flower'. Time and space seem to spread out sideways indefinitely to the extent of an awareness of great vastness and great and endless time.[26]

---

[26] Extract from Account 200025 in the Alister Hardy Archive of Religious Experiences held at the University of Wales Trinity Saint David. Account from 49-year-old female, no religious allegiance reported in 2005.

The second extract is taken from a 1500-word account written as a letter to Hardy in which numinous experience played a significant role in guiding the respondent (a Christian male) to a career as an artist and ordained minister. The letter was written in May 1974, and although the artist's age at the time of writing is not known the reference to war service suggests that he was in his middle fifties.

> Painting and 20th cent[ury] art movements absorbed all my thought, and I had the inevitable fantasies of becoming a successful artist. At about 16 I was working hard to develop my work and also was striving to grasp the significance of the work of the most admired artists such as Picasso and the Surrealists. One evening I was drawing, struggling with perhaps more than my usual intensity, and feeling that I didn't really know what I was doing, when, quite suddenly, I had a totally new sensation that I had broken through a kind of barrier of incomprehension. I had a surge of elation that I was getting through my problems. I felt everything was going to be alright, though I equally realised that the drawing I was doing was nothing very wonderful. The strangest thing to me then was that I found myself praying, thanking God for my experience,—the God who had, in the previous three years or so, completely disappeared from my life [...] After war service I attended College of Art full time, and qualified as an art teacher, and, while training, I many times had the feeling that my best work, especially abstract work, came, as it were, 'out of the blue'. I would literally clear my mind of previous ideas and try to work almost without conscious control, and there was growing in my mind the notion that one had to have a kind of humility and honesty for whatever 'design' was emerging to have its fullest realisation. I would not suggest, nor did I then think that the resultant work was 'received' in the sense of a Christian fundamentalist's view of the scriptures, but rather that the need for an openness and honesty came from outside one's general understanding of the requirements of artistic training and were not normally expected in the usual modes of artistic development. A quotation in your article in the 'Times' speaks of 'the humility of helplessness' and of

responding 'to this power'. I would say, looking back, that that expressed my feelings at that time very closely. While at School of Art my religious awareness was also developing and eventually I was ordained [...]

I based my 'college sermon' on the relationship between the roles of the prophet and the artist, since it seemed to me that in both cases there was a quality of revelation in their inspiration and work. It seems to me that both for the 'true' artist (as against one working for commercial ends, or the amateur artist whose art is a mode of escape), and the man of religion, he has to see himself as a vehicle, expressing in words or visual imagery, concepts that come from right outside himself, apparently. Both have to be honest and humble enough to reject any previously held ideas and modes of expression, if they do not seem appropriate to the new idea that is borne in upon him. In this context Roger Fry said somewhere that the art critic has to be prepared to abandon any or all previously acquired notions when faced with some new form of art. And both prophet and artist may find themselves having to reflect or comment on aspects of life around them that will not readily be accepted by their audiences. Thus the artist, like the prophet, may not just be a 'barometer' of the contemporary scene and its ethos, but also finds himself creating an ordering of reality unrealised by others who are totally immersed in living through the seeming shaplessness [sic] and meaninglessness of day-to-day life [...]

The 20th cent. artistic scene may in one sense reflect only the dehumanising of man and the breakdown of all accepted values and traditions, and yet some abstract work, as you suggest, does seem to have a 'Mystery', a timeless quality of underlying order, and that is not without precedents. Looking back on the many aspects of art of the past that seemed important to me at various times, I now find only a very few things that have these qualities, and which suggest that the artist was motivated by more than merely fulfilling a commission or giving a slightly new expression to some well worked style from the past. I think now of some Byzantine work, some Russian icons, some portraits by Rembrandt, and some of his drawings and etchings, Piero della Francesca's 'Resurrection', and some of Blake's works, and all have in one way or another a quality of abstraction, I find. They have, too, I think, an ability to point one outside themselves and outside one's own personal and artistic consciousness. They seem, in short, to point one towards what may be called religious experience.[27]

The account below is of an experience (recorded by a female of unknown age writing in February 1991) induced by seeing prehistoric cave paintings in two locations and separated by many years. The experiences of viewing these paintings seemed to have enabled the respondent, who had read Blake and Kathleen Raine (1908–2003), to appreciate fully the meaning of spirituality:

> I read widely: mysticism, Eastern religions, the strange and inexplicable, and poetry—Blake, who said that the world of imagination was the real world and perception was infinite; Emily Dickinson, who expressed so concisely her contact with that wider universe of awe; and Kathleen Raine, who actually wrote about experiences like my own of expansion and awe, evoked by contact with nature. Eventually I came to realise that the 'scientific' and 'spiritual' perceptions give different views of the world which are complementary and not in opposition. They are describing the world from different aspects and each is true in its own realm; the external scientific view for the world of practical action, and the spiritual view for inner understanding of the inter-connectedness and unity of the universe. I had experienced a little of this inter-connectedness in contact with nature; but I also felt drawn to the past, to the roots and this is the context of the following experiences. Many years ago I had a very vivid experience in the prehistoric painted caves in Altamira in Northern Spain. In spite of the guided tour and the other tourists I felt linked, over 20,000 years, with the painters of these images; I was filled with a great sense of the wholeness of human life, of expansion and freedom, and a feeling that I can only describe as love, not for any individual but for the whole of humankind. I remained exultant for three days after this. It was a joyful experience very much connected

---

[27] *Ibid.*, Account 003163, Christian male reporting in May 1974, age at the time of writing unknown but possibly of around 50–60 years.

with human life. Many years later in Ireland I visited the
Celtic and prehistoric remains at Tara. There, peering into
the carved chamber called the 'Tomb of the Hostages'
I had a vivid impression of the huge figure of a woman
giving birth. It occurred to me that these carved chambers
(officially called 'tombs') may have been birth chambers
in the days when birth was revered. What could be more
sacred than the bringing forth of new life to be celebrated
with reverence and awe? These experiences were both
joyful and life-affirming. In contrast with many religious
philosophies which oppose the carnal and the spiritual they
were experiences of reverence for life on the earth. It is this
reverence for life which I find lacking in religious systems
which see the physical world as an inferior realm to be
overcome in the search for 'spirituality'. Such beliefs have
led to the exploitation of the earth and to the denigration
of women who make men aware of their bodies and, in
the process of birth, bring new flesh into the world. I have
never felt drawn to religions with an external 'heavenly
father' but find the holy within all life. Spirituality is then
a spontaneous consciousness of living, a joy in life, not in
withdrawing from the world which is seen as a prison for
the soul. I see spirituality as including a responsibility for
my own integrity, a recognition of myself as part of the
whole of humankind and the living earth, a reverence for
the holy in oneself, others and the world which makes the
whole of life a sacrament.[28]

This next extract is a much-shortened account which expresses
a vision inspired by nature and a painting by Caspar David
Friedrich, possibly *The Wanderer above a Sea of Mists* (1818) or
Chalk Cliffs on Rügen (after 1818):

> After the good God had become for me without a dwelling-
> place, I often felt how strongly life pulsates in nature, in
> gentle moods as well as in thunderstorm and tempest, by
> day and by night, through thoughtful solitude as well as
> when two are together, in myself, too, when a rhythm carried
> me away. I do not hesitate to regard such an experience
> as religious. Beauty is something originally divine and a

---

[28] *Ibid.*, Account 005067, female of unknown age, sent in 23 February 1991.

heart that beats in tune with nature with its harmonies as with its contrasts, is bound up with everything that comes to pass in blossoming and flourishing, in the love dance as in the struggle of rivals, in dying as in being born. The daily course of the sun with its rosy dawns, with its shining high noon, with its crimson evening symphonies, is for me a religious manifestation, and I experience the work of Nolde, which gives expression to this motley colouring, as a religious empathetic collection and re-creation of a high order. Clouds wander and somewhere there is a lake or the sea, and the sun and the moon are mirrored in their infinite depths. Yonder is a mountain or glacier, and my eye ranges over the world of mountain, over everlasting snows and peaks, and I lapse into contemplation as to the fascination itself. Another time I travel in a storm across the black sea, everything is tossed up, and the ship is snatched down into a valley in the waves and hurled up onto a foamy peak. There are the dunes, like waves benumbed they stand in the sun, like phantom images of sand they dream beneath the moon. Up above the stars twinkle, the big yellow-golden ones, the little tiny white ones, they are ordered in galaxies, they are clustered in nebuli. And then someone stands before it like Caspar David Friedrich in the great silence of the chalk cliffs and contemplates the vault of night, and the friends both feel the same thing, their hearts pound their way into this holy outflow. It is a song without words that they repeat within themselves, a blissful hymn before the horizon back there, which delimits their view, lest they become giddy with delight.[29]

The following account is a letter to Hardy, which muses on art, beauty and visions and the paintings of Samuel Palmer:

> Dear Professor Hardy, In spite of my academic background (MA Oxon Theology 2nd Cl. 1936) religious experience is for me not intellectual at all but visual. Austin Farrer had pointers to this approach in his Bampton Lectures, 'Glass of Vision', but that is only rationalising what is to me real

[29] *Ibid.*, Account 003733, sent in from Germany. Christian respondent of unknown gender. Date of writing: 1977. Age at time of writing: 82 years.

and direct experience. By 'visual' I mean two different things: A. Sudden unplanned visualisations during periods of quiet or prayer. One, of a splendid bird, came years ago as a message from outside self of the fact and truth of God—the Spirit, perhaps—caring 'even for me' that left me in its grip for longer than I usually meditated. Similarly an actual vase of flowers, 'Those flowers are praising God by their nature, as I long to do, though I shall have to will to do it—they just do it!' These have lived powerfully as memories. B. Is a long-term result (perhaps) of interest in art, or was it vice versa? A watercolour, if I can see it, remember it, or paint it myself, which conveys a sense of light (from mystery) is a real religious icon. I have only pulled this off two or three times in my own work, but Turner had it supremely. Such pictures stay with me as a central focus in the mind of all I most deeply experience. The Samuel Palmer drawings in the Ashmolean strike me as evidence that he knew my experience from within, though as icons Turner is nearer my own visual imagery. This is not just 'an interest' but a way in which 'God' lives as truly Wonder. I believe this experience to be quite common, though not readily articulated. I mix much in Isle of Wight art circles and find ordinary people readily know. I am due to talk to a young group in Shanklin next Sunday after church by invitation. Do I articulate it as I do because I am a theologian? (I do local ordination training.) How can one tell. There are visual memories of wonder with me from early childhood. Perhaps all I have done is to treasure and preserve something from preverbal [sic] experience? I would discard my library rather than lose it. Mostly the visualisations are not in the least ecclesiastical. I am also a fly fisherman with a reputation for skill in that sport—the sense of direct contact with beauty and the mystery of underwater life convey the same things in the silence the sport demands. This is terribly ordinary—but life itself to me.[30]

This final extract looks forward to one of the later chapters in this book when I shall be examining the role of paintings

---

[30] *Ibid.*, Account 003641. Christian male writing in December 1975 at the age of 59 years.

as aids to devotion and their use within a church service. The female Christian respondent clearly found in her experiences a profundity that was akin to worship:

> Other instances that come to mind are the overwhelming sight of Tintorettto's Crucifixion in San Rocces in Venice; & the Giotto frescoes in the Scrovegni Chapel in Padua were almost a parallel to the Revelation of St John—a new experience of worship. I have present in mind, always ready, the experience of Klemperer's conducting of Beethoven's Missa Solemnis & of [Benjamin] Bri[t]ten's War Requiem & the Church Dramas, especially the Prodigal Son—One could mention many other instances which have opened another world or a moment of great intensity & complete self-forgetfulness & absorption.[31]

Summary

This chapter has shown the progression of an approach to intuition and religious experience which began with Schleiermacher and was developed to a further and more disciplined stage by Otto. Practical examples of religious experience were then recorded by James, with the analysis being built on by the reflections of Happold. The work of Hardy was then highlighted with extracts from a number of accounts of religious experience, sent in to the Religious Experience Research Centre at Lampeter, which relate to the experience either of creating or of viewing a work of art. This chapter closes the part of the book concerned mainly with theology, philosophy and the philosophy of art. The following chapters will be set mainly in the discipline of iconology; I examine in detail such artists and their works as induce, in my estimation, a state of experience in the appropriately susceptible viewer which approaches or equals that of the mystical state described above.

[31] *Ibid.*, Account 003436, female Christian of unknown age writing in November 1974. The chapel at Padua is almost certainly the Cappella degli Scrovegni, which contains perhaps the greatest collection of Giotto frescoes. See: http://www.cappelladegliscrovegni.it/index.php/en/.

The Spiritual and Literary Background to Samuel Palmer's Paintings

Introduction

From an early age, Samuel Palmer showed signs of considerable sensitivity. At the age of three he was standing one evening with his nurse, Mary Ward, and looked out of the window as the rising moon cast a shadow of an elm tree onto a white wall. As the branches moved in the wind his nurse recited this couplet from Edward Young's *Paraphrase of Job*:

> Fond man, the vision of a moment made,
> Dream of a dream, and shadow of a shade.

This chapter begins by setting Palmer in the milieu of Romanticism, and includes some brief biographical notes to set his work in context; I then examine the way in which he endeavoured within some of his paintings and drawings of nature to create characteristics that point towards the transcendent. A sense of the transcendent may lie deep within the psyche or it may exist in some other way, but beyond our ability to detect using either the five senses or any instrumentation currently available. Palmer tried to express the immanence of God, the God within, to show His glory; he would have been quite content with the suggestion of the late Archbishop of Canterbury, Michael Ramsey (1904–88), that 'Man exists to glorify his Creator'.[1] It is important to highlight that glory is a biblical word with a special meaning, which Ramsey defines as follows:

[1] M. Ramsey, *Canterbury Pilgrim* (London: SPCK, 1974), p. 56.

To glorify God is to reflect the radiance of God like a mirror, in a life of righteousness, justice and compassion. But the nearer to God man comes in so reflecting him, the more he is aware of his creaturely dependence, his unworthiness, his need for forgiveness, and the more he finds his joy in God himself in praise and gratitude.[2]

Palmer could not have known this definition but it epitomises the understanding of his artistic aims; it will be argued that Palmer used his talent to fulfil this objective to glorify God and in so doing produced paintings which point to the transcendent.

Palmer in the context of the philosophy of the age— A short recapitulation

Samuel Palmer stood at a pivotal point in the age of Romanticism. It can be argued that the Age of Reason began with Isaac Newton and David Hume during the first half of the eighteenth century. As a counterpart to this emphasis on scientific reason, which it was thought could obviate any need for religion, William Blake (1757–1827) stressed emphatically the need for the continuing use of the imagination, an emphasis which was one of the characteristics of the age of Romanticism. This is summarised by the historian Jacques Barzun (1907–2012): 'The deism and atheism (of the Enlightenment), its scepticism and materialism left many earnest souls seeking an outlet for piety, a surrogate for the *infâme* [infamous] church that had been discredited.'[3] The philosopher most associated with the beginning of this age is Jean-Jacques Rousseau, who moved in his thought from 'a Platonic position involving a theoretical condemnation of art' to a position where the artist 'expresses his or her creativity through nature.'[4] The German Idealists (for example Schiller,

---

[2] *Ibid.*
[3] J. Barzun, *The Use and Abuse of Art* (The A. W. Mellon Lectures in the Fine Arts, 1973) (Princeton: Princeton University Press, 1974), p. 27.
[4] For a full treatment of the philosophy of Rousseau see J. H. Brome, *Rousseau: A Study of his Thought* (London: Edward Arnold, 1963). For

Schleiermacher, Schelling and Hegel) endeavoured to bridge the gap between reason and Romanticism and were rather more open-minded in their thought, with Schleiermacher regarding the universe as divine. 'You lie directly in the bosom of the finite world. In that moment you are its soul. Through one part of your nature you feel, as your own, all its power and its endless life.'[5]

A similar view is expressed by Schlegel: 'The universe we can neither explain nor conceive, but only contemplate and reveal.'[6] Schlegel saw philosophy

> as 'logical beauty' and the way to knowledge therefore as through art. The artist is himself a mediator of truth, aesthetic truth, with the power at his command of reconciliation and unity: [The artist] is the higher organ of the soul, where the living spirits of all outer humanity meet and in whom the inner man acts immediately.[7]

This is not altogether surprising because there are some obvious similarities between art and religion in terms of inspiration and contemplation. As Gordon Graham indicates when discussing art and religion in relation to the philosophies of Søren Kierkegaard (1813–55) and Friedrich Wilhelm Nietzsche (1844–1900):

> There is a good case to be made for thinking that Art and Religion are closely allied in some way or other. In their most developed forms both make important use of three concepts, namely 'creation', 'inspiration' and 'contemplation'. God is a creator, and his creative acts both invite our contemplation and inspire us. Something very similar is said of art and artists—that artworks are also the outcome of creativity and objects worthy of studied contemplation. They are also commonly said to be both inspired and inspiring.[8]

the relationship between Rousseau's thought and art see pp. 183–207.
[5] B. M. G. Reardon, *Religion in the Age of Romanticism* (Cambridge: Cambridge University Press, 1985), p. 4, quoting Schleiermacher.
[6] *Ibid.*, p. 19.
[7] *Ibid.*
[8] G. Graham, *The Re-enchantment of the World* (Oxford: Oxford University Press, 2007), p. 17.

The Romantics, theologians and idealist philosophers regarded experience as very important: as Reardon points out—'faith has its roots in feeling and intuition, of which theological doctrines can never be more than an imaginative symbolism, historically determined.'[9] This viewpoint is very much in accord with Schleiermacher—'in neither the Bible nor the doctrinal tradition does the ultimate authority reside, but in the vital momentum of religious experience itself.'[10] In summarising Schleiermacher's influence, Reardon states the logical development of this idea— 'immanentism brought the divine into the world-process itself, God, man and nature coming together in a cosmic harmony in which each blends with the other in the soul of the believer.'[11] To quote Barzun again, who emphasises that the 'power of art to evoke the transcendent [...] is what has led artists and thinkers in the last two centuries to equate art and religion, finally to substitute art for religion.'[12]

There were two main philosophical approaches to the way in which art may represent the numinous. The philosopher Hegel 'forecast the very evolution of art from the time that it assumed the role of religion [...] and proclaimed in his own day by Blake, whose figurative art results from the conviction that nature and the senses are a veil that conceals the Divine.'[13] Wordsworth, Schubert, Goethe, Friedrich and Runge all endeavoured in their work to show that the representation of nature could embody the divine. This was the philosophical and theological background of the world into which Samuel Palmer was born. He occupied a position where he was influenced by Blake, but expressed his

[9]   B. M. G. Reardon, *Religion in an Age of Romanticism* (Cambridge: Cambridge University Press, 1985), p. 29
[10] *Ibid.*, p. 56.
[11] *Ibid.*, p. 58. This was not a universally accepted viewpoint and Karl Barth was opposed to the liberal theological views expressed at this time—referring to this liberal era as 'Schleiermacher's century'. However the views of Schleiermacher would have the support of demythlogising theologians such as Paul Tillich
[12] J. Barzun, *The Use and Abuse of Art*, p. 26.
[13] *Ibid.*, p. 30.

own ideas through the depiction of nature. The spirit of this age is very well summarised by Warner:

> The yearning for faith remained; it simply became a hopeless yearning. Art responded by becoming a religion of its own, its sacred object not the God who may or may not be there in the darkness above the great world's altar stairs, but a deity created in the beholder's own eye, beauty. Almost all the best of Victorian art could in some sense be called religious, a sign of anxious, doubting, times, constantly aspiring to the condition of faith.[14]

The early influences—
The Dissenters and the High Anglicans

Palmer was born into a Baptist household; two great influences were his father (who became a Baptist preacher on his retirement from bookselling) and his nurse (his mother died when he was twelve). He was also influenced by a grandfather, another staunch Baptist. However, in spite of this background, from an early age (around 12 years) Palmer developed a 'passionate love [...] for the traditions and monuments of the [Anglican] Church; its cloistered abbeys, cathedrals and minsters which [he] was always imagining and trying to draw'.[15] The reason for this allegiance to the Anglican rather than Baptist Church is not known (many of his early letters and papers were destroyed by his son, A. H. Palmer) but possibly he was influenced by his short spell at the Merchant Taylors' School, or maybe it was owing to the earlier family background; his great-grandfather and another grandfather were Anglican priests. David Cecil suggests that the

> English Baptist Church in the early nineteenth century was not a congenial place for an artist, especially one with a romantic sense of the past. It was too bleak, too

---

[14] M. Warner, *The Victorians: British Painting 1837–1901* (Washington, DC: National Gallery of Art, 1997), p. 39.

[15] G. Grigson, *Samuel Palmer: The Visionary Years* (London: Kegan Paul, 1947), p. 5.

puritan, too unfurnished with historical associations. The Church of England, on the other hand, was ancient and sacramental: its music and ceremonies and magnificent liturgy were the outward and visible signs of an inward and spiritual sense.[16]

While this argument has some merit, is not totally convincing since John Linnell, who became Palmer's father-in-law, was a very determined Baptist and, of course, Blake came from a dissenting family and was happy to remain in that tradition. In addition, John Milton with *Paradise Lost* and John Bunyan with *Pilgrim's Progress*, both of whom came from the Puritan tradition, were two very great influences in Palmer's life, a subject which will feature later in the analysis of some of his paintings. The importance of the Bible must also be emphasised—his father read extracts to him every day and encouraged him to remember many significant passages.[17]

Perhaps, then, the key to Palmer's belief was that 'the deity he prayed to was not a featureless spirit but the post-resurrection Jesus.' Cecil quotes John Betjeman, who states 'That God was Man in Palestine/ And lives today in Bread and Wine'.[18] Palmer, then, with his appreciation of drama, would feel at home in a Church where this life today 'in Bread and Wine' was celebrated, as in the High Anglican Church, by the involvement of all the senses rather than the one sense, as in the dissenting churches, where the emphasis was placed on listening to the Word. Palmer showed his talent at an early age and, following instruction in painting from William Wate (d. 1832), he had reached such a standard that he was able to exhibit four paintings at the British Institution.[19] Whilst this early success should have boosted his confidence he still experienced feelings of inadequacy:

[16] D. Cecil, *Visionary and Dreamer: Two Poetic Painters: Samuel Palmer and Edward Burne-Jones* (Princeton: Princeton University Press, 1969), p. 16.
[17] R. Campbell-Johnson, *Mysterious Wisdom: The Life and Work of Samuel Palmer* (London: Bloomsbury Publishing, 2011), p. 17.
[18] *Ibid.*
[19] Grigson, *Samuel Palmer*, p. 6.

I cannot execute at all [...] I feel ten minutes a day, the most ardent love for art, and spend the rest of the time in stupid apathy [...] and restless despondency; without any of those delicious visions which are the only joys of my life—such as Christ at Emmaus; the repenting thief on the cross; the promise to Abraham; and secondary visions of the ages of chivalry, which are toned down with deep gold to distinguish them from the flashy and distracted present.[20]

Perhaps Palmer's feeling of frustration at his inability to express the sense of the God within was, in part, due to his very limited knowledge of art history and particularly the lack of opportunity to visit the art galleries in the company of someone who was knowledgeable about the artists whose works were on show. In answer to this, in 1822 'It pleased God to send Mr. Linnell as a good angel from Heaven to pluck me from the pit of modern art.'[21] Linnell introduced Palmer to a much wider range of art than he had previously experienced—German, French and early Italian works, with Palmer being, like Blake, particularly impressed by Albrecht Dürer. These older artists of the fifteenth and sixteenth centuries 'wonderfully express the spiritual and the supernatural', their angels and saints being 'more convincing than those of later artists.'[22] These Renaissance artists were a considerable influence on Palmer, who eventually was able by the use of his imagination to express his visions of that which lay 'beyond the veil' through his images of nature rather than through biblical illustration.

The important roles played by William Blake and John Bunyan

In 1824, Linnell introduced Palmer to Blake, who would become perhaps the most important mentor and influence in his life. Although in his depictions of his visions Blake painted very much from the imagination, he nevertheless helped Palmer in his

---

[20] *Ibid.*, p. 17, quoting Palmer.
[21] W. Vaughan, *Samuel Palmer, Vision and Landscape* (London: British Museum Press, 2005), p. 11b, quoting Palmer.
[22] Cecil, *Visionary and Dreamer*, p. 19.

quest to use nature as a way of expressing the glory of creation. As Vaughan points out,

> Palmer [...] was fascinated by Blake's powers. He believed, moreover, that they were relevant for landscape. Accepting—like Wordsworth and Linnell—that nature provided the visible proof of divine creation, he felt that it could be further used to provide an intimation of the 'higher reality' beyond it, if viewed with the transforming powers of the visionary.[23]

The significance of the book of Job, illustrations to which Blake was working on when they first met, lies in its references to God's immanence—the most direct of these being Job 33:4, 'The spirit of God has made me, and the breath of the Almighty gives me life'.[24] At this time Palmer was reading John Bunyan's allegorical *Pilgrim's Progress* (1678), Virgil's *Georgics* (c. 30 BCE), Milton and Shakespeare, and it is almost certain that Blake would have helped in the interpretation of these works. Indeed, Palmer and some of his friends soon began to regard Blake as the 'Interpreter', a reference to the guide to Christian in *Pilgrim's Progress*.[25]

Such was his importance during the formative years of Palmer's creativity that consideration must now be given to Bunyan. He

[23] Vaughan, *Samuel Palmer, Vision and Landscape*, p. 12a.
[24] In this passage Elihu appears to be acting as interpreter or intermediary and tries to explain God's behaviour—defending 'the pedagogical value of suffering, and praising the omnipotent wisdom of God'—O. Odelain and R. Séguineau, *Dictionary of Proper Names and Places in the Bible* (London: Robert Hale, 1991), p. 112b.
[25] Grigson, *Samuel Palmer*, p. 19. Palmer and his friends, as they got to know Blake in those three years, came to think of his rooms as 'The House of the Interpreter'. In *Pilgrim's Progress*, Christian came to the House of the Interpreter and knocked: "'Sir,' said Christian, "I am a Man that am come from the City of Destruction, and am going to Mount Zion, and I was told by the Man that stands at the Gate, at the head of this way; that if I called here, you would shew me excellent things. Such as would be a help to me in my Journey.'" This exactly describes how Palmer came, knocked and saw, and felt about things—the excellent things which he was shown, things which would be a help on the journey of the next few years.

was a Dissenting preacher whose major work, *Pilgrim's Progress Part I*, was published in 1678, some time after his spiritual autobiography, *Grace Abounding to the Chief of Sinners*. *Part II* of *Pilgrim's Progress*, a much happier work, was published six years after *Part I*. Bunyan's reputation varied over the years; in his own time his work was regarded as not intellectual by the educated theologians of the day. During the eighteenth century his reputation seemed to follow two parallel paths: he was despised and admired equally. By the end of that century his position was much more secure—he was enthusiastically supported by Blake, Crabbe Robinson, Wordsworth, Keats, Hazlitt and Emerson.[26]

Pilgrim's Progress is a long narrative poem—an allegory for the relationship between mankind and God—describing Christian's route via many vicissitudes to salvation; it is based on many of Bunyan's own difficulties occasioned by his living at the time of the Restoration and of the 1662 Act of Uniformity (which effectively denied the Dissenters their existence and led indirectly to the imprisonment of Bunyan).[27] The experiential 'quality of Bunyan's belief is reminiscent of Luther, who suffered a similar crisis of despair and forgiveness, and it is not surprising that reading Luther in translation was one of the formative theological influences in Bunyan's life'.[28] One thinks perhaps of the Puritans and Dissenters taking a very literal view of the Bible, but it is interesting to note that Bunyan comes to a more relaxed attitude when he learns that the Bible is not to be naively interpreted. 'Was not God's Laws [...] in olden times held forth by Types, Shadows and Metaphors?'[29] However, Bunyan was very clear that the 'Spirit worked through Scripture using ignorant men [...] and [he] had not much time for the intellect and the reason.'[30]

---

[26] N. H. Keeble (ed.), *John Bunyan Conventicle and Parnassus Tercentenary Essay* (Oxford: Clarendon Press, 1988), p. 254.
[27] M. Furlong, *Puritan's Progress: A Study of John Bunyan* (London: Hodder and Stoughton, 1975), p. 86.
[28] *Ibid.*, p. 141.
[29] *Ibid.*, p. 94, quoting Bunyan, *Pilgrim's Progres Part I* (1678).
[30] *Ibid.*, p. 148.

This was, of course, in the period before the Enlightenment, but one sees a close parallel here between this expressed opinion and Blake's view and indeed that of the Romantics generally that the imagination, both visual and literary, was all-important. With all this influence from the Puritan and Dissenting tradition derived from parents, friends and reading, it is perhaps indeed surprising that Palmer became a member of the High Anglican Church—a Church which at that time espoused the views of the Latitudinarians—'religion is about two things, reason and morality'.[31] Maybe Palmer was able to bring the 'enthusiastic nature of the Puritan religious experience' to the drama of the High Anglican services. In addition the Anglican Church would have suited Palmer's conservative attitude, opposed to the acts of Parliament giving relief to Dissenters, and 'a political conservative who deplored the *Reform Bill* of 1832'.[32]

The influence of John Milton

Another very important influence on both Blake and Palmer, and indeed other artists of the period, such as John Martin, was John Milton—to the extent that Blake wrote his own versions of some of Milton's works, endeavouring to make them relevant for his own age: *Songs of Innocence and Experience* (1794) and the long narrative poem *Milton* (1811).[33] In *Milton* Blake introduced the land of Beulah—'a place where Contrarieties are equally true [...]

---

[31] Keeble, *John Bunyan* (I. Rivers, *Essay Bunyan and Restoration Latitudinarianism*), p. 69.

[32] M. Yorke, *The Spirit of Place* (London: Constable, 1988), p. 110.

[33] P. Kitson, writing in T. Corns (ed.), *A Companion to Milton* (Oxford: Blackwell, 2001), p. 472: 'The most rigorous rewriting of Milton's work was, however, that of William Blake. His *Songs of Innocence and Experience* (1794) arguably demonstrate the pattern of Natural Supernaturalism, placing Eden and the Fall in symbolic states of the human mind. For Blake redemption is available in this world and the divine attributes are found in human forms [...] These ideas are given a more complex form in Blake's poem *Milton*, which adapts his mythological system of division, dispersal and reorganisation, as enunciated in the Four Zoas, to personal and narrative concerns.'

It is a pleasant lovely Shadow where no dispute can come'[34] Beulah, according to Sloss and Wallis, was 'either as something a little lower than the perfection of Eternity, or, though less distinctly, as the proximate highest, if not the highest mode of communication possible to mortals.'[35] Beulah is a Hebrew word meaning 'Married' and occurs in the Bible—Isaiah 62:4. Blake elaborated this concept of Beulah in Bunyan's *Pilgrim's Progress* and doubtless influenced Palmer with the image of Beulah in *Milton*.[36] The images conjured up by the phrases 'moony habituations of Beulah' and 'Beulahs moony shades and hills' must have exerted a power on Palmer, as one can trace this influence within many of the works of Palmer completed during and immediately following the period when he was in thrall to Blake.[37]

Palmer's move to Shoreham— Early works—The Oxford Sepia Series

Some three years after Palmer's meeting with Blake, ill-health forced a move into the country. Having visited and been inspired

---

[34] D. Bindman (ed.), *William Blake, The Complete Illuminated Books* (London: Thames and Hudson in association with The William Blake Trust, 2001), p. 441.

[35] Grigson, *Samuel Palmer*, p. 144, note 51.

[36] Bindman, *William Blake*, p. 441: 'But Beulah to its Inhabitants appears within each district / As the beloved infant in his mother's bosom round encircled / With arms of love & pity & sweet compassion, But to / The Sons of Eden the moony habituations of Beulah, / Are from Great Eternity a mild and pleasant Rest.'

[37] Space does not permit a full discussion here of the influence of Milton's narrative poem *Paradise Lost* (1667), concerned with the age-old battle between good and evil and told through a reinterpretation of Genesis and the Fall followed by the story of the coming of the Messiah, his death, resurrection and ascension. For a helpful commentary on Milton see Corns (ed.), *A Companion to Milton*. For a short summary of *Paradise Lost* see M. Drabble (ed.), *The Oxford Companion to English Literature* (Oxford: Oxford University Press, 1994), p. 736b. For the full poem: B. Lewalski (ed.), John Milton, *Paradise Lost* (Malden, Mass.: Blackwell, 2007), pp. 5–332. Each part of the poem (book) is preceded by Milton's helpful statement of the argument.

by the Darenth Valley, he chose to live in the nearby village of Shoreham. Coincidentally, at this time (1827) Palmer received a significant legacy from the estate of his grandfather, which enabled him to work free of the need for an income. This was a formative period in his life, when he was able to produce work that had only to satisfy himself and to enjoy a life of sketching, painting and discussing the meaning of life with a group of friends (known as the 'Ancients') of much the same age as himself, all of whom had been influenced by Blake and lived for a while in Shoreham. The result of Palmer's fascination with Blake, Bunyan and Milton was the series of studies, produced in 1825 in brown ink and sepia mixed with gum arabic, of pastoral twilight or dawn scenes.[38]

A very clear link with these writers was given by Palmer, who inscribed the mounts of these works with appropriate quotations, in addition to which an extract from the Harvest Festival Psalm 65 appears appropriately on *The Valley Thick with Corn* (1825). A common theme in these sepia works was that of the moon—usually it was drawn, often as a sickle shape, low down in the sky, where its size was very dominant. Possibly Palmer was exaggerating the optical illusion when the moon is viewed low down, near the horizon, where it is seen amongst trees or buildings and appears very much larger than when it is high in the sky with no land-based reference points. For Palmer the moon was very significant and even personified—'Sometimes the rising moon seems to stand tiptoe on a green hill top to see if the day be going and the time of her vice-regency be come.'[39]

Palmer was totally enraptured by the countryside around him; from the way in which he expressed his love of that countryside one can deduce that his relationship with the scenery was akin to that of a religious experience. For example, he writes: 'How happy are those who find Him and adore Him everywhere, as they investigate His beautiful creation.'[40] As Rachel Campbell-Johnson

---

[38] These are now in the Ashmolean Museum, Oxford and are known as the Oxford Sepia Series.
[39] Cecil, *Visionary and Dreamer*, p. 30, quoting Palmer.
[40] R. Campbell-Johnson, *Mysterious Wisdom*, p. 155, quoting Palmer.

points out, he saw nature as evidence of the divine presence in the world—a presence which he expressed in words as 'the translucent amber [...] the purple sunset blazoned with gold' and so on.[41] In expressing these views Palmer may have been referencing William Paley's *Natural Theology* (1802), where the teleological basis (the design argument) for the existence of God is presented. While all such proofs are now discredited, Palmer would have been influenced by the satisfaction expressed by Paley that the whole of nature was interdependent and designed to realise an overall state of well-being.[42] A logical conclusion to be drawn from Paley is that his conception of God is that He lies outside time and space and hence is transcendent. It is the immanence of God—the God within—that enables Palmer to suggest what may lie beyond the veil to those whose beliefs and cultural background would enable them to detect such connotations.

A paragraph from one of the meditations of Thomas Traherne (1636–74) seems very relevant to the style and content of the Palmer Oxford Sepias, particularly *A Rustic Scene* (1825) or *Early Morning* (1825):

> The corn was orient and immortal wheat, which should never be reaped, nor was ever sown. I thought it had stood from everlasting to everlasting [...] all things abided eternally as they were in their proper places. Eternity was manifested in the Light of the Day, and something infinite behind everything appeared. I saw all in the peace of Eden [...] All time was Eternity and a perpetual Sabbath.[43]

The divine presence, the ultimate reality or God cannot be pictured because, unless one uses the anthropomorphic image or metaphor for God as the Father, God is not a depictable object. One can only suggest from one's experience a signpost

---

[41] *Ibid.*, p. 129.

[42] An on-line version of *Natural Theology* can be found at https://archive. org/details/naturaltheologyoopale

[43] Reginald Askew, 'The Church in Constable's Landscape', *Theology* (January/February 1996), quoting Traherne, *Centuries of Meditations* (1665). Whilst the subject of this essay was Constable, the quotation applies equally to Palmer.

pointing towards that reality that one senses but cannot prove. Palmer's solution to this problem as set out in the Oxford Sepias is to create a veil (the 'something infinite behind' of Traherne) by making some of his images of nature less clear, placing them in the evening with the characteristic large moon or church steeple pointing towards the infinite. In this way he is presenting the viewer with a signpost which suggests a Transcendence which can then be perhaps instrumental in furthering the faith of a receptive viewer. In addition, if one looks at the *Lonely Tower* (1879), a work which was produced towards the end of his life, he is suggesting the limitlessness of the ineffable in the way in which he combines the idea of a veil with the infinite immensity of the night sky. As Harvey suggests:

> For Palmer, the natural and the supernatural were almost indivisible, as they had been in Eden. The natural world was like a transparent curtain through which, vaguely, we might perceive the greater splendour of the heavenly or supernatural world.[44]

Of this period in Palmer's life Grigson suggests 'The three years in which influence in the form of borrowing from Blake are visible, as distinct from an enlargement and energizing of spirit, are 1824, 1825 and 1826—naturally enough.'[45] These works point towards the transcendent and could be regarded as sacramental inasmuch as they assist the receptive viewer towards a closer relationship with Ultimate Reality.

A brief dalliance with politics

After about 1832, Palmer's work became less intense; it was a period when, on a personal level, he had to start thinking about the need for an income, and for a while he became involved in politics. The country was in turmoil with Corn Law problems and with consideration of the Reform Bill, and

---

[44] J. Harvey, *The Bible as Visual Culture* (Sheffield: Sheffield Phoenix Press, 2013), p. 59.
[45] Grigson, *Samuel Palmer*, p. 25.

in the religious domain there were many changes, the most significant of which was the tolerance being shown both to Dissenters and to Catholics.[46] Palmer was very conservative in his views, even to the extent of being concerned about the Acts of 1828 and 1829 granting relief to the Dissenters and Catholics. In a letter to George Richmond he refers to thinking the 'best of the old high tories, because I find they gave most liberty to the poor, and were not morose, sullen and bloodthirsty like the Whigs, liberty jacks and dissenters.'[47] It seems that Palmer was able to separate the visionary views of the Dissenters and their tremendous influence upon him from their political views. Indeed so concerned about the political situation was he that he wrote an extreme paper— 'The Address to the Electors of West Kent'—in support of the conservative position. His beloved countryside was in turmoil, ricks were being burned and the Anglican Church, whilst remaining the established Church, no longer held the position of exclusive authority in matters of religion. Harrison notes that 'the political changes profoundly affected Palmer's art, as religious subjects gave way to the pastoral' and there are no longer the obvious references to Bunyan, yet a similarity with the more obvious visionary works can still be seen in such paintings as *Moonlight: A Landscape with Sheep* (c. 1831–2), *The Golden Valley* (c. 1833–4) and *A Pastoral Scene* (1835), where surely Palmer is still 'reflecting the radiance of God.'[48] After 1835, Palmer began to travel; in 1837 he went with his new wife to Italy and as a consequence his work changed radically, with his focus from this time on and for the next thirty years or so being on earning a living. Transcendence and the attempts to capture the glory of God were no longer uppermost in his thoughts. However, as Cecil suggests, his

---

[46] Dissenters were permitted to stand for Parliament in 1828 and the Roman Catholic Relief Act was passed in 1829.

[47] Grigson, *Samuel Palmer*, p. 103, quoting Palmer.

[48] C. Harrison, writing in Vaughan, *Samuel Palmer, Vision and Landscape*, p. 137b.

faith was always informing his art: 'Certainly it was his faith that vitalized his art. For, as he saw it, it was his faith that made his vision imaginative and therefore aesthetic.'[49] In addition, Blake was always in his thoughts; in a letter to Alexander Gilchrist in 1855, Palmer writes of Blake: 'In him at once you saw the Maker, the Inventor [...] He was energy itself, and shed around him a kindling influence, an atmosphere of life, full of the ideal. To walk with him in the country was to perceive the soul of beauty through the forms of matter.'[50] In 1864, Palmer writes of looking again (with the Gilchrists) at a number of Blake's drawings: 'and [we] were so riveted and unaware of the time, that a first look at the watch told three in the morning!'[51]

The Valley Thick with Corn

As a foretaste of the next chapter, below is an analysis of one of Palmer's best-known spiritual paintings, *The Valley Thick with Corn* (1825). This small painting is annotated with an extract from one of the traditional 'harvest' psalms—no. 65: 'Thou crownest the year with thy goodness.'

In the immediate foreground there is a figure reading a book (or at least contemplating it: the light comes only from the rather exaggerated moon), who is connected visually by the ascending stems of the remaining standing corn to the church, with its steeple pointing to the (harvest?) moon. There has been much speculation on the reader's identity—Harvey suggests it is Palmer himself with a copy of the Bible, while another school of thought suggests that it is Bunyan reading *Pilgrim's Progress*, and others have speculated that he is a Shakespearian character or even Shakespeare himself.[52] Harvey agues strongly that with

---

[49] Cecil, *Visionary and Dreamer*, p. 90.
[50] M. Abley, *The Parting Light. Selected Writings of Samuel Palmer* (Manchester: Carcanet Press, and Mid-Northumberland Arts Group, 1985), p. 179.
[51] *Ibid.*, p. 205.
[52] Harvey, *The Bible as Visual Culture*, p. 62.

the typological influence evident in the painting there is much to support his view that the reader is to be identified as the artist, but given Palmer's interest in *Pilgrim's Progress*, the suggestion of Bunyan is not unreasonable. Vaughan suggests that owing to the style of the dress, the suggestion that this figure is Christian from *Pilgrim's Progress* has much to commend it.[53] He writes:

> Malins has associated the figure with Christian, the protagonist in Bunyan's *Pilgrim's Progress*, dressed in his new coat, resting and reading in the 'arbour' halfway up the hill called 'Difficulty'. Even though certain other features in the landscape (such as the gate and the two paths to the right) could be related to this interpretation, it seems difficult to match the details exactly. The general inspiration of the landscape invested with religious meaning that Bunyan's book provided for Palmer is not in doubt.[54]

This is speculation, and many hills are shown, any of which could be the Delectable Mountains overlooking Beulah. To the left of the figure above the stooks of corn there is a shepherd watching over his flock (an allusion to Christ the good shepherd, as exemplified particularly in Psalm 23), beyond which there is a wooded area and, in the far distance, a horse and cart, presumably returning to the farm. The road beyond the cart disappears over the brow of a hill, beyond which there is another wooded hill: overall there is a suggestion of tremendous distance. This is reflected also on the right-hand side of the painting, where there is a road leading to a high cliff, which takes the eye through a bridge and a wood, and out of the picture. In the centre of the picture, there are two farm workers pausing to look at the cattle on their way back to the village, represented solely by the church, whose steeple, as mentioned above, leads the eye upwards to the moon and the sepia sky with its hovering birds, which, following a reference to Palmer's sketch book, could be owls.[55] In this particular work

---

[53] Vaughan, *Samuel Palmer, Vision and Landscape*, p. 93b.

[54] *Ibid.*, p. 93 b and c.

[55] B. Butlin, *Samuel Palmer. The Sketchbook of 1824* (London: Thames and Hudson, 2005), pp. 9 and 39.

there is religious or spiritual significance and the influence of Blake, for, as Vaughan observes,

> The reclining figure in a landscape, with head resting on arm (as the reading figure in this work is so doing) is a traditional image of melancholia. Palmer may be alluding to this tradition and perhaps revising it in the Blakean manner as a means of returning imaginatively to the times of plenty in olden days through reading the Bible.[56]

While there cannot be a definitive answer to the identity of the book which is being read, perhaps there is further evidence in support of the Bible from Palmer's 1824 sketch book. Wilcox refers specifically to the reclining figure in the pastoral sketch on p. 9 of the 1824 book, where quite clearly the book being read is the Bible, and there is, as mentioned above, reference to Psalm 65 in a sketch of the harvest moon with reclining people and the open Bible with the extract from that psalm visible.[57]

The enthusiastic nature of religious experience is clearly evident in Palmer, and he is surely endeavouring to overcome the difficulty of validating that conviction through his presentation of such scenes as this. The composition creates an impression of a tremendous expanse (meeting one of Otto's criteria), encouraging the viewer to contemplate the far distance as well as the bounty provided by the world that God created; Palmer 'fuses the real (Shoreham) with the ideal (the Promised Land)'.[58] The approach to the perspective is generally accurate, with the church steeple and the receding hills all shown in their correct relationship. The only obvious distortions are of the birds, which are not directly overhead but shown to be in the distance yet rather large for that distance, and the exaggerated moon. The moon in reality always appears to be large when close to the horizon, where it is seen in relatively close proximity to trees and buildings, but even

---

[56] Vaughan, *Samuel Palmer, Vision and Landscape*, p. 93c.

[57] Butlin, *Samuel Palmer*, pp. 63, 206, 41 and 202, referring to sketchbook original pages nos. 9 and 39. See also T. Wilcox, *Samuel Palmer* (London: Tate Publishing, 2005), pp. 13–17.

[58] *Ibid.*, p. 60.

taking this into account Palmer is making a point to emphasise the importance of the moon, possibly representing the Mother of Christ. It can then be argued that Palmer links this image to the infinite-beyond, as suggested by the vast panorama which can be inferred from the visible tops of the hills receding into the distance. This is speculative, and I prefer to see a reference to the 'moony habitations of Beulah'. As Colin Harrison writes, 'the literary sources, in Bunyan's *Pilgrim's Progress* and the Book of Isaiah, were well known to Palmer and to Blake, and it is possible that all six of these (sepia) designs were intended to be evocations of specific passages.'[59]

The use of light and dark is interesting inasmuch as the moon has been given prominence but there is obviously still much light coming from the setting sun. The light from the sun is shining on the stooks, the front of the person reading, the book, the hill in the central background and the white cow. It is obviously late in the evening because work has stopped and the people are going home (during harvest time this would not happen at the end of the afternoon or early evening) and I doubt that in reality there would be as much light as Palmer has suggested. This tactic certainly leads to a very strong contrast with the deep shadow, which suggests mystery or, perhaps, shows that the artist discerns mysticism within the scene that he depicts. This contrast is, of course, a characteristic which has been highlighted by Otto as indicative of the endeavour to portray the numinous.

Palmer has used dark brown ink and sepia mixed with gum arabic. As well as enhancing the air of mystery or even mysticism, this medium when the picture itself is viewed (rather than as a print in a book or on the screen) has a solidity, and a three-dimensional quality which enhances the perspective discussed above. This three-dimensional quality almost suggests that the ink and sepia have been applied to a shallow ivory carving of the scene.

The Valley Thick with Corn achieves the objective of pointing to the transcendent, not through the size of the work but with subtlety through its representation of the mystical through symbolism,

---

[59] C. Harrison, *Samuel Palmer* (Oxford: Ashmolean Museum, 2010), p. 24.

particularly in the church steeple pointing to the moon. The abundance of God's creation is represented by the harvest scene itself, aided by the inscription from Psalm 65. Thoughts of 'what lies beyond' are induced by the use of perspective and the far-distant hills. The reading figure suggests contemplation—the book is not known but both the Bible and *Pilgrim's Progress* would be consistent with the interpretation that this is a work of art that points towards the transcendent. The painting as a whole could be an allegory representing Christ's care for his flock, symbolised by the shepherd and his flock, with the idealised rural scene providing a symbol for the Kingdom of Heaven. Transcendence is being suggested in three ways; first by great distance to the horizon, encouraging the viewer to think of that which may lie beyond the veil. Secondly, there is an evocation of the past by the presentation of a current scene with allusions to history. Thirdly, the past is also evoked by recalling a biblical quotation that has resonance with the depicted harvest scene.

6

The Spiritual Paintings of Samuel Palmer

This chapter will continue the examination of a number of works by Palmer, analysing those aspects of the iconography which suggest the transcendent. Most of the comments made at the end of the previous chapter about *The Valley Thick with Corn* could be applied to all six of the Sepia Series, but to examine one further drawing in more detail, *Late Twilight* (1825) is chosen. Instead of a biblical passage, this is inscribed with a quotation from Shakespeare's *Macbeth* (misattributed by Palmer to Milton): 'The west yet glimmers with some streaks of day' (*Macbeth*, Act 3, Scene 3, line 5).

In comparison with the previous work, the moon is shown with sickle shape, on this occasion with a halo, usually indicative of an approaching warm front some 400 miles distant with its approaching rain. It is late summer with stooks of corn standing in an enclosed field. Maybe this scene is, again, representative of John Bunyan's Beulah—the land that lies beyond the Valley of the Shadow of Death.[1] As mentioned previously, Blake was working on Bunyan's *Pilgrim's Progress* at the end of his life and could very well have influenced Palmer's evocation of that imaginary land. It is very late in the evening with the sun having just set,

---

[1] Beulah first occurs in Isaiah 62:4, in reference to the marriage between Yahweh and Zion and the land that they will occupy being no longer desolate or abandoned but called Married (Hebrew: Beulah). In *Pilgrim's Progress*, when the Pilgrims were in sight of the Heavenly City, 'they heard continually the singing of birds and saw every day the flowers appear in the earth.' Beulah is also used in a similar sense by Blake, to represent a state of light (often associated with the third state of vision and sexual love): its symbol is the moon. See Drabble, *The Oxford Companion to English Literature*, entry on Beulah, p. 97a.

and, with a fog having settled in the valley beyond the cottage, the suggestion of a village is just discernible in the centre of the picture. A particular and unique characteristic of this sepia work is the fog, which, to invoke an element of eisegesis, could be indicating a separation between heaven and earth, encouraging the viewer in contemplation of what may lie beyond.

In terms of composition, the moon is central, set above figures presumably returning home. In the left foreground appears a shepherd (the usual symbol for Christ), resting with his sheep, one of which has a rather owl-like face, perhaps representing wisdom. The village is just discernible in the gloom, the church with its spire pointing directly to the moon—a typical Palmer iconographic motif—and in this case looking towards heaven above the sea of fog. Although not easily seen in reproductions, there is an owl on the fence, maybe representing wisdom, while the shepherd with his sheep is possibly a reference to the Gospel of John 10, which describes the shepherd acting as the door to the fold, the better able from there to defend his sheep against intruders.

Although the pictures are very different, it is interesting to note that Caspar David Friedrich uses fog as a means of pointing towards the transcendent in *The Wanderer above a Sea of Mists* (1818), to be discussed in a later chapter. Both of these works achieve the effect of requiring the viewer to look ever more closely at the picture, endeavouring to see beyond the veil, the very ground upon which the pictures have been painted. In the *Late Twilight* and *The Valley Thick with Corn*, there is a narrative which can help to focus the mind of the susceptible viewer on thoughts of that which lies outside and beyond the scene depicted. But the strongest characteristic of *Late Twilight* is its contrast between light and dark, with the whole scene about to be plunged into absolute darkness, the sun having set and the moon about to dip below the western horizon. In addition to this shadow/light contrast, there is in this painting the suggestion of vast space and tremendous distance across the fog, another characteristic which Otto regards as indicative of the numinous.

All the Sepia Series works are imbued with a sense of the numinous created by the contrast between light and dark, as well as with the sense that the viewer has to look ever deeper into the painting, an effect created by the far-distant horizons. In addition most of the drawings connote particular passages from the Bible. As Harvey writes: 'The biblical ethos is evoked when the formal and intrinsic aspects of the drawing(s) intersect with the requisite biblical texts to enable the subject to transcend the genre of rural landscape.'[2]

The Repose of the Holy Family

This next significant painting, *The Repose of the Holy Family* (*c.* 1824–8), is very different from the Sepia Series, which he completed during the course of its composition. This painting demonstrates that a work of art that points towards the transcendent does not necessarily need to conform to the Sepia Series pattern. The analysis will be split into sub-sections as follows: the biblical context, artistic influences and the analysis of the painting itself.

The biblical context

The flight into Egypt and return occur only in St Matthew's Gospel, as part of the infancy narrative (Matthew 2:3–23). The infancy narratives themselves which occur in Luke as well as Matthew are contested, with many scholars regarding them as symbolic rather than as literal history. There are a number of reasons for this scepticism but one difficulty is the comparison of the timing of the flight from Egypt in Matthew with the return to the house at Nazareth in Luke.[3]

As Vaughan suggests, while this narrative is probably apocryphal it is nonetheless important for the messages that it

---

[2] J. Harvey, *The Bible as Visual Culture* (Sheffield: Sheffield Phoenix Press, 2013), p. 60.

[3] For further details see for example the website: http://www.oxfordbiblical studies.com/article/opr/t94/e939

contains.[4] First of all the writer of the Gospel has Joseph warned in a dream to travel to Egypt to avoid becoming a victim of Herod's stated intention of murdering babies aged below two years. There is a tradition of Jews escaping to Egypt to avoid persecution, and it would have been quite logical therefore for Joseph to take his family to one of the Jewish enclaves in an Egyptian city. The writer links this story to fulfilment of the passage in Hosea 11:1: 'When Israel was a child, I loved him, and out of Egypt I called my son'. Whilst this has no reference to Jesus, it does emphasise the deliverance of God's chosen people out of slavery in Egypt. It has a typological application, where the writer of the Gospel of Matthew is making use of an Old Testament prophecy to comply with his narrative. Matthew, writing for Jews, 'knew that almost the only way to convince the Jews that Jesus was the Anointed One of God was to prove that he was the fulfilment of Old Testament prophecy'.[5] Regarding the intent of the passage, deliverance is the main theme—in another dream Joseph is advised by God not to travel back to Bethlehem, where Herod's equally ruthless successor, Archelaus, now ruled, but to Nazareth in Galilee, where Herod Antipas, a much more benign king, reigned. This move to Nazareth established Jesus as a Nazarene.[6]

Although the infancy narratives are no longer regarded by most scholars as historical fact, the question of interest in the context of Palmer is whether or not they were considered true in his day, when research into the historical Jesus was only just beginning.[7] The extent to which Palmer would have been

---

[4] Vaughan, writing in *Samuel Palmer, 1805–1881*, ed. William Vaughan, Elizabeth E. Barker and Colin Harrison (London: British Museum Press, 1995), p. 106. This was published to accompany the exhibition of Palmer's works held in 1995 and 1996 in the British Museum and Metropolitan Museum of Art (New York).

[5] W. Barclay, *The Gospel of Matthew* (Edinburgh: Saint Andrew Press, 1991), p. 36.

[6] For a detailed discussion see C. E. Laymon, *The Interpreter's One Volume Commentary on the Bible* (Nashville: Abingdon Press, 1992), p. 612a.

[7] The quest for the historical Jesus could be said to have begun in earnest

aware of this research, much of which was being undertaken in Germany, is difficult to assess, but he would probably have known of the work of such influential theologians as William Paley, writing of his view of God as the creative designer of nature.[8] The idea of God in nature (the whole of the natural world) is a theme which seems to be prevalent in the early works of Palmer, only a few of which are directly linked to the biblical narrative. There were, of course, at this time those who would have taken a very conservative if not literal view of the truth of the Bible, an example being Ernest Renan, who saw in the Bible an infallible authority which must never to be seen to be in error, 'for if the basis of the church's dogma is detected to be thus insecure what can be said for the security of the superstructure itself?'[9] This does not seem, however, to be the approach of Palmer, most of whose works employ the imagination in the representation—his works are certainly not literal illustrations of biblical passages.

So far as a non-biblical reference is concerned, Palmer, together with many of the other artists who have depicted this scene, refers to the Qur'an, suras 19–24, which describe the collection of dates from the palm tree 'and if you shake the trunk of this palm tree it will drop fresh ripe dates in your lap. Therefore rejoice. Eat and drink.'[10]

Artistic influences on Palmer's *Holy Family's Flight into Egypt*

This narrative of the *Holy Family's Flight into Egypt* has been selected for depiction by many artists, one of the earliest being Giotto di Bondone (*c.* 1300) with Sydney Nolan (1917–92) and John Swanson (b. 1938) providing more recent images.[11] The

---

in 1778 with the publication of works by G. E. Lessing. The quest has continued since that time with a major study produced by Schweitzer in 1906 and currently with works published by for example Ludemann.

[8] W. Paley, *Natural Theology*, first published by Paley in London in 1802.

[9] B. M. G. Rearden, *Religion in the Age of Romanticism* (Cambridge: Cambridge University Press, 1985), on Renan, p. 253.

[10] *Qur'an (Koran)*, trans. N. J. Dawood (London: Penguin Books, 4th rev. edn, 1981 [1956]), p. 33.

[11] www.textweek.com/art/flight_into_egypt.html

artists have very different approaches to the prominence of landscape in paintings that are essentially family scenes or portraits, with perhaps Claude (1600–82), who may well have influenced Palmer, placing the emphasis very much on landscape, particularly so in his version of 1666.

In an interesting essay, essentially on the subject of ecology, Kate Rigby argues that not only did the painting of landscape (nature) provide an antidote to the 'modern constitution' inaugurated by Bacon and Descartes, which severed the human from the non-human and determined their relationship in terms of mastery and possession, but also led to a rebirth of nature through the deployment of poetic imagination.[12] Neil Everden argues that even before Bacon there was this change in the attitude towards nature which began with Leonardo, who regarded 'the artist as "Lord and Creator", a person who is able to constitute an ideal world and from whom "abstraction" and "vision" collaborate intimately.'[13] As Everden continues,

> The artist presents an ideal world that can be taken in by the viewer in 'a single glance' through a 'proportioned harmony'. Leonardo gives the viewer *a whole landscape* as a visual object. As E. H. Gombrich notes, Leonardo's landscapes are conceptual, owing less to the painter's eye than to the imagination. Leonardo directs his viewer's eye to the beauty of his *abstraction*, and away from a world 'contaminated' through *empathy*.[14]

This is very much in accord with Palmer's own view. 'Sometimes landscape is seen as a vision, and then it seems as fine as art. But this is seldom, and bits of nature are generally improved by being received into the soul.'[15] For Palmer, the new vision

---

[12] K. Rigby, *Topographies of the Sacred: The Poetics of Place in European Romanticism* (Charlottesville: University of Virginia Press, 2004), pp. 4 and 23.

[13] N. Everden, *The Social Creation of Nature* (Baltimore: Johns Hopkins University Press, 1992), p. 64.

[14] *Ibid.*, p. 66.

[15] J. M. Moore, *The Green Fuse: Pastoral Vision in English Art* (Woodbridge: Antique Collectors' Club, 2007), p. 30, quoting Palmer.

he sought might open the door to some hoped-for synthesis of earthly nature with the continuing worship of God. This longing or nostalgia, perhaps best articulated by the Welsh word *hiraeth*, for an idealised countryside, is expressed by Palmer in the form of an earthly Kingdom of Heaven. Transcendence is at work in the mind of Palmer as he tries to express the Kingdom in terms of an idealised, imagined countryside which contains the lush pastures of Kent with the palm trees of the Middle East.

Apart from the influence of the Bible and the Qur'an, Palmer was certainly influenced by the artists Blake and Claude, both of whom had produced works on this subject of the visit of the Holy Family to Egypt. Claude's influence in general is highlighted by Lister and of course the influence of Blake is very well known, as is that of his peers, known as 'the Ancients'.[16] One of the 'Ancients', Edward Calvert, could almost have been echoing Palmer when he wrote 'Earth spiritualised, not Heaven naturalised [...] I feel a yearning to see the glades and nooks receding like vistas into the gardens of Heaven'.[17]

Analysis of the painting

Palmer's painting gives almost more prominence to the landscape than to the family, but his landscape is clearly not that of the Middle East, but of Kent, probably the area around his cottage, but with the addition of a large palm tree. The work was begun in 1824 and was for Palmer experimental; it was only completed after further experimentation and advice from the Blakes, which resulted in *In a Shoreham Garden* (1829). 'Quite suddenly, Palmer found he was able to complete his oil and tempera painting of the Holy Family (laid aside in 1824) with an ideal background which he found about a Shoreham paddock'.[18] Harrison quotes evidence of Palmer's despair in 1825—'I have laid by the Family in much distress, anxiety and fear: which had plunged me into

[16] R. Lister, *Samuel Palmer and his Etchings* (London: Faber and Faber, 1969), p. 30.
[17] Lister, *ibid.*, p. 29, quoting Calvert.
[18] Moore, *The Green Fuse*, p. 55.

despair but for God's mercy [...] but rather, distress (being blessed) was to me a great arousement; quickly goading me to deep humbleness, eager, restless inquiry, and diligent work.'[19] The landscape is imaginary, very much in accordance with the words of Leonardo mentioned above. There is a cave in the middle distance on the left, which possibly suggests an allusion to the legend of the Holy Family resting overnight in a cave. A spider weaves a dense web over the entrance to the cave; it shields them from the view of Herod's men as they go past looking for them, so they ignore this cave, the web covering the entrance suggesting that no one could have entered recently. The use of a dark cave is an established pictorial iconography which occurs frequently in the works of Palmer. The presence of a palm tree is a reference, as mentioned earlier, to the Qur'an, suras 19–24, the tree being a source of food for the journey.

Many artists have based their works closely on the literal biblical narrative, whereas others have tended to paint their interpretation of the narrative using their imagination and skills of exegesis (textual interpretation). Palmer is to be counted among this latter group, where the work as a whole, although based on a biblical story, has been constructed out of Palmer's imagination, where the English countryside has been conflated with Palestinian or Egyptian scenery.

So far as the interpretation of the work is concerned, there is consistency with the biblical theme of deliverance. Palmer is almost wrapping the Holy Family in the embrace of the landscape—God's creation, and God's providence in supporting the family with food (the palm tree) and shelter (the cave and the cottage with its warmth). It would seem that this interpretation comes very close to meeting Schelling's ideal that art should be an emanation of the absolute (God). Regarding the Holy Family itself, both parents are concentrating, although in a rather dream-like way, upon Jesus, with the donkey quietly grazing beside them. The whole scene suggests a relaxed, restful security—security provided by God. Without too great a stretch of the imagination,

---

[19] C. Harrison, *Samuel Palmer* (Oxford: Ashmolean Museum, 1997), p. 12.

one could suggest an ecological interpretation, along the lines of the interpretation of the Covenant with Noah—if mankind looks after the natural world to the best of its ability then God will never again flood mankind out of existence. Whilst this may be an interpretation that could be placed on the work in the twenty-first century, this would not have been an approach that Palmer would have recognised. His own view of the land was a very conservative one, concerned with the preservation of what he saw as a way of life in the countryside that should not change—faith in an unchanging landscape and faith in God. This is what he endeavoured to express in his art.

This work certainly points towards the transcendent. First, although the countryside is based on Shoreham, it has been extended by the addition of distant mountains, inviting the viewer to look into the far distance, thus meeting the 'great distance' criterion of Otto. Secondly, although the light/dark contrast is not so marked as in the Sepia Series, there is a significant contrast between the bright clothing—especially the cloth upon which Jesus is lying—and the darkness of the valley below, thus meeting the second of Otto's criteria. In addition to meeting these two criteria, a sense of mystery and the supernatural has been evoked by the extraordinary juxtaposition of the Shoreham landscape and the features of the Middle East—the palm tree and the distant mountain.

The work completed at Shoreham

During the time spent at Shoreham, Palmer produced some of his best works and certainly those which, as has been shown, enable the sensitive viewer with a cultural background in Christianity to discern something of the numinous. An indication of Palmer's thoughts at this time can be gleaned from the following extract from a letter which he wrote to John Linnell at the end of 1828. From this extract it can be seen that Palmer saw the glory of God reflected in nature, and endeavoured through his art to meet Ramsey's injunction mentioned above to 'glorify his Creator'.

Every where curious, articulate, perfect and inimitable of structure, like her own entomology, Nature does yet leave a space for the soul to climb above her steepest summits: as, in her dominion she swells from the herring to the leviathan [...] so divine Art piles mountains on her hills, and continents upon those mountains.

However, creation sometimes pours into the spiritual eye the radiance of Heaven: the green mountains that glimmer in a summer gloaming from the dusky but bloomy East; the moon, opening her golden eye or walking in brightness among innumerable islands of light, not only thrill the optic nerve, but shed a mild, a grateful, an unearthly lustre into the inmost spirits, and seem the interchanging twilight of that peaceful country, where there is no sorrow and no night. After all, I doubt not but there must be the study of this creation, as well as art and vision; tho' I cannot think it other than the veil of heaven, through which her divine features are dimly smiling; the setting of the table before the feast, the symphony before the tune, the prologue of the drama; a dream of antipast and proscenium of eternity.[20]

Palmer, in this passage gives an insight into his understanding of the Immanent (manifestation of the divine in the material world) and its relationship with the Transcendent (the sense of the divine being beyond the veil of heaven). This letter, perhaps more than many others in his extensive correspondence with John Linnell and the members of the 'Ancients', particularly George Richmond, gives an insight into the thought processes underlying the work of Palmer. These thoughts are brought out very strongly in the two Sepia Studies discussed above as well as being characteristic of many of Palmer's works during the period 1824 to 1834– the moon, the lustre, the green hills in the summer gloaming (twilight) and the interchanging twilight of that peaceful country. Although many of Palmer's letters contain rather mundane details of daily life in Shoreham, in

[20] R. Lister (ed.), *The Letters of Samuel Palmer, Volume I, 1814–1859* (Oxford: Clarendon Press, 1974), p. 50, letter to John Linnell, dated 21 December 1828.

one, written this time in 1834 to George Richmond, there is an interesting statement which rather confirms Palmer's own relationship to Christ:

> I have a slowly but steadily increasing conviction that the religion of Jesus Christ is perfectly divine but it certainly was not only intended to be enthroned in the understanding but enshrined in the heart, for the personal love of Christ is its beginning and end.[21]

While this was probably Palmer's thinking since his teenage years, there is a parallel here with Blake's emphasis on the imagination being given precedence and not usurped by the need to understand by rational thought and logic—which was very much the characteristic of the British approach to the Age of Reason. Perhaps Palmer's thoughts as a young man were confirmed and reinforced by his contact with Blake.

Ruth Returning from the Gleaning (c. 1828)

Palmer's work became rather more diverse during the Shoreham period, but strangely, in view of his feeling towards painting the human form ('the great edifice of the divine human form'), there are very few drawings or paintings involving primarily the human. A notable exception is *Ruth Returning from the Gleaning*—produced around 1828. This ink, wash and gouache over graphite work is based on the story in the book of Ruth (Ruth 2:17–18). In this story, Ruth (a gentile) worked so assiduously and humbly that she was actually given grain from one of the sheaves as well as the gleanings that were traditionally gathered by the poor—eventually Ruth is accepted into the Jewish community. Ruth finally marries Boaz, gives birth to a son Obed, the grandfather of David, ancestor of Christ. In the painting Ruth is shown walking back home with half a bushel of grain. In Shoreham, at the time, Palmer would have observed gleaners working in the fields and although they were unlikely to have been as well built as Palmer's

---

[21] *Ibid.*, p. 63, letter to George Richmond dated 14 October 1834.

Ruth and carrying as much grain—he may have been trying to say to the poor that if they were humble and conscientious, then God would provide and they would become as fit and healthy as Ruth. He may also have been keen to make a statement with regard to the changes in agriculture at that time, leading to greater efficiency and less gleanings, as well as drawing attention to the controversies regarding the Corn Laws, but it is more likely that Palmer is expressing the idea that the divine is immanent in the excess corn left over from the harvest. Vaughan makes a comment that 'The exaggerated forms of this figure emphasising power suggest Palmer's admiration for Fuseli, Michelangelo and the Italian mannerists.'[22] This exaggerated strength is also present in Blake's *Joseph of Arimathea* (1773)—maybe another example of Blake's influence.

Throughout this period at Shoreham, Palmer continued to create paintings and drawings which indulged his own almost child-like sense of wonder and awe (cf. Fascinens etc. in *The Idea of the Holy* by Rudolf Otto) in the panorama of nature which had been provided by the Creator. The words Honour notes in respect of an inscription by Calvert, 'Seen in the Kingdom of Heaven by vision through Jesus Christ Our Saviour', might 'equally well have been written by Palmer on any of his paintings and drawings of his Shoreham period.'[23]

Palmer's later work

After 1860 and the personal tragedy of the loss of his son, Thomas More, Palmer became a rather solitary figure and his work began to express a deeper vision—but a different vision from that of his Blake/Shoreham period. 'In the place of ecstasy and enthusiasm there was a more careful, meditative and richly laboured work.'[24] Three significant events occurred at the time

---

[22] Vaughan, *Samuel Palmer, Vision and Landscape*, p. 115c.
[23] H. Honour, *Romanticism* (London: Allen Lane (Penguin Books), 1979), p. 86.
[24] Vaughan, *Samuel Palmer, Vision and Landscape*, p. 224a.

which probably contributed to this return to visionary or more overtly transcendent art. First, with the death of Blake's first biographer, Alexander Gilchrist, Palmer came to be involved in corresponding with Mrs Gilchrist, not only in empathising in grief and mourning, but also in helping with the completion of the Blake biography, although in connection with the latter, Dante Gabriel Rossetti (1828–82) was the greater contributor. Secondly, he received a commission from Leonard Valpy to produce drawings to illustrate Milton's *Il Penseroso* ('the contemplative man') and *L'Allegro* ('the cheerful man').[25] Thirdly, while living at Redhill, his final residence, he had many discussions with a clerical family, the Wrights, one of whose sons became a prebendary at Hereford Cathedral. Whilst they did not frequently discuss art, they did discuss theology and morals.[26]

Il Penseroso is an 'invocation to the goddess Melancholy, bidding her bring Peace, Quiet, Leisure and Contemplation. It describes the pleasures of the studious meditative life, of tragedy, epic poetry, and music. *L'Allegro* is an invocation to the goddess Mirth to allow the poet to live with her, first amid the delights of pastoral scenes, then amid those of "towered cities" and the "busy hum of men".'[27] It is said that *Il Penseroso* influenced the 'graveyard poets', one of whom was Edward Young, whose extract from *Paraphrase of Job* had, as mentioned above, such an impact on the four-year-old Palmer. This incident with the shadow was of such significance in the work of Palmer that writing in 1871 to Frederick Stephens (1818–1907) (a founder member of the Pre-Raphaelite Brotherhood and an art critic) he quotes the famous couplet and then writes 'I never forgot those shadows, and I am often trying to paint them'.[28]

---

[25] http://www.yorku.ca/jprs/pdf/Allan_Life_with_Page_Life_28.pdf, for details of the commissioning by Valpy.

[26] R. Lister, *Samuel Palmer, A Biography* (London: Faber and Faber, 1974), pp. 257–8.

[27] Drabble, *The Oxford Companion to English Literature*, pp. 492a and 545a.

[28] Abley, *The Parting Light*, p. 220.

The Lonely Tower (1879) and The Bellman (1879)

Palmer produced eight watercolours for these two works and became so obsessed by them that, as with his early visionary works, they were financially very unrewarding. As Lister remarks, after some fifteen years following the award of the commission, 'the finest fruits of the venture were a couple of etchings, suggested by the watercolours, *The Bellman* and *The Lonely Tower*, the latter being Palmer's masterpiece in this medium.'[29]

Later in his biography of Palmer, Lister refers to *The Lonely Tower* as 'one of the greatest works ever made in this medium by an English artist.'[30] This view is corroborated by Vaughan, who quotes the view of Palmer held by Yeats (1865–1939), that 'The lonely light that Samuel Palmer engraved' was 'An image of mysterious wisdom won by toil.'[31]

The theme of the lonely tower occurs in at least two watercolours, the first (51cm × 70.5 cm) with a slightly different arrangement of landscape and figures being produced in 1867–8, and the second much smaller (16.5 × 23.5 cm), with an identical arrangement of figures as the etching, being produced later and probably just after the etching.[32] In the etching, the crescent moon sits low down in the centre of the picture, with the lonely tower lit from within through one window, located on a high bank to the left of the etching. On the right-hand side of the picture is a flock of sheep overseen by a reclining couple gazing at the tower, which is surrounded by the stars of Ursa Major, whilst on the left there is a wagoner with his ox cart negotiating a narrow stone-built pathway on the edge of a chasm, which separates the roadway from the hill on which the tower has been built. Trees to the right of the picture and one tree in the foreground complete the composition.

[29] Lister, *The Letters of Samuel Palmer*, p. 266.
[30] *Ibid.*, p. 273
[31] Vaughan, *Samuel Palmer, Vision and Landscape*, p. 224a, quoting from W. B. Yeats, 'The Phases of the Moon' (1919).
[32] *Ibid.*, p. 233c.

The watercolour (shown in 1868) on which this etching is based was accompanied in the exhibition by a quotation—this time not from the Bible but from Milton's *Il Penseroso*. In this narrative poem, set in his mind, Milton embraces the goddess Melancholy and asks her to take him on a journey where he may find peace and quiet and the opportunity for contemplation. The extract from the poem with which Palmer annotated this painting is:

> Or let my lamp at midnight hour,
> be seen in some high lonely tower,
> Where I may oft outwatch the Bear,
> with thrice great Hermes.[33]

Edward Cummins interprets this passage as meaning: 'There, he would contemplate the constellation known as Ursa Major (commonly called the Bear or the Plough) or consider the profound views of Plato. There he might also reflect on a great tragedy, such as that which befell Troy or that which was enacted on the stages of ancient Greece.'[34] This is the background, also, to a number of other paintings produced at this time (for example *The Prospect* (1881), and *The Bellman* (before 1881)), all based on Milton's poem. One can perhaps assume that Palmer was contemplating the end of his own life at this time, which may explain why he has returned to the style that he departed from at the time of his marriage and very close relationship with his father-in-law, John Linnell.

As with *The Valley Thick with Corn* the moon features strongly, being shown symbolically (because it is below the line of the horizon in the painting based on the etching) in the middle distance, and in the right-hand foreground there is a shepherd and (presumably) his wife or lover contemplating the scene and looking towards the tower. On the left-hand side there is a bullock cart being led homeward along a stone-flanked road leading upwards and out of the picture. As the eye is taken

---

[33] *Ibid.*, p. 232a.
[34] M. J. Cummins, *Study Guide to Milton's Poem 'Il Penseroso'*, available at http://www.cummingsstudyguides.net/Guides8/Penseroso.html.

upwards along this lane it is turned inwards towards the tower itself with a very bright line burning within. The prominent stone wall on the left is balanced by the hay rack on the right and the tower on the left by the prominent group of trees on the right. In the immediate centre foreground there is a stream visible below the stone walling; it flows into the valley in the middle distance and then away into the very far distance beyond the moon. In the centre of the painting there is a rather short (and hence symbolic) length of fencing, preventing the sheep falling into the stream below. The hill, surmounted by the tower, forms a diagonal, which leads the eye down towards the sheep lying at the base of the group of trees. Many stars are shown shining quite brightly, suggesting that is it quite late in the evening, although this is not consistent with the bright light coming from behind the viewer and illuminating the backs of the recumbent sheep and particularly the white shirt of the shepherd's companion. The constellation of the Great Bear (Ursa Major) is shown prominently, picking up the reference in the extract from *Il Penseroso*. Finally mention should be made of the 'Palmer bird'—presumably an owl—to the left of the centre foreground. Some commentators have suggested that the tower is that located on the top of Leith Hill in Surrey, which is very close to the farm where Palmer's son Thomas is buried. This, of course, would fit with the overall theme of melancholy, death and resurrection.[35]

There does not appear to be any distortion in the perspective, with the foreground figures and receding sheep all shown to their correct scale. As with *The Valley Thick with Corn* there is the impression of a tremendous distance to the far horizon—an effect emphasised by placing the bottom of the moon below the line of the horizon. If one assumes that the moon is the symbol for Christ (or Mary) then its positioning suggests that the Savour is coming towards the painter—maybe an allegorical rendering of the resurrection. The message here is that Palmer is contemplating a distance far beyond the moon, possibly even

---

[35] W. Vaughan, E. E. Barker and C. Harrison, *Samuel Palmer 1805–1881, Vision and Landscape* (London: British Museum Press, 2007), p. 232.

a world beyond death, Palmer's vision of heaven. The brightly lit tower is surrounded by sky and replaces the church steeple shown in a number of other Palmer paintings, a feature in the painting that takes the eye upwards perhaps in contemplation of heaven.

Aerial perspective is apparent, particularly emphasising the far-distant horizon and encouraging contemplation of the world beyond. The clarity of the foreground is contrasted with the mistiness of the distant horizon, but the tower which is some distance away from the foreground is also shown in sharp focus, confirming the importance Palmer is attaching to the significance of that tower. The use of very dark shadow gives rise to a sense of mystery, but the light brings particular attention to the crescent moon, the distant horizon and the light in the tower. The foreground is in sharp focus and quite bright, with the source of this light being unexplained. Examining the shadows in the painting in more detail, inconsistency is apparent; for example the shepherd's back is in deep shadow when with the same angle the nearside edge of the hay rack and the stone wall are very clearly lit from this unknown source of light. Palmer, one can only assume, is using this light to draw particular attention to those parts of the painting he wishes to emphasise—those parts which point towards the transcendent, namely the moon, the tower, the wall leading to the infinity beyond the edge of the painting and the infinity of the universe beyond the Great Bear.

While the colour range of the painting is greater than that of the *Valley Thick with Corn*, the palette is still limited, with the overall effect being sepia. The other main colour is the blue of the sky, which is reflected in the stream and the accoutrements of the shepherd and his companion. These dark colours are then contrasted with the bright white on the moon, the shirt of the companion and the bullock being led out of the picture. In the etching the deep shadows are emphasised but the unknown light coming from behind the viewer adds a symbolic mystery to the picture. The overall theme of the painting and the etching is contemplation—of life and death, of the firmament and of resurrection. The quotation from *Il Penseroso* points the viewer in this direction, reinforced by the special effects discussed above. The positioning of the moon gives it tremendous importance and the lighting effects all contribute to a sense of transcendence. The use of young people adds a more positive outlook to what could otherwise be a rather melancholy picture. The eye is taken in three directions—upwards towards the sky, to the left with the roadway, and outwards into the distance beyond the moon— and this constant looking outwards and beyond is the main characteristic pointing to the transcendent.

At the end of his life Palmer had returned to the visionary work of his youth—perhaps not with the same energy but with a more mature, considered expression of his vision as can be seen in *The Lonely Tower* and in his other Milton etching, *The Bellman*—a mature depiction of Shoreham and its countryside conflated with the Land of Beulah. Palmer wrote of *The Bellman* to his fellow-artist Philip Gilbert Hamerton (1834–94): 'It is a breaking out of village fever long after contact—a dream of that genuine village where I lost, as some would say, seven years of musing over many strings, designing what nobody would care for, and contracting among good books, a fastidious and unpopular taste.'[36]

To the end of his life, Palmer maintained the intention always to reflect the glory of God's creation in his work—to provide works of inspiration for contemplation. His God-given talent was his ability to draw, to paint and, at the end of his life, to etch. That his extraordinary ability to depict his visionary outlook was not recognised during his lifetime was disappointing and for him rather disheartening, but he did not allow this lack of recognition to detract him from his purpose. As Cecil points out:

> To respond to life was, for him, to respond to God as the author of life. This meant that religious experience was the mainspring of his creative vitality [...] His faith was strengthened by the habit of religious practice. He recognised this and drew his conclusions. Palmer was a

[36] Abley, *The Parting Light*, p. 230.

religious existentialist before his time, who discovered that the best way to maintain his faith was to act on it.[37]

In conclusion one can surely say that the words which Palmer applied to Claude apply equally well to Palmer himself: he should be considered the 'genius, equally tender and sublime, who re-opened upon canvas the vistas of Eden.'[38]

---

[37] Cecil, *Visionary and Dreamer*, p. 90.
[38] *Ibid.*, quoting Palmer.

7

German Romanticism and the Spiritual Paintings of Caspar David Friedrich

The previous chapter analysed a number of the works of Samuel Palmer that signposted the transcendent. Caspar David Friedrich was one of his contemporaries in Germany and although there is no evidence that they met, they were subject to many of the same influences. Both produced work that pointed towards the transcendent and both regarded their Christian faith as fundamental to their way of life. While Palmer's churchmanship was influenced by both Baptists and High Anglicanism, Friedrich came from a Pietist background, an influence that remained with him throughout his life. This chapter will analyse a number of Friedrich's works that point towards the transcendent, including biographical notes as appropriate to establish the context within which he was working.

The place of Friedrich within German Romanticism

Around the turn of the eighteenth to the nineteenth century, artistic creativity in the German-speaking part of Europe was very dominant. As has been shown in Chapters 1 and 2, German philosophers were in the ascendency, to which can be added musicians such as Haydn, Beethoven and Weber, and artists such as Friedrich himself, Runge and Peter von Cornelius (1783–1867). Germany at this time consisted of a large number of independent states, and although unification in the form of a German empire did not take place until 1871, the process could be said to have begun in the time of Friedrich Wilhelm I (1688–1740) and to have been developed by his son Friedrich the Great (1712–86), both of whom concentrated on developing a nation, where conscientiousness and hard work became very important characteristics.[1] During the same period Pietism, the religious movement which sought to return to the values espoused by Martin Luther, was gaining influence, an influence that would have a profound effect on Friedrich.

The origins of Pietism can be traced back to the followers of John Huss (*c.* 1372–1415), who led a reform movement before Luther came to prominence. This reform movement flourished until the middle of the seventeenth century, when it weakened under the influence of the Counter-Reformation.[2] The actual beginning of Pietism itself is difficult to ascertain but the two most prominent leaders were Philip Spener (1635–1705) and August Hermann Francke (1663–1727). Spener called for 'Bible study, better theological education, lay activity, ethical awakening, and lessened polemics.'[3] Pietism was established in eastern Germany by Count von Zinzendorf (1700–60), who had encouraged a number of Moravian families to join him on his estate in the early years of the eighteenth century. Under his leadership, the Moravian Church became recognised as a rather outspoken form of European Protestantism, which nonetheless was noted for its support not only of great creativity in music and liturgy but also of ecumenism.[4] The movement, which embraced many of the ideas of the Moravian Church, emphasised the work ethic and the concept of the 'priesthood of all believers', advocating the importance of undertaking good works in the present life, which would be taken into account on the day of judgement. Pietism became prominent throughout northern Europe; its influence can be seen, for example, in the work of the theologian Friedrich Schleiermacher, who regarded intuition and religious experience as being of much greater importance than dogma.

[1] Watson, *The German Genius*, pp. 43–9, and N. Stone (ed.), *The Times Atlas of World History* (London: Times Books, 3rd edn, 1989), pp. 216–17.
[2] K. Crim (ed.), *The Perennial Dictionary of World Religions* (San Francisco: Harper and Row, 1981), p. 493a.
[3] *Ibid.*, p. 568a.
[4] *Ibid.*, p. 493b.

Another force for creativity in northern Europe and a strong influence on Friedrich was Romanticism. This movement began with Rousseau, Kant and Blake, and ended with the advent of abstraction at the end of the nineteenth century, although some would argue that it died out at the beginning of the Victorian period. A characteristic of the Romantic movement was the regard paid to nature poetry as well as a feeling for the spiritual life, countryside and landscape, as exhibited in the poetry of Wordsworth and Schiller, the landscape paintings of Turner and the spiritual works of the German artists Johann Friedrich Overbeck (1789–1869) and Cornelius, as well as, of course, Friedrich and Runge. The movement was also exemplified in the *Sturm und Drang* literature in Germany and in the apocalyptic paintings of John Martin in Britain.

Romanticism must be seen within the context of the Age of Enlightenment, which began in the seventeenth century (John Locke is usually quoted as one of the originators of the Enlightenment Movement) and continued until at least the French Revolution, or as others may argue, the advent of Post-modernism. An important characteristic of both Romanticism and the Enlightenment was the separation between the rational, as it might be described, and the spiritual. An interesting definition was produced by Novalis:

> By giving higher meaning to the mundane, a mysterious appearance to the ordinary, the distinction of the unknown to what is known, the guise of infinity to the finite, I romanticise it. The operation is reversed for those which are higher, unknown, mystical and infinite: they are elucidated by the association, gaining a colloquial means of expression.[5]

The objective, therefore, for the creative artist in the Romantic period was to capture, or elucidate from within, the sense of the numinous, rather than to produce a straightforward representation or copy of nature. In Chapter 1 this distinction between the phenomenal and the noumenal was described in

---

[5] Hofmann, *Caspar David Friedrich*, p. 244, quoting Novalis.

some detail and will not be reiterated here; suffice it to say that in Germany the noumenal was referred to as the 'conception of a *Bildungsstaat*—a state whose main ideal was to enrich the inner life of man.'⁶ Some Enlightenment scientists would, of course, have concentrated on the rational, sometimes to the extent of a reductionism that could lead to a restricted view of the totality of knowledge, but this was more of a problem in Britain than the mainland of Europe.

This then was the cultural milieu into which Caspar David Friedrich was born in the Baltic port of Greifswald in the western part of the state of Pomerania on 5 September 1774. Greifswald was a town under Swedish control and was enjoying a period of peace and relative prosperity—Friedrich's father was a soap boiler and chandler and had by the time of Friedrich's birth achieved moderate wealth. The town had a university with a poor reputation, but, nonetheless, Friedrich benefited for four years from the instruction of one of its drawing instructors, Johann Quistorp (1755–1835), a radical who allied himself 'to the Storm and Stress movement with its valorisation of originality over imitation'.⁷ Whilst studying with Quistorp, Friedrich came under the influence of Gotthard Kosegarten, a poet and theologian who preached 'a particular theology of the heart, in which the subjective experience of nature's primal, and therefore divinely created, beauty leads to a direct experience of God'.⁸ This relationship was to endure, with Kosegarten becoming one of Friedrich's earliest collectors. Some of Friedrich's paintings (for example *View of Arkona with Rising Moon*, 1805–6) could be regarded as illustrating some of Kosegarten's sermons, preached on the shore of the island of Rügen. It is not known whether or not Friedrich actually corresponded with or even met the philosopher Schelling, but there seems to be an accord between Schelling's statement that 'in landscape painting only subjective

---

⁶ Watson, *The German Genius*, p. 77, quoting Walter Hofer.
⁷ J. L. Koerner, *Caspar David Friedrich and the Subject of Landscape* (London: Reaktion Books, 1990), p. 76.
⁸ *Ibid.*, p. 77.

representation is possible, since landscape has only a reality in the eyes of the beholder' and the work of the artist who stated that the 'painter should not paint merely what he sees in front of him, but also what he sees within himself'[9]

The *Zeitgeist* for Friedrich would have been rather puritanical, with a strong work ethic but also permeated with a sense that the emotions or feelings could have full expression through the creative art of painting. As we shall see, all of these characteristics can be seen as contained within the work of Friedrich, and enable him to be described by Rosenblum with some hyperbole as embodying the 'German contribution to European Romantic art'.[10] However, in assessing Friedrich's position within German Romanticism one needs to mention, at least briefly, his contemporaries. First, I would highlight Philipp Otto Runge, whose work and ideas were similar to Friedrich's, but whose technical accomplishment, with the exception of *Times of the Day*, did not reach the standard of Friedrich. However, Runge's great achievement, as shown in Chapter 3, was to write the manifesto for Romantic art which helped to establish an understanding between philosophy and art history.

Next, I would mention the work of Friedrich's pupil and friend Carl Gustav Carus, whose subjective experiential aim within his art was similar to that of Friedrich—works here that I would highlight would be *Felsenkeller im Grünen* (1824) ('Rocky Cellar in the Woods'), which bears some similarity with the work of Samuel Palmer, and as an example of a *Rückenfigur* painting *Fenster am Oybin im Mondschein* (1820) ('Monastery Window in the Moonlight').[11] Ernst Ferdinand Oehme (1797–1855) is another important artist in this genre, whose *Gotische Kirchenruine im Walde* (1841) ('Ruined Gothic Church in the Woods') shows a strong Friedrich influence, but although these two artists were

---

[9]   *Ibid.*, p. 74.
[10] Hofmann, *Caspar David Friedrich*, p. 15, quoting Rosenblum.
[11] My translation: taken from Konrad Kaiser, *Caspar David Friedrich und die zeitgenossische Dresdner Landschaftsmalerei* (Schweinfurt, 1970), pp. 29 and 47 and plates 4 and 7.

working within the framework of the Romantic ideal, they did not attain the stature of Friedrich.[12] Finally, Friedrich Overbeck and Franz Pforr (1788–1812) founded the Lukasbund (Brotherhood of St Luke, also known as the Nazarenes), to be joined later by Peter von Cornelius; they were contemporary with this period of German Romanticism but expressed their spiritual ideals through a style of painting similar to medieval religious art. As Rosenblum writes:

> The artists who by and large pursued these Romantic goals [to reconstruct the heavenly in the earthly] most passionately, even desperately, were artists of Northern and especially Northern Protestant origin, artists who seemed to work, like Friedrich, Blake and Runge, not in the art-for-art's-sake ambience of Paris but in the art-for-life's-sake ambience of a private world in which the making of art was a means of communicating with the kinds of mystery that, before the Romantics, were located within the public confines of religion.[13]

The following pages will demonstrate that Friedrich was a fine exemplar of the artists of whom Rosenblum writes.

Friedrich's iconography—Some general comments on the characteristics of his system

Before examining some of Friedrich's paintings in detail, there are a number of characteristics which can be highlighted and applied to many of his works. In terms of the geometry of his works, often they are divided by a vertical axis and by horizontal bands. The vertical axis or axes usually divide the painting into halves, or thirds—in the latter situation there is a suggestion of the triptych as in *Garden Terrace* (1811–12) or sometimes, as in the case of the *Monk by the Sea* (1809), the vertical figure is placed at the position of the golden

---

[12] My translation: Kaiser, *Caspar David Friedrich*, plate 47.
[13] R. Rosenblum, *Modern Painting and the Northern Romantic Tradition* (New York: Harper and Row, 1975), pp. 70–1.

section (roughly, just under than two thirds of the way across the picture).[14] Another characteristic arrangement of form which occurs frequently is for the painting to be divided by an inverted 'V' or circumflex accent with the arms extending from the lower corners of the painting and a 'V' with the arms extending downwards from the upper corners of the picture. Examples here include the *Cross in the Mountains* (1811–12), where the mountain forms the circumflex accent and the rays of the sun the 'V', and the *Chalk Cliffs on Rügen* (after 1818), where the composition includes the 'Vs' but in a reverse formation. Another frequent composition characteristic is the lack of continuity between the foreground and the distance—again illustrated in the *Chalk Cliffs on Rügen* (1825– 6), where the effect is to emphasise the height of the cliffs and the precipice beyond. Instead of the eye being led gradually through a painting there is discontinuity, which forces the mind into contemplating either the infinite distance or a seemingly bottomless chasm. As Hofmann indicates, by the use of these unconventional techniques, by not conforming to the modes of expression (Phrygian, Doric etc.) and avoiding the negativity associated at that time with Mannerism, Friedrich raised the status of landscape painting.[15]

So far as the colour palette is concerned, Friedrich began by using sepia (an interesting point of similarity with Palmer)— described by a correspondent as 'light, beautifully poetic, drawn with the utmost delicacy yet profound'—before eventually moving to oils (1806) when he could be assured of a market for his

---

[14] A more precise ratio is 1:1.618; for a full history of the theory involving both Plato and Euclid see *The Oxford Companion to Art*, ed. H. Osborne (Oxford: Oxford University Press, 1970), pp. 488a–489a, and for a very full discussion of the subject see P. Hemenway, *The Secret Code* (Cologne: Evergreen, 2008).

[15] Hofmann, *Caspar David Friedrich*, p. 24. 'Friedrich wanted to erect a bridge between simple imitation and style, in order to depict nature as a place for subjective experience, while simultaneously conveying the sense of the sacred. Although he was building this bridge he was not a Mannerist except in the positive neutral meaning it had for Poussin.'

works.[16] Sepia is a brown ink wash and can be very appropriate when line and form are a major consideration. It was inexpensive and was popular in Dresden, not a wealthy town, in the early part of the nineteenth century.

When Friedrich moved on to oils, blues, greens and browns generally predominated in his palette. Many of his works depict winter scenes, and for these in particular, lead white, red earth and smalt predominate. Smalt is a 'glass-like material which is used on its own in shades that range from pale, translucent grey to deep blue. A few particles of red earth pigment have been added to greyish smalt and white to make the pale mauve of the sky.'[17] Smalt was used in Germany and in Dresden in particular during the first quarter of the nineteenth century, and from Friedrich's point of view the transparent translucence enabled him to achieve the effect that he desired as, for example, in the *Cross in the Winter Landscape* (1811), sometimes known as the *Cross and Cathedral in the Mountains*. As Aviva Burnstock writes, particularly in respect of *Winter Landscape* (1811):

> The physical characteristics of smalt in oil and the use of stippled brushstrokes, especially in the hills and sky, enhance the transparency and light scattering of the paint surface. This technique effectively creates the texture of a shimmering, bleak misty landscape, in which hills and sky merge into the space beyond the church. Stippled paint appears in paintings throughout Friedrich's career, for example in 'The Cross in the Mountains' in the Kunstmuseum, Düsseldorf, painted in about 1811 and the later and much larger '*Riesengebirge*' (1830–5) now in Berlin. Stippling is used in translucent parts of the painting, especially in the skies and grey-blue parts of the landscape. The paint in these areas may contain smalt, although no

[16] W. Vaughan, *Friedrich* (London: Phaidon Press, 2004), pp. 82 and 95. The correspondent was Duke Emil August of Sachsen-Gotha-Altenburg writing to the Dresden musician and artist Therese aus dem Winckel (1779–1867).

[17] J. Leighton and C. J. Bailey, *Caspar David Friedrich, Winter Landscape* (London: National Gallery Publications, 1990), pp. 52–3, essay by Aviva Burnstock.

analysis is known to have been done. Friedrich is likely to have adopted the technique of stippling in order to achieve effects which would be similar to his early sepias.[18]

The pigment cobalt blue was developed at the time and can be found in some of Friedrich's later paintings, possibly as a replacement for smalt. Many of Friedrich's works have been underdrawn, with pen and pencil being clearly visible when paintings are viewed under infra-red lighting.[19]

People were very important in Friedrich's landscapes and should not be regarded as mere staffage. They fall into two categories: autochthonous, where they are indigenous to their surroundings; or as visitors or wanderers, recognisable, as Schelling points out, 'by their general disposition, appearance or even clothing, all of which is alien in relationship to the landscape itself'.[20] 'Autochthonous' has a Greek derivation which suggests 'born of the soil', and a good example by Friedrich is *Summer (Landscape with a Pair of Lovers)* (1807) where the two lovers blend so well into the scenery, whilst the visitor category could be represented by the *Wanderer above a Sea of Mists* (1818), which will be the subject of detailed analysis later. Schelling observed that the people (autochthonous or stranger) in a painting allow themselves to be 'combined in the landscape in a different sense, and the unique feelings attendant on our conception of such juxtaposition can be elicited'.[21]

A final, general, point should be made regarding Friedrich's depiction of clouds. Unlike Constable, who made such a careful study of clouds as they had been classified by Luke Howard that they were used as illustrations to identify the particular cloud types, Friedrich's representation of them was much vaguer, but his intention was not to show scientific accuracy but to add an

---

[18] John Leighton, Anthony Reeve and Aviva Burnstock, 'A "Winter Landscape" by Caspar David Friedrich', *The National Gallery Technical Bulletin*, 13 (1989).

[19] *Ibid.*, pp. 53–4.

[20] F. W. J. Schelling, *The Philosophy of Art*, trans. D. W. Scott (Minneapolis: University of Minnesota Press, 1989), p. 146.

[21] *Ibid.*, p. 146.

ethereal quality to the landscape or to symbolise a mistiness between heaven and earth.

The remainder of this chapter will be concerned with the analysis of some of Friedrich's works, including some of his mystical paintings as well as those which demonstrate one of the attributes of his genre—their openness to being interpreted in many different ways. By selecting mainly the *Rückenfigur* paintings I will be omitting from this chapter discussion of perhaps Friedrich's best-known painting, *The Cross in the Mountains*; however this work will be discussed in Chapter 9, which considers the sacramental nature of works of art. Where paintings, many of which were not named by Friedrich himself, have been given two possible titles I will initially mention both titles and then continue with the one which has the wider usage.

The Rückenfigur paintings

Whilst the back view of figures was not an innovation, the way in which Friedrich used them was quite novel. In previous uses of the back view, for example, Raphael's *St Paul Preaching at Athens* (1515), where the emphasis is on St Paul preaching to the crowd, or *The Rainbow* by Jan Luyken (1649–1712), or *Affected Feeling* (1780) by Daniel Nicolas Chodowiecki (1726–1801), where the emphasis is on the reaction of the person depicted to what they are seeing, the concern is with the intention of the person in respect to their position in the painting. Often such figures are standing to one side of the landscape, perhaps gesticulating to draw attention to a particular feature, whereas Friedrich's figures are often placed in the line of sight of the viewer and are undemonstrative in themselves, but invite the viewer to join in the contemplation. The use of a figure or figures looking out of a window was perhaps more frequent, such as in *Madonna of the Chancellor Rolin* (*c.* 1435) by Jan van Eyck (1389–1441), or Johann Heinrich Wilhelm Tischbein (1751–1829) showing *Goethe at the Window of his Lodgings in Rome* (1787); *The Draftsman at the Rock* (1640) by Allaert van Everdingen (1621–75) shows the artist in a corner of a painting sketching the scene. These all show the back of a figure, but with a different purpose from that of Friedrich.[22]

Vaughan cites Friedrich as speaking to a visitor to his studio, saying of his *Rückenfiguren* that he 'liked the device because "in Life it deceives the least"'.[23] Vaughan suggests that the intention behind Friedrich's *Rückenfiguren* is to stress 'what you see before you is dependent upon what is within you', which is, of course, consistent with the artist's stated view that he tries to portray the inner man.[24] Prettejohn rightly emphasises that the *Rückenfigur* is 'unlike any previous figure in the history of art in one crucial respect: he [...] is not just a represented object in the picture, but also the embodied subject of the aesthetic experience of the picture—we look *with* rather than merely *at* the *Rückenfigur*'.[25] She draws out here the consistency with the Kantian viewpoint and the aesthetic experience but carefully and correctly points out that Friedrich would not deliberately have set out to demonstrate that theory; it should be remembered that Friedrich, unlike Runge, was not keen on philosophising about theories of art. Although he was not prepared to fetter his approach to art with theories, one can see in Friedrich's art a consistency with the views expressed by Schelling in the latter's approach to landscape and nature, and also, as we shall see when examining the *Monk by the Sea*, existential tendencies.

I should at this juncture introduce the concept of *Eigentümlichkeit*, applied often to the German Romantics. Essentially it means a unique approach to one's identity. In the words of Koerner, *Eigentümlichkeit* 'locates truth as property of the unique, particular, experiencing, and radically autonomous Self'.[26] In a rare statement of his approach to aesthetics, Friedrich wrote of a Temple of *Eigentümlichkeit*, whose power is essential to creativity:

[22] More details on the back-view figures will be found in Hofmann, *Caspar David Friedrich*, pp. 256–7.

[23] Vaughan, *Friedrich*, p. 178.

[24] *Ibid.*, p. 203.

[25] Prettejohn, *Beauty and Art*, p. 57.

[26] Koerner, *Caspar David Friedrich*, p. 59.

The spirit of nature reveals itself differently to each individual, and for that reason nobody can burden anyone else
with his own teaching and rules as if they constituted an
infallible law. No man is the yardstick for all, each is the
yardstick only for himself and for minds more or less
kindred to his.[27]

Friedrich emphasises the need to listen to the God within, and
to adhere to the Ten Commandments. In a sentence that would
resonate with William Blake, he writes:

Beware of the superficial knowledge of cold facts, beware
sinful ratiocination, for it kills the heart, and when heart and
mind have died in a man, there art cannot dwell. Preserve
a pure and childlike understanding within yourself, and
follow the voice of your inner self unconditionally, for it
is the Divine in us and does not lead us astray.[28]

The rule of life expressed here is very much in accord with that
of Friedrich's friend and confidant Friedrich Schleiermacher,
who wrote that

It necessarily follows that the ground of our feeling of
absolute dependence, i.e. the divine causality, extends
as widely as the order of nature and the finite causality
contained in it; consequently the divine causality is posited
as equal in compass to finite causality. And further, the
feeling of absolute dependence stands in exactly the same
relationship with the partial dependence-feeling as with
the partial freedom-feeling, and so in that relationship
the antithesis between the two last disappears; but finite
causality is what it is only by means of its contract with
finite passivity, so it is to be inferred that the divine
causality is contrasted with the finite.[29]

In a coincidence of thought with Friedrich and Blake, Schleiermacher emphasises the duality within all human beings—freedom

[27] Extract from *Friedrich's Journal* (1803)—*On Art and the Spirit of Art*
contained in Hofmann, *Caspar David Friedrich*, p. 269.
[28] *Ibid.* p. 269.
[29] F. Schleiermacher, *The Christian Faith*, English translation ed. H. R.
Mackintosh and J. S. Stewart (Edinburgh: T. & T. Clark, 1928), p. 201.

and dependence on the God within—and Friedrich is saying make sure that it is the God within that is being followed. Perhaps surprisingly these statements of Friedrich and Schleiermacher accord well with the view of the pre-Enlightenment Leonardo da Vinci (1452–1519), who, writing three centuries earlier, stated that 'the divinity which is the science of painting transmutes the painter's mind into a resemblance of the divine mind'.[30]

It is my contention that in the *Rückenfigur* paintings Friedrich is inviting the viewer to look with the *Rückenfigur* at the scene or landscape and then have their own experiential relationship with the scene presented. This view, which I would describe as a sense of quiet contemplation of the depths of existence, resonates with the concept of *Innigkeit*, a process, as Vaughan notes, of contemplation seen as 'being typically German in its inwardness and depth'.[31]

The next chapter will offer an examination of a number of Friedrich's paintings which point to the transcendent but this chapter concludes with a detailed look at one of the best-known *Rückenfigur* works—the *Wanderer above a Sea of Mists* (1818).

Wanderer above a Sea of Fog or Mists (1818)[32]

In terms of its composition, the picture exhibits the V formation, with a strong verticality established by the figure himself. There is a very strong inverted V formed by the rock in the foreground, which has no link with the middle or background other than through the figure which stands at the apex of the mountain. This lack of linkage emphasises the precipice on which the wanderer is standing—he can go no further. In the middle ground there is a shallow V formed by the distant hills, which just rise above the fog, with both arms of the V meeting just below the heart of the figure. The background is formed from another inverted V mountain, offset to the left of the figure,

[30] Quoted by Rachel Campbell-Johnston in *The Times*, 5 November 2011.
[31] Vaughan, *Friedrich*, p. 178.
[32] The title is of doubtful authority.

139

balanced by a stack on the right above which is the horizontal banding of the clouds.

The emphasis is very clearly on the figure; he divides the picture both vertically and horizontally, with the diagonals of the picture crossing at the centre of his waist. He is dressed in the uniform of the volunteer rangers, 'detachments called into service by King Friedrich Wilhelm III of Prussia to war against Napoleon.'[33] Some historians have suggested that the wanderer was Colonel Friedrich Gotthard von Brincken of the Saxon Infantry, but Friedrich has rendered him anonymous through his placing within the painting, which indicates a more general representation and an encouragement to the viewer to place him or herself as the wanderer. The painting dates from around 1818, which is after the defeat of Napoleon, when anti-French feeling in the German-speaking world was running high but before any movement towards building a truly unified German nation had really become established.

There are three main interpretations of this painting—as representative of the sublime, of the leap of faith or of a political force for a unified German nation. In terms of the sublime, two techniques are employed here: there is the precipice over which the figure is looking into the unfathomable depths and there is the fog itself, giving an ethereal quality to the painting overall with a suggestion of limitlessness both in the horizon and in the depths. Although there are no linking pathways taking the viewer onto the distance, there is a considerable variation in detail of the vegetation, which gives an indication of distance. There is significant detail in the painting of the trees to the left and immediately beside the figure; to the right there is less detail and on the two hills which seem to radiate out from the figure there is still less; and finally in the far distance there is no detail at all. The ethereal quality of light depicted in the fog and the sky is very much in line with Schelling's observation that 'the true object, the idea, remains formless, and it is up to the observer to discover it from within the fragrant, formless essence before

[33] Koerner, *Caspar David Friedrich*, p. 179.

him'.[34] The use of the *Rückenfigur* in this landscape encourages the viewer to try to see beyond the veil towards the ineffable. In her discussion of this painting, Prettejohn draws a parallel with the Kantian aesthetic experience, highlighting the uncanny symmetry around the figure and the inability to measure the space in terms of post-Renaissance perspective, 'but only in relation to the figure itself'.[35] However, whilst agreeing that this is so, as Kant's remarks were concerned more with nature in reality rather than in representation I see an even closer accord with Schelling than with Kant. In Kantian terms, for the sublime truly to be represented by the work of a creative artist, that artist needs to be a genius—maybe Friedrich can be regarded as such, but Schelling does not demand such a quality from the artist endeavouring to elucidate in a work of art the divine mind from within the self.

Koerner rightly compares the insubstantiality and obscurity in the representation of the landscape in this painting with Edmund Burke's aesthetic of the sublime, where he 'valorised obscurity and strength of expression over the Neo-classical ideal of clarity, precision and adherence to rule [...] Burke argued that terror, the passion associated with the sublime, is best aroused by things "dark, uncertain [and] confused" while vastness and infinity, the chief attributes of the sublime in nature can only be elicited by obscurity'.[36]

Friedrich himself said:

> When a landscape is covered in fog, it appears larger, more sublime, and heightens the strength of the imagination and excites expectation, rather like a veiled woman. The eye and fantasy feel themselves more attracted to the hazy distance than to that which lies near and distinct before us.[37]

---

[34] Schelling, *The Philosophy of Art*, p. 145.
[35] Prettejohn, *Beauty and Art*, pp. 55–6.
[36] Koerner, *Caspar David Friedrich*, p. 180.
[37] *Ibid.*, p. 181. This quotation appeared in Sigrid Hinz, *Caspar David Friedrich in Briefen und Bekenntnissen* (Munich: Rogner & Bernhard, 1968), p. 123.

Here the actual feeling of the sublime is located in the viewer and is not an objective characteristic of the landscape itself—or as Kant would have said, the sublimity is located in the mind of the beholding subject. The Wanderer, with his feet planted firmly on the ground, is so prominent in this painting that he is perhaps helping to mediate between the insubstantiality of the landscape and the artist himself, who may be the *Rückenfigur*. Is the Temple of *Eigentümlichkeit* located within the Wanderer who invites the viewer to ascertain the 'truth as property of the unique, particular, experiencing, and radically autonomous Self'? The answer here can only be—perhaps, but I do consider that the *Wanderer above a Sea of Mists* must be one of the greatest works by Friedrich to attempt to induce the feelings of the sublime within the viewer.

With its subject poised on the edge of a chasm, this picture poses another question—is the Wanderer contemplating a leap of faith, the Kierkegaardian leap? To digress, one can view an approach to belief in God in perhaps three main ways. First there is the propositional (or strong fideist) approach, where one's belief derives from dogmatic statements. Secondly, a faith can be derived from a particular experience like the calling of St Paul on the road to Damascus (Acts 9:3–19 and 22:6–16), and thirdly there is an approach derived as far as possible from enculturation, sometimes called the cultural-linguistic approach. These approaches span the spectrum of religious thought from the evangelical to the liberal or even radical—in Christian terms the evangelical could be represented by Billy Graham and his successors and the radical by Don Cupitt.

Wherever one places oneself on this spectrum there is, at some stage in the attaining of a religious conviction, a leap of faith, referred to as the Kierkegaardian leap. With those of a fideist persuasion there is an acceptance of the proposition without any need for further discussion or consideration: for one persuaded by a religious experience, there is a personal awakening or realisation, whilst the cultural-linguist approach will require much reading and learning the language of faith prior to making that leap.

In the history of the philosophy of religion many attempts were made to prove the existence of God (Anselm probably produced one of the better attempts but, nevertheless, was unsuccessful), but eventually the impossibility of the task came to be recognised. God then came to be described as, for example, the Ultimate Reality, the Ground of All Being and the Fifth Dimension—descriptions which each in their own way try to describe that which is beyond time and space and beyond the comprehension of the human brain.

As a mystic and painter who endeavoured to represent the ineffable, Friedrich would have been well aware of the concept of a leap of faith; this is evident in a number of his works, not only the *Wanderer above a Sea of Mists*. For example, the Kierkegaardian leap can be discerned in early paintings such as the *Tetschen Altarpiece* (1807–8), where the chasm is shown just beyond the frame with the mountains rising in the centre of the scene, to later works such as *Two Men at Moonrise* (1835–7), where the leap would be from the rock on which they are standing across the sea to the rising moon. This contemplative work in sepia was one of his last, and the rising moon was possibly meant to represent the risen Christ or the Holy Mother, with Friedrich maybe thinking of his own imminent death, with the hope of redemption and salvation.

The idea of viewing across a chasm occurs in many of Friedrich's works but the *Wanderer above a Sea of Mists* and the other two paintings highlighted above are typical of the way in which he points towards transcendence, towards Ultimate Reality.

Since this book is primarily concerned with portrayal of the ineffable or numinous, I will consider only briefly the third interpretation of *Wanderer above a Sea of Mists*—as representing a political force for a unified German nation. At the time this painting was produced, Germany, if one can really describe it as that, consisted of some 200 individual states—some, such as Pomerania, being very large and others, such as Lippe, very small.[38] Although the German nation was dispersed, there was a strong sense of nationalism within Friedrich—enhanced by the dislike

---

[38] Stone, *Times Atlas of World History*, pp. 216–17.

of France through the Napoleonic Wars and indeed the actions within France of Napoleon himself. A political interpretation of the *Wanderer above a Sea of Mists* can then be established in which the Wanderer can be seen as representative of the German people contemplating the future of their nation—is the nation going to fall into the abyss or is it going to soar into prominence as it moves into the middle distance and beyond into the infinity of the future? The relationship with France will be explored in more detail when *The Chasseur* is examined, but the *Wanderer above a Sea of Mists* was regarded as of such political importance that it was taken out of context by the magazine *Der Spiegel* (8 May 1995) and modified to show the Wanderer contemplating Germany's past—concentration-camp barbed wire, a uniformed soldier jumping over barbed wire to freedom and a group of soldiers marching out of the picture.[39] The message here was clearly to look to a future of freedom whilst not forgetting the past. The future that this wanderer would have been contemplating would have been one, approximately five years after re-unification day, when the topic of conversation in Germany was whether or not normality in the German context could ever be achieved or indeed was even desirable. In this context, normality meant on the one hand establishing a good relationship with the Jews and on the other the reinstatement of a 'positive German national identity'.[40] Of the former, there was no doubt that this should be promoted and achieved, whilst for the latter there were mixed views, with a number of politicians and philosophers concerned about the possibility of the rise of an aggressive German nationalism. The ramifications of German politics are clearly outside the scope of this book but for more information the reader is referred to Peter Watson's *The German Genius*, details of which are given in the bibliography. It is, however, interesting to note the similarity between the political interpretation of the *Wanderer above a Sea of Mists* in 1820 and the interpretation of the same painting in 1995—a nation contemplating its future.

---

[39] Hofmann, *Caspar David Friedrich*, pp. 9–13.
[40] Watson, *The German Genius*, p. 783.

→ 8 ←

Caspar David Friedrich's Later Works

This chapter examines a number of later works by Friedrich, concluding with a short section setting his *œuvre* in a theological context.

The Monk by the Sea (c. 1809)

This large painting shows the lone figure of a monk, deep in thought, with his chin resting on his hand, standing on a shallow cliff looking out to a sea surmounted by a dark, stormy sky in the distance, with blue sky immediately overhead. The composition of the painting shows a strong horizontal emphasis, with five bands, one representing the land, one the sea and three the clouds and sky. Whilst horizontality is the prominent compositional characteristic, there is also a typical Friedrich V structure present but only lightly stressed. There is the very shallow inverted V of the land, possibly sand dunes or more probably rounded grey rock, and then a slightly more prominent inverted V formed by the boundary between the grey and white clouds. There is an infinity of space between the apices of the two shallow triangles, with just the faint line of the horizon being visible between the almost black sea and the very dark clouds.

The monk, a lone, isolated figure located 64 per cent of the distance from the right to the left of the picture—close to the dimension of the golden section—is the sole vertical element in the work, other than the vertical brush strokes of the heavy clouds on the horizon. Above the horizon the dark clouds merge into a band of much lighter clouds, which then dissolve into the deep-blue sky above the monk. The choppy sea is shown to be black, reflecting the storm clouds, which themselves fade from black on the horizon up to grey, then white, before being gradually replaced by the blue of the clear sky. There is some vertical striation in the rendering of the clouds and sky which takes the eye up and down the picture. The monk is shown standing at the apex of the shallow triangle formed by the cliff, with his back to the viewer staring out to sea. The monk is shown as a small, isolated figure, emphasising the huge scale of the sea and sky.

The viewer here has the sense of sharing the viewpoint of the monk, staring into the scene as though looking for a vanishing point. It is this encouragement to try to look further and further into the painting that is one of the elements that point towards the transcendent—one is constantly trying to see beyond. The effect of this dark colour scheme in the lower part of the picture is to bring the horizon, with its dark storm cloud, forward towards the monk, whilst the aerial perspective of the light cloud gives the effect of a tremendous expanse of sky and cloud stretching towards infinity. There is a strong contrast between light and dark in the painting. The cliff-top is lit brightly beneath the bright sky immediately overhead. This is contrasted with the black sea, painted even darker than the storm clouds, which have been painted to have the effect of blurring the horizon in the middle distance and reducing the horizon on the right and left wings of the picture. This treatment elicits a similar reaction in the viewer to that of the aerial perspective inasmuch as it encourages the viewer to look deeply into the picture in an endeavour to discern what lies beyond. In a similar way to the works of Palmer which point towards the transcendent, Friedrich meets Otto's criteria of the contrast between light and dark and the suggestion of a tremendous distance or huge empty space.

In addition, two other features stand out in this picture that characteristically point towards the transcendent—the loneliness of the monk and his insignificance in the face of the storm brewing in the distance, and the treatment of the horizon, which encourages the viewer to stare into the distance, wondering what it is that could lie beyond. These features, combined with the size of the painting, give an impression of the sublime and emphasise the power of nature in very much the way Ward achieves with *Gordale Scar*—the insignificance of the powerful bull contrasted with the power of the Creator can be compared with the insignificance of the monk set beside the awesome power of the storm and its effect on the sea. The characteristic Friedrich discontinuity between the horizontal banding stops the eye of the viewer from roaming through the picture from foreground to background, the banding forcing the viewer to pause with the monk in viewing the vastness of the sky and contemplating the minuteness and insignificance of the monk himself. With this work Friedrich surely intends to represent mankind considering his own insignificance when compared with the God-created universe, a universe which Friedrich is suggesting lies beyond what is attainable by the monk alone—in other words, the Kingdom of Heaven itself. The art critic Kleist, a contemporary of Friedrich, wrote of this work:

> There can be nothing sadder or more desolate in the world than this place: the only spark of life in the broad domain of death, the lonely centre in the lonely circle. The picture, with its two or three mysterious subjects, lies there like an apocalypse, as if it were thinking Young's *Night Thoughts*, and since it has, in its uniformity and boundlessness, no foreground but the frame, it is as if one's eyelids had been cut off.[1]

It is interesting that Kleist quotes Edward Young's long narrative poem, *Night-Thoughts*, as this work was of considerable inspiration to the artist Samuel Palmer, the subject of Chapter 5.[2]

Kleist equates this work with sadness—I am not convinced of this and would argue that it represents another example of the German *Innigkeit*—deep thought but not necessarily sadness. Secondly, if he is a monk contemplating the infinite mystery of the divine and the possibilities after death, then he may well be excited and fearful at the contemplation of this which evokes the sublime, but not necessarily sad.

[1] Hofmann, *Caspar David Friedrich*, p. 56, quoting Kleist.
[2] E. Young, *The Complaint: or, Night-Thoughts on Life, Death, and Immortality* (London, 1743).

One obvious question to be asked in connection with this work is the identity of the monk—is he Friedrich himself? Friedrich kept his studio very much like a monk's cell (as shown in the portrait by Georg Friedrich Kersting (1785–1847)—*Caspar David Friedrich in his Studio*) and at times wore clothing that was not unlike that of a monk. Koerner remarks: 'For along with the cell-like bareness of his atelier, Friedrich's travelling cloak evokes both a sense of penitent self-denial for the sake of art and a notion of the artist as purgatorial wanderer, never at home and always in transit, even when he stands in his own studio'.[3] This, coupled with his feeling for Pietism, gives credence to the view that *The Monk by the Sea* is a self-portrait, the painter-monk contemplating the unfathomable, the immanence and transcendence of the Ultimate Reality. In addition to expressing a oneness with God, Friedrich is also highlighting the solitude of the human—who not only *is* alone, like other creatures, but also *knows* that he or she is alone. As Paul Tillich writes:

> God himself cannot liberate man from his aloneness: it is man's greatness that he is centred within himself. Separated from his world he is thus able to look *at* it. Only because he can look at it can he know and love and transform it. God, in creating him the ruler of the earth, had to separate him and thrust him into aloneness. Man is also therefore able to be spoken to by God and by man.[4]

In this painting, the painter-monk is fulfilling the role of priest by attempting to bring a concept of the Ultimate Reality to mankind—an eternal presence informing the lone receptive human being, and to give existential meaning to his or her life.

While the artist is endeavouring to suggest the numinous, the effects of pointing towards the transcendent are only going to be apperceived by those viewers who are susceptible to that experience—who are indeed 'his kindred spirits'. The writer, Marianne Rankin, who uses Friedrich as an exemplar of those

---

[3] Koerner, *Caspar David Friedrich*, p. 72.
[4] P. Tillich, *The Eternal Now* (London: SCM Press, 2002 [1963]), p. 4.

who endeavour to portray the numinous, suggests with regard to *The Monk by the Sea*:

> The palette is limited but effective—pale hues for the sand and clouds, blues ranging from deep, dark tones of the sea and nearer sky with lighter blue for the more distant scene. The light is muted, suggestive of evening. There is movement in the sky and sea. One can feel the wind, the cold of the evening and the aloneness of the figure on the shore. The emptiness of the painting appeals to me, it seems to enable the imagination to run free. There is more to it than just the natural scene.
>
> The monk stands on the empty sea-shore gazing out at eternity and as he is turned away, we look out with him. So we too contemplate infinity—the empty sand, dark sea and scudding clouds in the vast sky.[5]

At the time of this painting, *The Sorrows of Werther* by Goethe had just been issued, which contains the passage: 'It is night; I am alone, forlorn on the hill of storms [...] no hut receives me from the rain; forlorn on the hill of storms.'[6] Hofmann emphasises the influence of Burke: 'What Burke says there (in his *Philosophical Enquiry* [...]) about the "uniformity", "vastness" and endlessness of deserts, seashores and threatening clouds reads like a commentary on *The Monk by the Sea*.'[7] Highlighting these two characteristics, Hofmann continues by quoting Schiller:

> It is a compound of unease, expressed in the highest degree as terror, and joy capable of intensifying to delight, and although it is not really pleasure, it is much preferred to any pleasure by fine souls. This compounding of two contradictory sensations in one single emotion is an irrefutable proof of our moral independence.[8]

This independence is demonstrated when, instead of experiencing the sublime as a physical threat, we create it as the object of our own imagination, in an act of 'free contemplation'.

---

[5] From private correspondence.
[6] Hofmann, *Caspar David Friedrich*, p. 58, quoting Goethe.
[7] *Ibid.*
[8] *Ibid.*, pp. 58–60.

Friedrich does this when he paints his alter ego as a monk by the sea, exposed to the dangers of nature. When Schiller says that a person approaching the 'terrifying images of his own imagination' does so 'fearlessly with horrified pleasure', it applies to Friedrich, both as painter and monk. And it follows, in Schiller's words, 'that we ourselves stand in two different relationships to the object, and therefore that the two opposing natures must be united in us.'[9]

Thus, in this picture there is not only the suggestion of pointing toward the transcendent, but there is also an insight into the personality of the painter himself. This insight into the creative forces at work within Friedrich is very much in accord with the concept of the artist as co-creator, described by C. S. Lewis.[10] The style of *The Monk by the Sea* is not unique to Friedrich; the painting resonates, for example, with works of Turner, such as *Venetian Festival* (1846) or *Off the Coast: Seascape and Clouds* (unknown date but nineteenth century). The ethereal, impressionistic treatment is apparent in all these works. In both *The Monk by the Sea* and *Seascape and Clouds* there is a suggestion of the colour field paintings developed by the Abstract Expressionists in the twentieth century. Indeed, Rosenblum draws a very precise link between *The Monk by the Sea* and Mark Rothko's *Green on Blue*:

> If these paintings look alike in their renunciation of almost everything but a sombre, luminous void, is this merely an example of what Edwin Panofsky once called 'pseudomorphosis', that is the accidental appearance at different moments in the history of art of works whose close formal analogies falsify the fact that their meaning is totally different. Or does this imply that there may be a true connection between Friedrich and Rothko, that the similarity of their formal structure is the result of a similarity of feeling and intention and that, indeed, there may even be a tradition in modern

9   *Ibid.*, p. 60.
10   See A. McGrath, *The Intellectual World of C. S..Lewis* (Chichester: John Wiley, 2014), pp. 55–74.

painting that could bridge the century and a half that separates them?[11]

From his few writings, it is known that Friedrich believed in expressing his religious feelings or experiences through his art— 'Regard every pure mental impulse as holy, honour every devout presentiment as holy, for it is the art within us'—very much as a modern icon painter would regard it as essential to pray his images into existence.[12] Whilst it may not be possible to prove a similarity of feeling across a century and a half or even beyond, I would suggest that there is a similarity of intention that can be traced over the centuries of artistic endeavour. That endeavour to 'transmute the painter's mind into a resemblance of the divine mind' exhibited itself in many different ways as time passed, from the early medieval paintings with their images of Christ and biblical scenes, through landscapes of Runge and Friedrich, to the colour fields of the twentieth century, so I would suggest that there is indeed a similarity of feeling and intention rather than the similarities being a spurious serendipity.

In summary, three features stand out in this picture that point towards the transcendent—first, the loneliness of the monk and his insignificance in the face of the storm brewing in the distance; secondly, the contrast between light and dark; and thirdly, the treatment of the horizon, which encourages the viewer to stare into the distance, wondering what it is that could lie beyond, 'beyond the veil'. These features, combined with the size of the painting, give an impression of the sublime and emphasise the power of nature, very much as Ward achieves with *Gordale Scar*. *The Monk by the Sea* can be interpreted as an allegory of the power of the Creator and, furthermore, illuminates aspects of Friedrich's personality that may not be at all obvious.

---

[11] R. Rosenblum, *Modern Painting and the Northern Romantic Tradition: Friedrich to Rothko* (New York: Harper and Row, 1975), p. 10.

[12] Hofmann, *Caspar David Friedrich*, p. 269, quoting from Friedrich's *On Art and the Spirit of Art*, written in his journal in 1803. Aidan Hart speaks of praying his icons (images of Christ and his saints) into existence.

Two Men Contemplating the Moon (c. 1825–30)

There are a number of paintings with the back view of two men contemplating the moon or just looking at the landscape or seascape in the moonlight—the one I have chosen is generally called *Two Men Contemplating the Moon* (c. 1825–30). This is the third version which Friedrich painted, the first having been produced in about 1819.

Beginning with an analysis of the composition, there is a very strong V formation created out of the shape of the tree to the right of the picture merging into the hill on the left. This is sitting in another flattened V formed by the heavy rocks in the foreground, between which lies a pathway upon which the two men are standing. The path curves out of the picture at the place where the men are standing. The moon is located at the intersection of the two diagonals, which is at the same height as the waists of the two men. There is a distant inverted V formed by the hill on the right fading into the misty background. The vertical elements are formed by the two men located on the left some three quarters of the way from the right-hand border of the painting.

The Friedrich characteristic of looking over a chasm is achieved by there being nothing visible between the tree with its exposed roots and the moon, the pathway having curved out of the picture in the foreground. The leap of faith as described when discussing the *Wanderer above a Sea of Mists* is a possible interpretation but in this particular painting the air of mystery is created by the strange arrangement of the central tree, which is shown with the roots half-exposed. Friedrich effects an aerial perspective by lightening the mist around the moon, which emphasises the distance—unlike Samuel Palmer, who produced many 'moony' pictures, the Friedrich moon has not been exaggerated in size. In fact, the smaller moon has the effect in this picture of exaggerating the horizontal distance towards the far horizon hidden by the mist, but hinted at by the row of evergreen trees on the right-hand side of the picture. This, as with many of the paintings considered here, asks the viewer to look very deeply into the picture and to try to discern what may lie beyond. The comment on the Metropolitan Museum of Art website offers a rather wider role for the moon and summarises the Rückenfigur motif rather simplistically:

> The mood of pious contemplation relates to fascination with the moon as expressed in contemporary poetry, literature, philosophy, and music. Both figures are seen from the back so that the viewer can participate in their communion with nature, which the Romantics saw as a manifestation of the Sublime.[13]

So far as the figures themselves are concerned it has been suggested that the larger figure is Friedrich himself with a student, August Heinrich (1794–1822), leaning on his shoulder. It has also been suggested that Friedrich's uniform is that of the Lützower Corps (freedom fighters in the War of Liberation).[14] It was reported by the Dresden poet and translator Karl Foster (1784–1841) that when visiting Friedrich's atelier, with the highly respected but arrogant Peter Cornelius, a member of the Brotherhood of St Luke, they were told by Friedrich that the two figures were 'at their demagogic machinations'—an illegal activity at that time when Metternich was anxious to subdue those not in favour of the settlement achieved at the Congress of Vienna in 1815, which left Austria and Prussia as the two most powerful states in the German-speaking world.[15] This is a different approach to the interpretation of this work from that of Foster, who related that Friedrich always knew how 'to place his figures in a meaningful relation to the landscape [succinctly suggesting] contemplation of the infinite'.[16] It is just possible that Friedrich was endeavouring to fool Cornelius, who was initially so dismissive of Friedrich, but knowing Friedrich's political views, I would say this was unlikely and that the artist was being quite serious. As Koerner remarks: 'Demagogue was a derogatory term used by conservatives for someone who espoused

---

[13] http://www.metmuseum.org/toah/works-of-art/2000.51
[14] Vaughan, *Friedrich*, p. 158.
[15] *Ibid.*, p. 155, and Koerner, *Caspar David Friedrich*, pp. 239–43.
[16] Koerner, *Caspar David Friedrich*, p. 241.

the ideal of a unified German state established by constitution and governed with the consent of it citizens'.[17]

Friedrich was very keen on the establishment of a unified Germany; I would suggest therefore that the anti-*demagogen-verfolgung* (persecution of the demagogues) importance of this painting is paramount, indicated by Friedrich's own comment when he usually carefully refrained from giving any indication of the possible interpretations of his works.[18] Napoleon had been defeated; the returning soldiers were no longer particularly loyal to their old states and they might have expected that the king of Prussia and the leaders of the other states would have been keen to support the unity of Germany. This was not to be, which led those in favour of unity to form nationalistic bands 'or "German societies" with names like Teutonia, Vandalia, Germania and Arminia'.[19] Members of the societies wore clothes which resembled the attire (*altdeutsch* clothing) worn by German-speaking people of the Middle Ages, when there was supposedly strong support for a unified Germany: this out-dated attire is reflected in *Two Men Contemplating the Moon* and the other paintings with similar titles. This movement was a threat to the privileged establishment, and following a decree from Wilhelm III declaring that the Napoleonic War was a 'War of liberation rather than a Freedom War, so as to discourage any analogy to the American and French revolutions', a further decree was promulgated in 1819 which effectively outlawed the German freedom societies and forbad the wearing of the *altdeutsch* costume.[20] There is thus a sadness about this painting and some of the other *Rückenfiguren*; Friedrich was expressing the collapse of hope for a new future, as indicated by the fallen tree and the *altdeutsch* clothing.

However, apart from historical-political connotations, there is an intimacy about this picture both in the viewer feeling that

---

[17] *Ibid.*
[18] Vaughan, *Friedrich*, p. 158.
[19] Koerner, *Caspar David Friedrich*, p. 242.
[20] *Ibid.*, p. 243.

he or she may be taken into the confidence of the two speakers and in the close relationship of the speakers to the surrounding nature. There is the closeness of the gnarled roots immediately in front of the two men, and, on the right of the picture, the mossy pathway and the overall mistiness almost enable the viewer to feel and smell the atmosphere and to share that close relationship with nature.

The moon is sometimes used as a symbol of the risen Christ; whether it should be interpreted as such in this case remains open, but is merely a possibility. If so, then it would reveal an additional dimension to the painting of consideration of the future—be it a personal future beyond death or the two men contemplating a future Germany where the individuals would be free from any sort of oppression. Koerner suggests that the '*Rückenfigur* transposes the metaphysical yearning for union with nature into the contemporary political imperative of a unified state'.[21] I may be guilty of unjustified eisegesis, but I think the *Rückenfiguren* are open to a wider interpretation than this, with the invitation being to the viewer to join with the figures in contemplation of God's created world—both the world of nature and the world of human interactivity. It is true that there is evidence of much decay but decay in nature always leads to a nurturing of new growth, although for Germany that growth or resurrection was not realised until 1871 (or even, as some would argue, 1989)—but arrive it eventually did.

The Abbey in the Oak Wood (c. 1809)

Departing now from the *Rückenfiguren*, the large *Abbey in the Oak Wood* is divided into two halves by the presence of the entrance to the ruined abbey tower in the centre foreground, with a group of four aging, bare oak trees on each side. On the right-hand side only there is evidence of more of the ruined abbey, with one of the oaks almost appearing to be growing out of the structure. Visible through the doorway in the tower

---

[21] *Ibid.*

is a simple crucifix, which seems to have survived in spite of the decay which has occurred throughout the remainder of the abbey. In the immediate foreground, there are groups of black-clad people (mourners?) on the left, and on the right there is one conventional cross, marking a grave, with a number of markers with simple two-pitch roofs as well as on the extreme right a metal cross surmounted by a semi-circle, together with a small notice or marker. The cross is almost identical to the cross at the top of the window in the abbey tower. The addition of pitched roofs to grave crosses seems to have been a tradition in this part of Germany, as it is shown in other Friedrich paintings, for example *Graveyard under Snow* (1826–7). In the middle distance through the mist there is the suggestion of many more trees sloping down the hill into the mist and away from the viewer. The ground around the abbey is uneven, uncultivated and untended.

The upper branches of the oak trees are silhouetted against a bright sky gradually darkening to the point of being dark sepia immediately above the viewer. There is a crescent moon showing with the vague outline of the full moon. The misty horizon is shown at about one third of the way from the base of the picture. The overall mood depicted is one of gloom and decay imbued with mystery. The dark sepia of the land around the abbey is very similar in form to *The Monk by the Sea* (both of these large pictures were exhibited together) with its dark-blue foreground. This similarity is carried upwards with the light middle and dark upper part of the painting—again almost suggesting the colour field paintings of the twentieth century. Such is the similarity that these paintings could be called 'study in blue' and 'study in sepia'. The picture raises many questions, the main one being the activity of the people. The use of the many autochthonous, spread out, black-clad figures invites questions of the viewer: what are they there for, what are they doing, thus adding to the enigmatic atmosphere? If they really were a mourning party then would they not be grouped around a grave? But then, would an abbey in such a state of ruin still be used for funerals? Perhaps a more plausible explanation is that the mourners were attending the abbey on a day of some significance when they were remembering the dead of the past—perhaps the dead of the fourth and fifth coalition wars (1806–9). The ruined abbey could be said to represent the Catholic Church—in decline and, in Germany, being replaced by the Lutheran Church with its emphasis on the word rather than on the sacramental services conducted in grand churches or cathedral buildings. The retention of the crucifix, however, suggests that in spite of the decline of the Catholic Church, the cross is still there to be followed but within the context of the Lutheran or Moravian Churches.

Perspective is emphasised by the diminishing size of the oaks, beyond the eight oaks in the foreground. It is also evident from the diminishing size of the people and the grave markers. The overall effect of this is to give great depth to the picture. There is a general air of mistiness about this painting which is achieved by a combination of aerial perspective and the depiction of mist in the distance, lower down the slope. With regard to the use of mist (and this applies equally to the *Wanderer above a Sea of Mists*), Friedrich wrote:

> When a landscape is covered in fog, it appears larger, more sublime, and heightens the strength of the imagination and excites expectation, rather like a veiled woman. The eye and fantasy feel themselves more attracted to the hazy distance than to that which lies near and distinct before us.[22]

The overall effect of this combination of mist and aerial perspective is to imbue the picture with mystery. The lower third of this picture is dark, the remainder being light, punctuated by the eight oaks, with the exception of a small triangle of dark cloud in the top left-hand corner. The light sky emphasises the detail of the oaks and the cross in the window of the tower. This light contrast realises one of the characteristics that Otto highlighted as necessary to intimate transcendence. The unanswered questions in this picture highlight its ambiguity, which is brought out well in an ekphrastic (vivid description of a scene) sonnet by the Dresden poet Karl Theodor Körner (1791–1813), which begins:

[22] *Ibid.*, p. 181.

> The fountain of grace flows in death,
> And those there are comrades in bliss,
> Who pass through the grave into eternal life,

and ends:

> Here I can boldly trust my heart;
> Cold admiration I shall not have—no, I feel,
> And in feeling art completes itself.[23]

In this sonnet Körner moves from an interpretation of this painting as pointing towards the transcendent to a position where, as Koerner emphasises, by elevating 'us to the eternal [...] Friedrich's canvas justifies our faith in the redemptive powers of art per se, and in our subjective capacity to feel those powers.'[24]

Thus, there is the suggestion in this work that the viewer is being invited to partake of the existential angst of the participants in the painting. Whether or not one can agree with Koerner's suggestion that what Friedrich has created in his works can be translated into the redemptive power of art in general is open to question—I would argue that it is only true of those works which specifically include those characteristics which originated with Otto and have been refined further in respect of the paintings analysed in this book.

This particular painting certainly exudes an air of mystery, of the sublime and of transcendence. The decaying old abbey indicates not only that the Church of Rome has been replaced but also that the church building itself is not essential to the worship of God or the experience of the ineffable. The minute figures in this very large painting emphasise the inconsequentiality of mankind in comparison with the Creator, a characteristic common to many of the works which point towards the transcendent. The sense of something beyond death can be inferred from the dying oaks in the foreground, set against the younger vegetation in the middle distance, and justifies Körner's ekphrasis.

[23] *Ibid.*, pp. 109–10.
[24] *Ibid.*, p. 110.

This painting and the *Monk by the Sea*, with their blocks of dark and light tones, point towards the colour field works of the twentieth century; both have an indistinct horizon, encouraging the viewer to peer into the distance to try to see that which lies beyond, and both emphasise the insignificance of man compared with the creative power of God.

The Large Enclosure (c. 1832)

In this evocative painting of the River Elbe, near Dresden, Friedrich has taken the viewer into the very centre of the picture by an extraordinary use of distorted perspective, almost to the point of achieving a view of the transcendent itself. Not only is the horizon located very close to the point of the golden mean, but there is also a hyperbolic effect created by the curving lines, which emerge from the two foreground corners of the painting and then meet in the centre with the curve of the clouds just above the horizon completing the effect. Just above this meeting point is the low point in the curving horizon created by the rising hills to the right and the rising trees to the left. Vaughan refers to the 'strange urgency to this picture [given by] the oddly distorted perspective, the "fish-eye" view that the artist appears to have taken of the scene, so that, when standing before the actual canvas, we have to get very close indeed for it to fall into place'.[25] Werner Hofmann takes a more scientific approach to the hyperbola effect, referring to the curves, which

> do not lie two-dimensionally within the picture plane but bend through space. They correspond, but do not create any linear axes of central perspective. Friedrich leaves a gap to peer through (an isomorphic, Euclidian space, to be more precise), and invents an airy space which moves simultaneously towards us and away from us.[26]

Friedrich certainly achieves Otto's two criteria for producing an atmosphere in which the viewer may appreciate the numinous by

[25] Vaughan, *Friedrich*, p. 290.
[26] Hofmann, *Caspar David Friedrich*, p. 236.

creating the effect of a huge space as well as the light/dark contrast (chiaroscuro) of the water and the marshy grass. Friedrich here meets not only the Otto criteria, but also the third Podro criterion (see Chapter 1): 'The artist engages with the state of mind of the viewer to achieve an elevated or heightened emotional response to the work of art which may suggest a transcendence that lies behind the objects depicted.'[27]

In summary, this is a picture of a huge, desolate landscape, demonstrating, once again, mankind's infinitesimal status in the face of God's creative power, mankind being represented by the small boat sitting on the mud bank, perhaps awaiting the rising tide or perhaps abandoned for ever. In the ethereal nature of this work Friedrich is articulating that inner sadness, hinted at in many of his earlier works, with a strength that comes with knowing that his own departure from this world cannot be long delayed. Friedrich is here expressing 'the tragedy of landscape', a phrase from a comment by David d'Angers (1788–1856) which I believe so often underpins the works of Friedrich, for the artist seems to have found it impossible to come to terms with the death of his brother—without whose action Caspar would not have survived.[28]

Stages of Life (1834–5)

This painting was completed in 1835, just before Friedrich suffered a stroke from which he only partially recovered, thereafter producing only one major picture in oil, *Seashore by Moonlight* (1835–6), and a few pencil and sepia drawings, the most evocative of which were *Landscape with Grave, Coffin, and Owl* (1836–7) and *Window and Garden* (c. 1837).

The composition of *The Stages of Life* is typical of Friedrich, with a strong vertical symmetry about the mast of the tallest ship

---

[27] Podro, *The Manifold in Perception*, pp. 1–6.
[28] Vaughan, *Friedrich*, p. 295. Friedrich's brother died while rescuing the young Caspar from a frozen lake—a tragedy which surely contributed to Friedrich's melancholic outlook on life.

placed exactly in the centre of the painting. The horizon is placed 59 per cent of the distance from the top of the picture, very close to the dimension of the golden section—the divine proportion. The V formation is provided by the land in the foreground, with an upturned boat on the right being balanced by the open barrel and fishing tripod on the left. An inverted V can be seen in the arrangement of the various ships' masts with the angle formed by the masts of the ships on the right with the mast of the largest ship exactly equalling the angle formed by the mast of the ship on the left with the mast of the centre ship. Asymmetry is created by the ship nearest the shoreline, by the single ship on the left and by the people themselves.

The location has been identified as Utkiek, near to Greifswald, and the children depicted as Friedrich's son Gustav Adolf and daughter Agnes, both about the same age, with the elder daughter Emma looking on.[29] The suggestion is that the man in the top hat is Johann Heinrich (Friedrich's nephew) and surely the older man with the stick is Friedrich himself.[30] Friedrich has placed himself in the line of the mast on the ground with its pinnacle flag pointing to the figure in a way which encourages the viewer to join with the *Rückenfigur* in surveying the scene. Atypically the scene is not melancholic, with childhood represented by the two youngest, adolescence by the older daughter, young adulthood by Heinrich and the elderly adult by Friedrich himself, even though he was only sixty at the time. The two youngest children are playing with the Swedish flag. Mystery is provided by the five ships all sailing towards the harbour at Greifswald, leaving the viewer to decide what they are carrying, and by the inclusion of the nephew, who to me seems to be filling the gap between adolescence and mature adulthood, and then by the inclusion of the Swedish flag. An interpretation of the significance of the flag is given by Vaughan, who suggests that 'Friedrich and his family—like so many Pomeranians—retained a sense of loyalty to

[29] *Ibid.*, p. 297.
[30] Hofmann, *Caspar David Friedrich*, p. 240, and Vaughan, *Friedrich*, p. 297.

the Swedish crown!.[31] There was a tendency for the people within the various states to retain an allegiance to their state rather than to the new post-Napoleonic Prussia, and it is therefore possible that Friedrich was expressing this tendency, although, given Friedrich's lifelong wish for unification, I feel that this is unlikely. My belief is that Friedrich is expressing a nostalgic yearning for his very early happy life prior to the death of his brother, and he would naturally locate such a painting in the land of his childhood.

The setting sun is perhaps seen by Friedrich as representing his own life coming towards its end; although there is no obvious evidence that he had had a premonition of the stroke he was about to suffer, death at the age of 60 would not have been unusual for the early part of the nineteenth century. Certainly, once he had had the stroke Friedrich did not expect to regain a full and active life. He went to Teplitz to try to effect some sort of cure but a letter to Zhukovsky indicates that he did not entertain a 'hope [...] of ever recovering from the paralysis'.[32] However, he was not too depressed, because after receiving ten bottles of wine he expressed the hope that the effect of the grape would lead to 'new pictures, as different from those I have done up till now as wine is from beer'.[33]

It was not to be—he produced, as mentioned earlier, just one significant oil painting, a very dark, brooding picture with an extremely thin bright light of the rising moon seen as a slit between the black sea and the heavy blue-black clouds above. This arrangement is reminiscent of the dark tunnel ending in a bright white light so typical of near-death experiences—except that in this case the tunnel is flattened and the round light becomes a slit of light.

In summarising the meaning of *The Stages of Life*, I suggest that Friedrich is looking back over his own life, thinking about the happiness prior to the death of his brother, considering the

---

[31] Vaughan, *Friedrich*, p. 297.
[32] Hofmann, *Caspar David Friedrich*, p. 287.
[33] *Ibid.*, p. 241.

sadness of his young adulthood, which was then transformed into delight after his marriage and the arrival of children, whose play he enjoyed. His attitude to hard work, his support of Pietism and his determination to represent the Ultimate Reality through landscapes and seascapes was always uppermost in his mind when he was painting, leading to his setting his own painting of the Ages of Man in a scene with a distant horizon and vast sky, suggesting the infinite and eternal spiritual life.

Placing Friedrich in a theological context

Contemporary theologians of note working at the time of Friedrich were Schleiermacher and Kierkegaard, a Danish theologian who spent his life in Copenhagen. While it is impossible to summarise Kierkegaard's philosophy in a short chapter, John Bowden gives the essence of his thought as 'taking his focal point as that of the individual in his existence, relegating reason to the lowest level of human activity'.[34] It is known that Kierkegaard visited Berlin and listened to lectures by Schelling, who in turn may well have attended sermons or lectures by Schleiermacher. Both Kierkegaard and Schleiermacher were keen to establish a form of Christianity that followed what they regarded as the essence of the religion without the Catholic emphasis on ritual. Private contemplation and an experiential approach would have been espoused by both of these theologians. This way of thinking would, of course, have resonated well with Luther and Pietism. It was an approach that combined both existentialism (although not known by that name at the time) and ontology, a system that would eventually, via Bultmann, Rahner and Tillich, be written up formally by John Macquarrie as a methodology known as the existential-ontological interpretation. This methodology is derived from phenomenology, a school of thought taught by Edmund Husserl (1859–1938), and is, in the words of Macquarrie, 'letting us see that which shows itself [...] by removing, as far as possible, concealments, distortions, and

---

[34] Bowden, *Who's Who in Theology*, p. 70b.

whatever else might prevent us from seeing the phenomenon as it actually gives itself'.[35] The advantages of this method are that the phenomenon itself is the starting point, that the system leads to clarity of thought and 'that in proceeding by description rather than by deduction [phenomenology] moves upon a more secure ground'.[36] If we then apply this methodology to theological interpretation or hermeneutics, endeavouring especially to analyse revelation, two processes come into play. First, there is an experiential component—feeling—gained as a result of meditation or contemplation, and secondly there is the need to express logically, and carefully articulate, theological thought in a wholly coherent language. In setting out a systematic theology, Macquarrie argues that it is necessary to 'illuminate the symbolic language of revelation with an existential-ontological language drawn from contemporary philosophy'.[37] It may perhaps help to illuminate this if we think in terms of the self as consisting of both a temporal and an eternal component.

I am aware that with Macquarrie I have jumped over a hundred years into the middle of the twentieth century, but I consider that in the theologians Kierkegaard and Schleiermacher we have the expression of thought which can logically be developed and expressed as above and, indeed, an expression of thought that resonates well with Friedrich. It is known from the few writings that have come down to us that Friedrich felt intuitively that he had 'two poles of knowing and of feeling'.[38] As Hofmann writes:

> In one of his maxims [Friedrich] expressed a wish for himself: 'One painter knows what he is doing; another feels what he is doing. If only it were possible to make a single painter from the two!' In this statement he was expressing two factors, consciousness and unconsciousness, which dominated contemporary discussion of the preconditions

---

[35] J. Macquarrie, *Principles of Christian Theology* (London: SCM Press, 1966), p. 31.
[36] *Ibid.*, p. 32.
[37] *Ibid.*, p. 34.
[38] Hofmann, *Caspar David Friedrich*, p. 26.

and genesis of the creative act. Schiller, for example, invoked them in a letter to Goethe of 27th March 1801, with reference to Friedrich Wilhelm von Schelling's transcendental philosophy. Schiller disagreed with the 'idealist' Schelling's thesis that things in nature 'begin in unconsciousness and are raised to consciousness, whereas in art one proceeds from consciousness towards the unconscious', and asserted the contrary: 'In practice, the poet too begins with the unconscious alone.'[39]

At least they both agreed that there was interplay at work between the unconscious and the conscious. Expressing the principle another way, Friedrich wrote that the painter should be 'bringing what you saw in the dark into the light, so that it may have an effect on others as it shines in from outside.'[40] I see a parallel between this duality expressed by Friedrich and the existential and the ontological, which combine to form the theological methodology described above. The next step is to develop this argument further and make the claim that the art of Friedrich represents a form of symbolic theology. It is a truism that all imagery of the Ultimate Reality is analogous; the distinction between Friedrich and his predecessors is that whilst the latter used the imagery expressed in the Bible—Creation stories, Annunciation, Crucifixion etc.—Friedrich used the imagery of God's creation combined with an ethereal, enigmatic form of painting that expressed something of the infinite, eternal quality of that Ultimate Reality.

Vaughan highlights the curiousness of Friedrich's position 'that someone so committed to the understanding of nature as a manifestation of divine creation and so full of the hope of eternal life should find more to mourn than to celebrate the landscape.'[41] The explanation offered is that the 'mourning' is due to the death of his brother. While this is part of the explanation, surely the representation of the sublime (often an important component of paintings which point towards the transcendent)

[39] *Ibid.*, p. 26.
[40] *Ibid.*, p. 26.
[41] Vaughan, *Friedrich*, p. 295.

will always contain that element of the danger associated with dramatic landscapes, exhibiting elements of menace or peril either from the landscape itself or from the natural phenomena (for example thunderstorms or torrential rainstorms) that may be induced by the geological or topological characteristics of the landscape. One can see, therefore, how it is that Friedrich's landscapes, with their tragic overtones, have been linked to nascent existentialism—evidenced especially in the work of Friedrich's friend Schleiermacher, which was discussed earlier.

To summarise this chapter in a sentence, it has shown that the divine gift within Friedrich enabled him to express for the receptive viewer something of the transcendence of that divinity.

PART III

→ 9 ←

Art as Sacrament?

The meaning of sacrament

The word 'sacrament' is imbued with a number of meanings—it is a term of ecclesiology, of natural theology and of signification, and is an oath or pledge. In this chapter these meanings will be looked at in terms of whether or not a work of art may be likened to the sacred or be regarded as a sacrament.

First of all, to deal with the ecclesiological term, the Church is an organisation which on the one hand is concerned with celebrating divine action in the world—God's revelation and grace—and on the other with fulfilling a community or social function. Services of worship can be of many different forms and held in many different places but generally in each service there is a reading from Scripture (the Word) and in some there is a celebration of Holy Communion (the Eucharist). Within this context the sacraments are signs of grace to help to enable that Ultimate Reality called God to become manifest in human beings—'the growing points [...] at which the divine grace sanctifies the Church and conforms its life to Christ'.[1] In formal ecclesiastical terms there are seven sacraments: two primary or dominical sacraments that are said to have come directly from Christ—baptism and the Eucharist, and five lesser sacraments. The five lesser sacraments are confirmation, marriage, ordination, penance or sacramental confession and unction or healing with oils. So, strictly, within this precise category, a work of art cannot be regarded as a sacrament.[2]

---

[1]   Macquarrie, *Principles of Christian Theology*, p. 364.
[2]   For completeness, I include a definition of sacrament as used in

If, however, we examine the origin and derivation of sacrament then there is at least a discussion to be had. The Latin word *sacramentum*, which originally meant oath, was introduced into theological use by the early Latin Church fathers, where its meaning was changed from entry into military service to entry into a mystery religion. The Greek Church fathers used the Greek word *mysterion*, secret. The first recorded Church uses are by Tertullian (*sacramentum*) and Gregory of Nyssa (*mysterion*), who employed the term when initiating believers into the Church through the baptismal rite. Other Church fathers also used the word *sacramentum* to suggest a sign, or that which signifies, and eventually it was applied to the Eucharist and the Incarnation. Thereafter the sacraments came to be more closely defined, with Peter Lombard (*c.* 1095–1169) listing the seven sacraments in a summary of doctrine which became accepted as standard. This restricted definition of the sacraments persisted until the twentieth century, when a major contribution from the Second Vatican Council (*Lumen Gentium*) stated that the Church itself is in the 'nature of a sacrament, "a sign and instrument, that is of communion with God and of unity among all men"'.[3]
Setting aside this strictly ecclesiological meaning, within the discipline of natural theology there is an even broader approach to the use of the word sacrament, a meaning which was developed by Archbishop William Temple (1881–1944) in his Gifford Lectures of 1932 and 1934.[4] In these lectures Temple promoted the concept of a sacramental universe, which Macquarrie links to

anthropology: here, a sacrament may be defined as 'any rite which by way of sanction or positive blessing invests a natural function with a supernatural authority of its own [...] Of all ritual forms the sacrament is the most dynamic, coming to the aid of a given activity, at the point at which it finds itself baffled by nature in the shape of the contradictions of the sense world, so as to turn it into a super-activity by bringing into play the latent energy of the moral personality'. Taken from R. R. Marrett, *Sacrament of Simple Folk* (London: Clarendon Press, 1933), p. 1.

³ K. Crim (ed.), *The Perennial Dictionary of World Religions* (San Francisco: Harper and Row, 1981), p. 636b.

⁴ These lectures were written up in William Temple, *Nature, Man and God* (London: Macmillan, 1940).

a definition in the Anglican catechism, where a sacrament is said to be 'an outward and visible sign of an inward and spiritual grace given unto us, ordained by Christ himself, as a means whereby we receive the same, and a pledge to assure us thereof'.[5] In the use of the words 'inward and outward' we have the suggestion of both the immanence and the transcendence of God. It was, according to Temple, in things of this world that the reality of God was revealed, ultimately in the incarnation of Jesus Christ in human flesh, but also in the Scriptures and in the Church. Materiality was not the initiative of humans but the initiative of God. For Temple, the material was given a place of respect since it was created and used by God. All this affirms the idea that we live in a sacramental universe. Earlier Anglican thinkers had said much the same thing. The priest and poet George Herbert (1593–1633) had spoken of this sacramental principle in one of his well-known hymns. Herbert urges us to sing:

> Teach me my God and King
> in all things thee to see.

Herbert is here expressing a sacramentality which suggests that God is to be found and seen in all 'things', including the material things of this world. Very appositely, Temple uses the analogy of an artist when referring to the creative power of God, comparing the relationship of God to the world with the relationship of an artist to his or her work of art. Macquarrie emphasises the relevance of this analogy and in so doing comes close to defining immanence:

> The artist certainly transcends his work, for it is the artist who created it. But the artist is bound to the work so created and has poured something of his or her self into it so that from the work or through the work we can have a relation to the artist. Something of the artist is present in the work and revealed in the work. Clearly, the artist is not identical with the work or a mere aspect of the work, just as God is not identical with the world or a property of the world-process [...]

[5] Macquarrie, *A Guide to the Sacraments*, p. 4.

as Thomas Aquinas expressed it 'God exists in all things by presence, power and substance'.[6]

This viewpoint was also expressed by John Keble (1792–1866), a believer in nature-mysticism and joint founder of the Oxford Movement, who wrote poetry to suggest the idea that God is to be found not only in 'the depths of the human soul but in the natural world'.[7] A short extract from one his poems reads:

> The works of God, above, below,
> Within us and around,
> Are pages in that book, to show
> How God himself is found.[8]

In summarising Keble's mysticism, Macquarrie writes:

> If there is a word which best describes Keble's mysticism it is, I think, the word 'sacramental'. For him, the whole creation was a sacramental world. The material creation is not to be despised, for matter too belongs to God and owes its existence to God: it can be a vehicle for God's presence.[9]

If this argument is accepted, then all works of art have the potential to become sacramental, the question then being how to realise that potential. One needs to be careful to distinguish between the idea that everything in the world is a sacrament and those artefacts through which we can begin to have some appreciation of God's presence, leading to the third meaning of sacrament expressed in the first paragraph of this chapter—a term of signification or signposting. The previous chapters have examined, in case studies, how artists have intimated what lies beyond the veil—signifying that 'outward and visible sign of an inward and spiritual grace' referred to by Macquarrie. In some cases, such as Palmer's *The Bright Cloud* (1833–4), the artist

---

[6] *Ibid.*, p. 8.
[7] J. Macquarrie, *Two Worlds are Ours: An Introduction to Christian Mysticism* (London: SCM Press, 2004), p. 217.
[8] *Ibid.*, p. 220.
[9] *Ibid.*, pp. 222–3.

could be described as presenting the viewer with a vision of one of the traditional theophanies (visions or appearances of God) described in the Bible—Exodus 24:15: 'he called to Moses out of the midst of the cloud.' There are, of course other traditional theophanies described in the Bible which are clearly intended to demonstrate the presence of God—for example, the pillar of fire (Exodus 14:24), and these have been portrayed in art.

The contributions of Temple and Macquarrie facilitate a wider interpretation of sacrament, to which attention is now directed. Suffice it to say at this stage that the relationship is between the artist and the viewer, very much as the relationship is between the priest and the communicant in the service of the Eucharist.

Examining this thought further, a church service will normally be conducted by a minister using a particular form of liturgy. Liturgy is difficult to define but a good description is that of J. D. Crichton:

> Liturgy is the communal celebration by the Church, which is Christ's body and in which he with the Holy Spirit is active, of the paschal mystery. Through this celebration, which is by nature sacramental, Christ, the high priest of the community, makes present and available to men and women of today the reality of his salvation.[10]

In general, liturgy consists of both the ministry of the word and the sacraments; the relationship between these two aspects of a service is extremely important. In both Protestant and Catholic worship the two are considered essential and complementary. The Belgian Catholic theologian Edward Schillebeeckx (1914–2009), who has written widely on the subject of the sacraments, states:

> At its peak the word itself becomes sacrament [...] Because the sacrament is entirely fruitful only in the one who receives by faith the gift which Christ makes of himself in the sacrament, the ministry of the word (whose internal

---

[10] From an essay by J. D. Crichton in C. Jones, G. Wainwright *et al.*, *The Study of Liturgy* (London: SPCK and New York: Oxford University Press, 1992), p. 28.

effect is the obedience in faith to the salvation brought to us by God in Christ) is necessarily directed towards the ministry of the Sacrament. What is begun in the word is perfected in the sacrament.[11]

Until relatively recently, Protestant worship, in addition to accepting a much wider variation of the liturgy compared with the Catholic, gave more prominence to the word inasmuch as communion services were held less frequently than services of the word alone (for example, Matins or Evensong).[12] However, in the last thirty years or so the Eucharistic service has come into prominence, with the dual proclamation of God's presence being given in the two forms of 'preached and signified.' This revised approach to worship and the sacraments enables greater flexibility to be adopted in the definition of sacrament and, in addition to the seven formal sacraments, alternatives can be considered, providing that they have the essential defining factor of assisting in communicating ultimate spiritual reality. This duality is shown most clearly in the Eucharist, where there is a genuine re-presenting by the celebrant of Christ's work, which has an effect on the participant which is particular to that participant and usually has an element of mystery. But this is only one way in which the relationship between mankind and God can be maintained, and following the concept of the sacramental universe the possibility remains of establishing that relationship in myriad other ways, including ways beyond the confines of Church authority.

So the question of the relationship of a work of art to the sacraments need not be concerned with whether or not the work fits into one of the seven formal definitions given above, but can be rephrased in other ways as follows. The sacrament can be regarded as enabling the presence of God to be perceived, with

[11] *Ibid.,* p. 38 (essay by Carol M. Norén, quoting Schillebeeckx).
[12] This emphasis given to the word in Protestant services can be traced back to an error in a development from John Calvin, whose intention was always to regard the word and sacrament as complementary, but actually referred to the sacraments as *verbum visibile*, thus encouraging the prominence of preaching in Protestant services.

that perception being established through a work of art that acts rather like a conduit, permitting the viewer or communicant a sense of the spiritual realm that lies beyond the veil. It is to this proposition that the remainder of this chapter will be addressed, first examining the work of art in relation to the numinous and then examining, as an example, a work by Caspar David Friedrich.

Acts of worship and the numinous

To reiterate the meaning of the numinous: as explained in Chapter 4, this is a word introduced by Rudolf Otto in his book *The Idea of the Holy* and was intended to refer to the non-rational component in the concept of the Holy God. The non-rational in religions is very rarely defined but in the words of Otto it can include

> The empirical in contrast to reason, the psychological in contrast to transcendental fact, that which is known *a posteriori* in contrast to that which is determinable *a priori* [...] the obscure forces of the subconscious in contrast to insight, reflection and intelligible plan; mystical depths and stirrings in the soul [...]; or, in general, the uneasy stress and universal fermentation of the time, with its groping after the thing never yet heard or seen in poetry or the plastic arts—all these and more may claim the names 'non-rational, irrational.'[13]

In refining the description of the non-rational when applied to the conception of God, Otto introduces three terms which, taken together, add up to that for which he has introduced the term 'numinous'. The three terms are *Tremendum*, which implies awfulness (that is held in awe), majesty and energy; *Mysterium*— the mystery inherent in any concept of God, meaning blank wonder, stupor or astonishment; and *Fascinans*, referring to the 'bliss which embraces all those blessings that are indicated or suggested in a positive fashion by any "doctrine of salvation" [...] more than the intellect can conceive in them or affirm of

---

[13] Otto, *The Idea of the Holy*, p. 58.

them!'[14] So, the numinous is a term which refers to the bliss, the awfulness and the mystery involved in any appreciation of that Ultimate Reality, the 'Ground of All Being', that is generally known by the name God.

As worship is the 'response of the creature to the Eternal', it follows that the experience of the sense of the numinous could be felt in an act of worship.[15] As Otto writes, in devotional worship there is the 'numinous silence of Sacrament'.[16] For example, in an act of worship practised by the Quakers, the first part of the service is concerned with 'the instant when "God is in the midst", experienced as *"numen praesens"* [...] the experience of the transcendent in gracious intimate presence, "the Lord's visitation of His people"'.[17] This moment of transcendence or 'numinous silence of sacrament' can occur in many different types of service—a time of silence in morning prayer, when the minister invites the congregation to join a moment of silent contemplation, in the Eucharist at the time of the celebration or in the Catholic Mass at the time of consecration.

If we accept Otto's concept that there exists the numinous silence of sacrament, then if it can be shown that a work of art can help to focus the congregation by signifying the presence of God then it can be argued that such a work of art could, in itself, be regarded as a sacrament. The radical theologian Don Cupitt argues that the 'major artists of Modernism and after—roughly,

---

[14] *Ibid.*, p. 33–4. For a detailed description of each of these terms the reader is referred to pp. 12 to 40.

[15] Worship, as Evelyn Underhill writes, is the 'response of the creature to the Eternal [...] is rooted in ontology (Von Hügel) [... and] is an acknowledgement of Transcendence; that is of a Reality independent of the worshipper which is always more or less deeply coloured by mystery': E. Underhill, *Worship* (London: Nisbet and Co., 1936), ch. 1–9.

[16] *Ibid.*, p. 211.

[17] *Ibid.* In the religious context, transcendent suggests the idea of 'something beyond'. There is 'a passing beyond all media in the approach to the Deity containing an effort to establish by a discipline of the intuitive faculty, direct intercourse between the soul and God.' H. D. Gray, *Emerson* (Stanford: Stanford University Press, 1917), quoting from C. J. Woodbury, *Conversations with Ralph Waldo Emerson*, p. 110, note 9.

since the 1860s—can be viewed as prophets of a new religious order' and that in the 'Abstract Sacred we find an art which is both genuinely modern and genuinely religious.'[18] The previous chapters and this chapter are concerned with the question of the sacramental or numinous qualities of painters in particular who were of the pre-Modernist period and were influenced both by natural theology and revealed theology, and by the grandeur of the nature around them.

Sacramental qualities of works of art

Images have been used as an adjunct to worship since the time of prehistory—cave paintings have been found in France which are thought to be about 30,000 years old and were probably used as a basis for nature worship. However, if we concentrate on the Christian era, then from the earliest days of worship in church, painted images have played a part. Such images, or icons—usually showing the face of Christ or a saint—became widely used in worship, particularly in the Eastern Orthodox Church.

Macquarrie draws a parallel between the Eastern Orthodox 'appreciation of icons and the Western practice of praying in the presence of Christ in the reserved Eucharistic body. In both cases, a physical object, in the one an icon, in the other the consecrated bread, awaken(s) the spiritual susceptibilities of the worshipper.'[19] The question of whence the image, or, more pertinently the icon, gains its power remains open; did iconicity gain its sacred power from the spiritual qualities inherent in the artist, or did the image have to be consecrated by a priest, from whom it then received its authority? It should, of course, be noted that nearly all works of art when installed in a church building are dedicated—by a theologian, sometimes a priest or, with even higher authority, by a bishop. However, the church authorities had to be satisfied

---

[18] D. Cupitt, *Radicals and the Future of the Church* (London: SCM Press, 1989), p. 26, and W. Beckett, *The Mystical Now: Art and the Sacred* (New York: Universe, 1993), p. 1, quoting Cupitt.

[19] Maqcquarrie, *Two Worlds are Ours*, p. 105.

that the work of art had those qualities that were appropriate for its use in the enhancement of worship. Therefore it had to have inherent sacredness prior to its dedication or consecration. By common consent, the icons or holy images, produced from the early years of the Church through to the present day, have the quality of sacredness, but the question remains of whether or not narrative images, images of nature or indeed abstract works of art can have that quality or conducive property.

The conducive properties necessary for a work of art to have sacredness

As John Bowker has pointed out, developments in neuro-physiology will in time enable us to tie together in an objective way perception, emotion and rationality and hence be able to define the conducive properties of a work of art that can lead to consistent judgements of value. Such properties could be mimesis, synecdoche (part of a body used to describe the whole) and maybe moral uplift.[20] Bowker writes:

> [There] is the truly important conjunction in art, between skill and its competence to bring into being the conducive properties that evoke in the observer the emotion and the judgement of beauty or of other satisfaction [...], in the case of theology of contemplation because it is this that creates a real distinction between art and mere artefact.[21]

The need therefore is to identify those conducive properties that imbue a work of art with sacredness, to identify how it is that an artist can achieve such a depth of expression that it can lead to the work being appropriate for veneration. Peter Forsyth, in a series of lectures which eventually came to be published under the title of *Christ on Parnassus* and now established as a classic, gave us a clue to identifying this characteristic when he

---

[20] J. Bowker, *The Sacred Neuron* (London and New York: I. B. Tauris, 2005), p. 64. Here John Bowker is referring to a work by Holman Hunt.
[21] *Ibid.*, p. 51.

produced an argument for the importance of art in the worship of the Creator.[22] He emphasised that in Christian art the artist is able to achieve a depth of expression or transcendence of matter by soul that is greater than that of the Jew or Greek—it is a spiritual gift that is 'something fuller, more precious in every way. It is not transcendence, and it is not immanence. It is the immanence of the transcendent.'[23]

The emphasis that Forsyth places on the artist being a Christian can be contrasted with the view expressed by Peter Fuller (an atheist) in *Theoria* (an accepted standard work setting out Ruskin's views on art) that a work of art can have a 'spiritual orientation, a spirituality without God.'[24] Whether or not this was really the view of Ruskin, who was a committed Christian, will be discussed in a later chapter in the context of Turner's works of art. However, this view does accord with that of the philosopher Jacques Maritain (1882–1973), who argues that 'an artist is not called upon to love God or the world or humanity, but to love what he or she is doing.'[25]

Finally, in these general comments I would refer to the theologian and artist Paul Tillich. While, as we shall see later, Tillich was emphatic that Expressionism was the style that was best able to elucidate mankind's relationship with Ultimate Reality, nevertheless naturalistic forms of art were also able to stimulate the religious experience, as can be seen from his dramatic encounter with Botticelli's *Madonna with Singing Angels*:

> Gazing up at it, I felt a state of approaching ecstasy. In the beauty of the painting there was Beauty itself. It shone through the colours of the paint as the light of day shone through the stained-glass windows of a medieval church [...] As I stood there, bathed in the beauty its painter had

[22] P. Forsyth, *Christ on Parnassus: Lectures on Art, Ethics and Theology* (London: Hodder and Stoughton, 1911).
[23] *Ibid.*, p. 82.
[24] P. Fuller, *Theoria: Art and the Absence of Grace* (London: Chatto and Windus, 1988).
[25] R. Williams, *Grace and Necessity: Reflections on Art and Love* (Harrisburg: Morehouse, 2005), p. 15, quoting Maritain.

envisioned so long ago, something of the divine source of all things came through to me [...] That moment has affected my whole life [...] I compare it with what is usually called revelation in the language of religion.[26]

Clearly, for Tillich, the encounter with this work of art created an experience in which he felt closer in his relationship with Ultimate Reality and for him its power was such that it must have ranked on a level with the sacraments. Summarising this, I suggest that the criteria or conducive properties required for a work of art be viewed as a sacrament are the intention of the artist, the content of the picture and the experiential effect on the viewer. It may be that not all these properties are required but I suggest that it is probable that at the very least one will be required if the work is to meet the overall requirement that the work will assist in a person's contemplation of his or her relationship with Ultimate Reality. This broad claim will be examined through the work of Friedrich, concentrating on his altarpiece *The Cross in the Mountains*.

Friedrich and The Cross in the Mountains

It is clear that Friedrich regarded his religion as of the utmost importance, even arranging his atelier in a manner that resembled a monk's cell. I will therefore avoid any discussion of the religiosity of the artist and begin immediately with a discussion of the work I have chosen as a possible sacrament—the *Tetschen Altarpiece* or *The Cross in the Mountains* (1807–8).

This work is one of the most important produced by Friedrich and helped to form his reputation as one of the foremost painters in the German-speaking world. The work was originally produced for King Gustav IV of Sweden in his honour. Gustav IV was a pious Protestant Christian and the painting 'may have been designed to reflect and encourage Gustav's renewed piety'.[27] The

---

[26] G. Pattison, *Art, Modernity and Faith* (London: SCM Press, 1998), p. 101, quoting Tillich.

[27] Koerner, *Caspar David Friedrich*, p. 50.

work was intended as an altarpiece and, given Friedrich's pietistic outlook, there is little doubt that his intention was to provide a work of art that would provide a signpost to the sacred. This is further emphasised by Friedrich himself, whom I quote below in the analysis of the content of the altarpiece.

In compositional terms, the *The Cross in the Mountains* is slightly asymmetrical about the central axis and follows the Friedrich trait of a triangular arrangement, with the cross forming the apex and slightly offset to the right-hand side of the picture. The frame, designed by Friedrich and carved by the sculptor Gottlieb Kühn, is an essential part of the work as a whole. The perspective of *The Cross in the Mountains* is rather like that of a traditional icon, but not exactly so, as the ivy entwining the distant cross is as sharply focused as the trees in the foreground and there is no aerial perspective. The sun's rays are shown symbolically as emerging like the rays of several search lights located at the centre of the eye of God, which has been carved into the centre of the bottom of the frame. The frame is of such importance that I will quote Friedrich's own words:

> At the sides, the frame has two Gothic columns. Palm branches rise from them and form a curve above the painting. There are five angels' (or putti) heads in the branches, all looking down at the cross and worshipping. The evening star stands above the middle angel in purest shining silver. At the bottom, in an oblong panel, is the all-seeing eye of God, enclosed by the holy trigon, surrounded with rays. Ears of corn and vines on either side bow to the all-seeing eye and signify the body and blood of Him who is fixed to the cross.[28]

Friedrich added a further explanation relating to his thinking behind this picture:

> With the teachings of Jesus, an old world died, the time when God the Father walked directly on earth. The sun went down and the earth could no longer grasp the departing light. The Saviour on the cross shines in the gold

[28] Hofmann, *Caspar David Friedrich*, p. 44, quoting Friedrich.

of sunset with the purest, noblest metal, and reflects the light onto the earth with a gentler gleam. The cross stands on a rock, as unshakeably firm as our faith in Jesus. Fir trees grown around the cross, evergreen and everlasting, like the hope of men in Him, Christ crucified.[29]

Thus, there is an interplay between the frame and the painting as well as between the sky and the mountain and between the trees, the cross and the light of the setting sun within the painting itself. The clouds follow Friedrich's predilection for the triangle format, with the dark triangular bands of clouds rising higher and higher in the sky, eventually to disappear behind the putti at the top of the frame—perhaps suggesting a distance stretching towards the infinity of the heavenly realm. As Koerner remarks, 'the crucifix itself, composed of a vertical crossed with a horizontal, has always uncannily embodied the intersection of heaven and earth, God and man.'[30] The triangle itself as mentioned earlier could be said to be representing Christ and the Trinity. Another characteristic of Friedrich is the suggestion of an abyss in the immediate foreground, which Koerner posits is to articulate the disjunction between 'the finite and the infinite, the material and the spiritual, earth and heaven, or indeed between the whole host of opposing contraries whose synthesis was the stated task of Romantic art and the Idealist philosophy of identity.'[31] I would argue, therefore, that not only is there in this quotation a reinforcement of the intention of the artist to produce a work of art that signposts the transcendent but also its content suggests that salvation is available to those who accept the grace of God. This proposition, regarding the soteriological quality of the picture, is underscored even more strongly when it is recognised that Christ is presented as looking towards the eternal light which he reflects and, in Friedrich's words:

He beholds the light face to face [...] to us. He imparts but a reflection of the same! Thus as herald of the salvation

[29] Hofmann, *ibid.*, quoting Friedrich.
[30] Koerner, *Caspar David Friedrich* p. 142.
[31] *Ibid.*, p. 128.

that awaits us, He becomes simultaneously mediator between earth and heaven [...] Here I felt the need to celebrate that commemorative rite which, itself a secret, is symbol of another: the Incarnation and the Resurrection of the son of God.[32]

The picture departed from the landscape tradition established by Claude Lorrain and aroused controversy when it was first shown—one critic, F. W. B. von Ramdohr (chamberlain at the court of the king of Saxony), was so vehement in his criticism that it became known as the Ramdohr dispute.[33] Answering Ramdohr's criticism of the lack of perspective, Friedrich acknowledged that he did not follow the exact perspective of the icon makers and could not therefore take every advantage of the illusion caused by that effect—the effect which has been described by Panofsky as 'where the work of art itself works the miracle.' Instead, he painted the symbols themselves where they were available for meditation by the viewer. In this way, Hofmann writes, 'Friedrich gave the *Altar* access to "the realm of the dogmatic and symbolic" [...] The noble human being [the painter] finds God in everything. He [Friedrich] goes on to explain that the sun is to be understood as the "image of the eternal Father, giver of all life"'[34]—a resonance here with the view of Turner, about which more in the next chapter.

It is clear from this that the intention of Friedrich was that the work should be regarded as enabling landscape and the symbols of the Eucharist to be used as the icons of the Middle Ages would have been used. Perhaps, furthermore, Koerner is correct when he suggests that Friedrich, in vowing to infer the celebration of the mass, presents us with the *The Cross in the Mountains*. 'Through its symbolic frame and planned chapel setting, the natural scene evocative of the Eucharist's meaning

---

[32] *Ibid.*, pp. 128–9.
[33] The whole of this critique is set out as an appendix to Hofmann, *Caspar David Friedrich*, pp. 276a–280a; it is cited here only when relevant to the discussion of the sacredness of Friedrich's work.
[34] *Ibid.*, p. 45.

becomes an actual altar for the sacrament.'[35] Whilst that was his intention, the question that must now be answered is: to what extent was Friedrich's ambition achieved?

At the time Friedrich was painting, there was considerable turmoil within Christianity, with the effects of the Reformation and the need to come to terms with the scientific endeavour of the Enlightenment still much in evidence. Expressed another way, there was one school of thought which espoused the idea that rationality must be applied to religion even to the extent of trying to prove the existence of God, and another which espoused the idea that religion and belief should be based on intuition and the experiential dimension. In addition, Friedrich saw the influence of the formal doctrines of the Catholic Church and its hierarchy in decline and reflected this in his paintings. He would have supported the concept of a priesthood of all believers; he was influenced by Schleiermacher, who promoted the experiential nature of religion and who saw an important role for art within religion, without going so far as some contemporaries, who might have suggested that art could replace religion. As Schleiermacher wrote in the third of his *Speeches on Religion to its Cultured Despisers*:

> The greatest work of art is that whose material is humanity that the universe forms directly and the sense for this must soon open up in many. For even now it is creating with bold and powerful art, and you will be the modern Caryatides when new structures are set up in the temple of time [...] Let past, present and future surround us, an endless gallery of the most sublime works of art eternally reproduced by a thousand brilliant mirrors.[36]

The suggestion here is that the greatest art can be like columns supporting the whole of religion. As David Klemm writes, 'for

[35] Koerner, *Caspar David Friedrich*, p. 129.
[36] F. Schleiermacher, *On Religion: Speeches to its Cultured Despisers*, trans. Richard Crouter (Cambridge: Cambridge University Press, 1996), p. 71. The Caryatides were the columns (six elegantly draped female figures) who hold up the entablature of the porch of the Erechtheum in the Athenian Acropolis (note 25).

Schleiermacher art is a medium for religious communication, but it is distinct from the substance of religion itself [...] Art therefore plays its appropriate role in culture by evoking and sustaining religious apprehensions.'[37]

Two of the criteria—the intention of the artist and the content of the work—for a painting to be regarded as a sacrament have clearly been met in *The Cross in the Mountains* and I would assert that this particular painting could be equivalent to a sacrament inasmuch as it assists in mankind's contemplation of his or her relationship with Ultimate Reality.

There remains, however, the third criterion, that of the experiential effect on the viewer, which is almost impossible to judge without undertaking ethnographical research beyond the scope of this book. However, there is some evidence: the quotation from Tillich above, and, for example, the case histories taken from the Alister Hardy archive of accounts of religious experience described in Chapter 4, indicate that the viewing of works of art such as *The Cross in the Mountains* may well assist the viewer with some religious susceptibility in their relationship with that Ultimate Reality. Thus, to reiterate, in considering *The Cross in the Mountains*, the three criteria or conducive properties for sacramental equivalence are met— intentionality, content and probable experience felt by the viewer—and hence the work of art helps to communicate the sense of Ultimate Reality to the communicant, worshipper or, indeed, anyone open to spiritual experience.

Summary

This chapter began with a discussion on the meaning of sacrament, ascribing to the word a much wider meaning than is indicated in the strictly ecclesiological approach. In the context of art, it has been argued that a work of art which assists in helping the

---

[37] J. Marina (ed.), *The Cambridge Companion to Friedrich Schleiermacher* (Cambridge: Cambridge University Press, 2005) (an essay by David E. Klemm), p. 267.

human being become closer in his or her relationship with the Ultimate Reality may be regarded as a sacrament. The particular characteristics required of such a work were then evaluated, with the conducive properties of intentionality, content and experiential effect on the viewer being the salient criteria. Finally in this chapter, as an example, the only work which Friedrich actually designed as an altarpiece was examined, the conclusion being that *The Cross in the Mountains* acts as a work of art which indeed meets all the criteria to be regarded as a sacrament.

Classical Art as Religious Devotion

Introduction

From the age of the painted icon (approximately 400–1300 CE) to the present day, art has been used as a medium in which to express the relationship between mankind and God. From around the fourth century, icons were produced as an aid to worship—to concentrate the mind on the divine. As Paul Johnson emphasises in *Art: A New History* (2003), 'the icon, a comparatively cheap and small representation of the everyday form of Orthodox devotion, constituted the commonest form of art throughout a vast region embracing nearly twenty modern countries'. He continues:

> It is important to grasp [...] that [the icon] is a physical part of the act of worship, like the altar furniture, vestments, banners and sacred vessels. Painting is thus itself a spiritual act. The painter realised the divine within himself and re-created, in a real sense, the image of Christ or the events depicted: the Incarnation, the Nativity, the visit of the Three Kings.[1]

The icon continued to have a major role in worship, particularly in the Orthodox Church, up to the beginning of the Renaissance, when in the West that form of art began to give way, for example, to paintings with much more diverse scenes and more particularly large altarpieces displaying events such as those mentioned above. However, icons are still produced today; the modern iconographer Aidan Hart, at a lecture given in 2008, referred

---

[1] P. Johnson, *Art: A New History* (London: Wiedenfeld and Nicolson, 2003), p. 113.

to 'praying an icon into existence'.[2] In addition, during the pre-Renaissance period, art endeavouring to express the spiritual was exhibited in architecture in the building of the great cathedrals, in sculpture, in needlework and in the production of beautifully illuminated manuscripts and printed editions of the Bible.[3] All of these forms of visual cultural production were aimed at aiding devotion and assisting in the contemplation of the divine.

The previous chapter developed the argument that works of art could be regarded as sacraments, using as an example a work by Friedrich. In this chapter and the next I will be examining the development of the changing subjects chosen for devotional art from the depiction of biblical scenes through to the use of landscape and eventually on to the use of abstraction. This is a vast subject and I will be restricting my consideration to a small number of artists who represent some of the various types of art that could best be said to point towards or suggest a timeless transcendence and to induce in the sensitive viewer a religious experience, defined by Ninian Smart as an experience which involves some kind of 'perception' of the *invisible* world, or involves a perception that some visible person or thing is a manifestation of the invisible world.[4]

William James endeavours to be more specific in relating religious experience to salvation, referring to a two-part process of experience. First there is a lack or uneasiness at there being something missing in an individual's life and then a sense that there is a solution, that the individual has some connection with a power beyond or outside him or herself. James summarises this in terms of a man who identifies his real being as follows:

---

[2] Aidan Hart, lecture given in 2008 at the School of Art, Aberystwyth University.

[3] In addition to Johnson, *Art: A New History*, pp. 153–82, see also H. De Borchgrave, *A Journey into Christian Art* (Oxford: Lion Publishing, 2001), which includes a succinct summary of Christian visual art prior to the Renaissance (pp. 9–40).

[4] Rankin, *Introduction to Religious and Spiritual Experience*, p. 12, quoting N. Smart, *The Religious Experience of Mankind* (New York: Scribner's Sons, 1984), p. 20.

He becomes conscious that this higher part is coterminous
and continuous with a MORE of the same quality which
is operative in the universe outside of him, and which he
can keep in working touch with, and in a fashion get on
board of and save himself when all his lower being has
gone to pieces in the wreck.[5]

The analyses which follow will describe works of art that, whether
in use as an altarpiece or as a small painting in a private chapel,
help the viewer towards an appreciation of that higher power or
Ultimate Reality. The earlier chapters of this book are particularly
concerned with the Romantic age. This chapter will be more
discursive and will follow a chronological order; while still
focused on artists of that time, to aid contextualisation reference
will be made to earlier and later painters.

My starting point is the period when the approach to perspective had been explored and established (the fifteenth
century). Two of the greatest artists of this period to create
sacred art to be used as aids to devotion were Dürer and Raphael;
one work from each will be examined. Then, with Peter Paul
Rubens (1577–1640) and Claude Lorrain (1600–82) we move to
the period in which landscape became acceptable and indeed
began to be used to suggest the sacred; an examination of one
painting of each of them will be included.

Albrecht Dürer, The Adoration of the Magi

The story that *The Adoration of the Magi* (1504) depicts occurs
only in Matthew 2:7–11. The legend has been considerably
elaborated over the centuries—with the Magi being established
as three in number (the Bible does not give a number) and even
given names—Balthazar, Melchior and Gaspar (or Caspar).
Even later legends gave the three Magi descriptions of their
physical appearance, with Balthazar being black with a newly

---

[5]   W. James, *The Varieties of Religious Experience* (London: Fontana Library
of Theology and Philosophy, 1971), p. 484 (The Gifford Lectures delivered
at Edinburgh 1901–2).

grown beard, bringing the gift of myrrh, Melchior being very old, grey and bearded and bringing the gift of gold and Gaspar being young, beardless and very swarthy and bringing the gift of frankincense. The significance of the gift is that gold is for a king, frankincense is for a priest and myrrh is for one who is to die.[6]

This later description can be read into the picture by Dürer, although Gaspar has been given a beard and is not very swarthy, and Balthazar has no beard. Some versions of the legend have it that the three came from Persia (Iran) whilst others suggest that they came from further afield, with one of the kings representing India. Closest to the biblical version is that they were wise men who came from Persia and were invited to interpret dreams, this latter version being consistent with the need to interpret Joseph's dreams.[7]

The picture itself, possibly the central panel of a polyptych, shows the human characters all exquisitely drawn, with Melchior and Gaspar wearing very expensive decorated clothing, emphasising the importance of their status, and Balthazar dressed more simply. Mary with Jesus is sitting just outside the stable with a cow and a donkey clearly visible. There is a controversial opinion that Joseph was once included in this picture and subsequently removed. Beyond the significance of the aforementioned gifts, there is much additional symbolism in this picture. Butterflies have been included to represent the soul or spirit. Two crosses have been included as part of the crumbling structures, above one of which Dürer has included two doves of peace. The crumbling building itself could be said to suggest the beginning of the end of the Old Covenant. On the right-hand side of the picture in the middle distance are various people on horseback waiting around—presumably these are the servants or guards who would have accompanied Melchior and Gaspar on their journey with Balthazar's turbaned assistant

---

[6] For full discussion, see, for example the commentary by William Barclay, *The Gospel of Matthew*, vol. 1 (Edinburgh: Saint Andrew Press, 1991), with the legend of the three Magi being on pp. 31–3.

[7] http://ireport.cnn.com/docs/DOC-906514

just on foot, carrying a bag which could have contained their provisions. Further into the background there is a steep hill rising, presumably from the Dead Sea, although this is about 25 km from Bethlehem. However, most importantly there is a city on this hill stretching upwards right to its pinnacle, which I would suggest is the Kingdom of Heaven—that eternal state which is available to all who are willing to accept the gift of the grace of God. Finally, we come to God, represented traditionally in the form of the rising cumulus cloud—the Shekinah—the symbol for God which reaches back to the giving of the Law to Moses, described in the Book of Exodus.

So in this picture we have an elaborated biblical illustration of the story of the Magi, with added symbolism extended to the point of the suggestion of transcendence with the inclusion of the Heavenly City and the cloud representing God, all set in the far distance, away from the immediate focus on the birth and significance of Jesus and the future role he is to perform. As a focus for devotion this picture offers in the immediate foreground a biblical story with much detail, upon which the eye can rest, as well as having a tremendous depth through to the Heavenly City, all of which gives great opportunity for meditation on both the physical as well as the spiritual world.

Raphael, *The Sistine Madonna*

This next picture, by Raphael, is known correctly as *Virgin, Child appear to the Saints Sixtus and Barbara*, but is also known as *La Madonna di San Sixtus* and generally referred to as *The Sistine Madonna*. It was commissioned by Pope Julius II for the abbey church of the Benedictine convent dedicated to St Sixtus, and is one of the greatest of Raphael's later works.

The composition of this painting is that of a triangle in the foreground formed by the heads of the three main characters, with distance only being suggested by the building just discernible on the right of the painting behind Barbara. The palette is limited, being mostly blue for the Virgin's and Barbara's dresses and the curtains, and white and gold, the traditional colours for a pope.

The painting is possibly the result of a dream, and shows the Virgin Mary located at a position between heaven and earth supported by clouds (meaning that she is upheld by God). She is accompanied on her right by St Sixtus I, a Roman who lived around the turn of the first century and whose papacy lasted about ten years.[8] On her left she is accompanied by St Barbara, patron saint of artillerymen.[9] The usual position of the putti has in this picture been reversed, with Raphael grounding them at the foot of the painting in the central foreground.

The painting was designed to be placed above the high altar in the abbey which supposedly contained the relics of both Sixtus I and Barbara; this could explain why Raphael placed them both in a position suggesting the spiritual world. The faces of both the Madonna and Jesus look troubled—the reason for this being a source of controversy for many years. The most plausible explanation was produced by Prager, who is quoted as follows on the Safran Arts website:

> As recent research by A. Prager has shown, the key to the mystery [of the troubled expressions] lies in the position in which the altarpiece originally stood. Taking again the intriguing question of what the Pope is pointing at and what the Mother and Child are looking at, the answer is as astonishing as it is persuasive. It has long been forgotten that, as in many churches, opposite the altarpiece in S. Sisto

---

[8] http://www.catholic.org/saints/saint.php?saint_id=917. The inclusion of this saint was a requirement of the commission.

[9] Barbara was reputed to be a virgin martyr, who may have lived in the second century CE. Legend has it that she converted to Christianity and decided to live in her father's bath house. Whilst he was away she asked the workman to install a third window to represent the Trinity. Her father was furious at her conversion to Christianity and threatened to kill her. Instead he handed her over to a judge who then condemned her to death (this was the time of the Maximian persecutions). As Farmer writes: 'Her father was then struck by lightning and died. This was the basis of her patronage of those in danger of sudden death, first by lightning, then by subsiding mines or cannon-balls. Hence her patronage of miners and gunners': D. H. Farmer, *The Oxford Dictionary of Saints* (Oxford: Oxford University Press, 1997), p. 39a.

and above the rood screen at the far end of the chancel there stood a crucifix. The expressions of horror on the faces of Mother and Child are thus their reaction to the sight of death. It is interesting to note that, long before this successful interpretation, it was a writer, and not an art historian, who came closest to understanding the mystery: R. A. Schröder saw the 'deepest horror' written in the face of the child, 'before which even Death itself is frightened to death'.[10]

It is intriguing to note the claim that Raphael has given Pope Sixtus I five fingers as well as a thumb. The pointing finger is of considerable importance inasmuch as it is indicating the destiny of the future Christ—perhaps in adding this as an extra finger he is suggesting the role beyond the human within the physical world. In other words, he is using this feature to emphasise the divinity of Jesus. As the picture is no longer in the position for which it was commissioned, it is possible that the figure was designed to point to something within the church, for example to the crucifix to which reference has already been made. The pope has left his mitre on the ground, perhaps suggesting that he is leaving the signifier of his office back in the physical world. The faces within the clouds may represent all those who have passed beyond the half-opened veil. The use of the veil in this way suggests that there is a spiritual world beyond, the world which the putti seem to be so seriously considering. There is therefore much to contemplate in this devotional picture; as with the Dürer picture described above there is an immediacy of the three pyramidal figures in the foreground and there is the suggestion of transcendence in the array of faces in the clouds and in the idea of glimpsing the whole scene through a veil which has been temporarily drawn back. This painting can have a profound effect on those who view it but I will leave the final comment to the English essayist Henry Crabb Robinson, who was contemporary with many of the artists and philosophers considered in this book: it was after

---

[10] http://www.safran-arts.com/42day/art/art4mar/raphael/sismadon.html

listening to a lecture from Schelling which included the subject of Raphael that Robinson visited the Dresden gallery and on viewing the Sistine Madonna wrote:

> Of all the Paint[ing]s I have ever seen none equals the Paint[in]g by Raphael representing the virgin with Jesus in her Arms. 2 side ffigures And below 2 Angels look[in]g upwards—The latter par[ticu]larly had on their count[enance]s such an expression of devotion and love.[11]

As Vigus writes, this painting and many others in the Dresden gallery were 'a source of inspiration for many of the early German Romantics.'[12]

Peter Paul Rubens, Landscape with a Rainbow

Landscape with a Rainbow (1636) was one of a pair of paintings which, towards the end of his life, Rubens painted for his own pleasure, both to be hung in his country house called Het Steen in Belgium. The other painting forming the pair is called *An Autumn Landscape with a View of Het Steen* (1636), now hanging in the National Gallery, London; it too could be said to have qualities which suggest the transcendent but for this chapter I will confine my comments to the picture with the more obvious biblical and typological connections.

To begin by setting the biblical context, there were three covenants which are set out in Genesis, between God and Noah, between God and Abraham and between God and Jacob. The last two are not relevant to this painting, so I follow the theme by considering just the covenant with Noah. After the story of the flood God says: 'Behold, I establish my covenant with you and your descendants after you, the birds, the cattle and every

---

[11] From notes on Schelling's aesthetics by James Vigus writing about Robinson, with this particular quotation taken from Robinson's travel diary dated 29 September 1801. See Vigus, *Essays on Kant*, p. 65. Robinson's 'Travel Diary', June 1801 to January 1802, is in four parts and can be found in Dr William's Library, 14 Gordon Square, Bloomsbury, London.
[12] *Ibid.*, p. 65.

beast of the earth with you as many as came out of the ark.'[13] Later on, referring to the rainbow, God speaks again: 'This is the sign of the covenant which I make between me and you and every living creature that is with you, for all generations: I set my bow in the cloud, and it shall be a sign of the covenant between me and the earth.'[14] One modern interpretation of these passages is that the essence of this covenant is that mankind is required to exhibit a basic reverence towards all life and, in return, God promises never again to flood creation out of existence. There is a typological link here with the New Testament book of Revelation, where the writer (possibly John the Apostle) states: 'And he who sat there appeared like jasper and carnelian, and round the throne was a rainbow that looked like an emerald.'[15]

Unlike the two earlier paintings considered above, the *Landscape with a Rainbow* was not designed as an altarpiece, but the question can nonetheless be asked—could it be used as an altarpiece? Whilst the link with the New Testament is fairly tenuous, the modern interpretation of the Genesis creation stories together with the covenant with Noah suggests a concern for stewardship of the world (the first creation story) and care for all living creatures (the second creation story), which is entirely consistent with the overall message of the New Testament, that one should worship the one true God and love one's neighbour. I therefore argue that this painting is certainly capable of being used as an aid to worship in a church building and could even be used as an altarpiece.

The painting is a celebration of rural life and the bounty that is provided by mankind acting as a steward on behalf of God. A storm has just passed, emphasising the need for water (rainfall provided by God) to encourage the crops to grow—haymaking which has halted for the rain is about to start again, with the workers building ricks in the middle distance. The cows are being moved, perhaps towards a milking point in a field as they

[13] Genesis 9:9–10.
[14] Genesis 9:12–13.
[15] Revelation 4:3.

are accompanied by the milkmaids; this perhaps highlights the need for careful husbandry of the cattle in order to ensure an ample supply of milk.

However, more important than all of this detail is the significance of the rainbow, which was painted to provide a bridge from the dark brooding woods into the much lighter distance—an area of the countryside whose distance is emphasised by the aerial perspective and perhaps represents, or at least could represent, the heavenly kingdom. It must be remembered that this picture was painted about thirty years before Newton established precisely the colours of the rainbow, and hence the rainbow at that time would have been regarded as a sign from God. In the particular reproduction that I have examined the colour green is prominent, and it is possible that Rubens is alluding to the above-mentioned passage in Revelation, but whilst some of the colours appropriate to jasper have been reproduced there is no suggestion of the red of carnelian, so one would have to be cautious about reading a reference to Revelation in this painting, particularly as in the other Rubens pictures showing rainbows, the colour scheme is the same, with the predominance of yellow and/or green. I suggest a more plausible typological link for the rainbow is with Pentecost. Just as the Passover has always been linked with the Exodus, the rainbow, the covenantal sign, has been associated with the Feast of Weeks, which occurred fifty days after the harvest; hence the name Pentecost, when the *Paraclete* (Comforter or Holy Spirit), promised by Christ just before his ascension, actually arrived. The possibility that this painting has a connection with the promised Holy Spirit cannot be ruled out and gives a further reason for its use to assist with meditation or devotion. John Drury has a rather different interpretation of the detail of this picture:

> This is a picture which implies God as an appreciative spectator within it of his latest artefact, the rainbow, and of his whole creation. It is also Rubens's own offering of thanks for his fulfilment as painter and *parvenu* landowner, in a country restored to economic prosperity under benevolent Christian regents after war and depression.

As spectators we stand before it as receivers of blessings. We should hesitate to advance and tangle with the cows. Better to stand still and let all this abundance pour into our laps—or rather eyes.[16]

I agree with many of Drury's comments but would disagree with his first sentence. I see God as the Creator and Rubens as the spectator bringing God's creation to the attention of the viewer. The concept of God as spectator almost suggests God as a physical reality somewhere 'out there' rather than as a spiritual reality, beyond time and space and greater than anything of which we can conceive. Certainly as spectators we stand before this painting as receivers of God's blessing and for this reason, if not for a number of others, I would argue strongly that this picture could easily serve to inspire devotion in the viewer.

As this painting and its companion piece, *Autumn Landscape with a View of Het Steen*, were painted towards the end of his life, one can speculate on whether or not the change of scene signified a change of outlook in Rubens. Many of his earlier works were of traditional altarpieces but maybe by this time in his life he wished to express what Drury argues was the mind-set of a devout Christian in the mid-seventeenth century, when, as he writes:

> In the two-world structure of apocalyptic cosmology and in paintings based upon it, heaven was the predominant realm of value and the fulfilment of vision, earth a subordinate place. Rubens could do that too, whether with a moral generosity or a bourgeois biddability to aristocratic commands [...] But in the freedom of his final years the balance was, without the least trace of apostasy from the Catholic Church, the other way. If cosmologies and systems have their day and cease to be, love, as St Paul taught, abides. Its descent into mundane existence is the dynamic of Christ's story, the Christian arch-myth with the world as its destination. Taken on by Christ's followers, it survives and finds plenty of work to

---

[16] J. Drury, *Painting the Word: Christian Pictures and their Meanings* (New Haven and London: Yale University Press, 2000), p. 151.

do in our world [...] In Christian doctrine and devotion, dying (metaphorically including any kind of loss) is a gate to new life when love is its motive. It applies as much to Christianity itself as an historical phenomenon as to the individual Christian such as Rubens.[17]

To examine this quotation in more detail, at the time of Rubens heaven would by most people be seen as a physical place above the sky (it must be remembered that it was in 1632 that Galileo was imprisoned for supporting the Copernican view of the universe), which explains Drury's use of the phrase two-world structure of apocalyptic cosmology.

This, of course, is consistent with Rubens painting the two worlds (earth represented by the dark woods and the foreground subjects, and the kingdom of heaven towards the distant horizon) joined by the rainbow. The word love needs explanation for it is a translation of the Greek word *agape*—Christian love, which I always equate with the concept of wanting the best for one's fellow human being—and it is not to be confused with *eros* or *philia*, sexual love and brotherly love respectively. Drury is extending the use of love (which is sometimes used to define God) into the idea of human destiny as being to look after the world to the best of our ability—acting as regent or steward on behalf of God and of being 'in Christ', to use St Paul's expression.[18] If we accept this argument, then it follows that Rubens was—by using his God-given talent and experience—'infused with the

---

[17] *Ibid.*, p. 153.

[18] Whole treatises have been written on Christian love, particularly in connection with God loving the world so much that he sent his only son to expiate for the sins of the inhabitants of the world. See, for example the first letter of John 4:9–10: 'In this the love of God was disclosed to us, that God sent his only son into the *kosmos*, that we might live through him. In this is love, not that we loved God but that he loved us and sent his son as a *hilasmos* for our sins'. *Kosmos* relates to the whole of the sinful community whilst *hilasmos* refers to forgiveness, but with also a sense of sacrifice. For a more detailed exposition see, for example, K. Grayson, *Dying, We Live: A New Enquiry into the Death of Christ in the New Testament* (London: Darton, Longman and Todd, 1990), pp. 276–82.

divine', expressing the ensoulment of creation in his landscape paintings and particularly in *Landscape with a Rainbow.*[19] It is then a very small development of the concept of ensoulment to suggest that the painting has just as much relevance to be used for devotional and meditational purposes as the traditional altarpieces depicting the Madonna or Christ.

Claude Lorrain,
Landscape with Ascanius Shooting the Stag of Sylvia

It may seem somewhat superfluous to include Claude Lorrain in a chapter concerned with sacred art when he is not renowned for his religious or transcendent works. However, he is considered of major importance when the development of landscape art is being considered, and for this reason I am including the artist in this section. Whether or not his great skill in landscape painting derived from the fact that he found such trouble in figure painting, it is difficult to say, but certainly he was one of the earliest artists in whose work the landscape came first and the staffage (the subordinate people) second. The very accurate treatment that he gives to clouds has some similarity with Constable's approach, and, as Johnson writes, 'Claude looked forward to the eighteenth century, its serenity and stasis'.[20] More importantly from the perspective of this study, Claude had an influence on Palmer, who wrote, in connection with the endeavour to achieve timeless transcendence in his own works, that

> I do not think that it is either the truth of his colour or the charm of his trees (unrivalled though they be,) or the gold of his sunshine, that makes CLAUDE the greatest of landscape painters, but that Golden Age into which

---

[19] Oskar Bätschmann introduces the concept of ensoulment when he refers to Gustav Carus's description of the ultimate in landscape painting when 'science and art combine to produce an image that aims at nothing less than the all-embracing ensoulment of nature'. See Carus, *Nine Letters on Landscape Painting*, p. 7.

[20] Johnson, *Art: A New History* p. 338.

poets' minds are thrown back—on first sight of one of his [...] pictures.[21]

To emphasise this timeless quality in Claude Lorrain, Palmer writes (to L. R. Valpy) that 'ordinary landscapes remind us of what we see in the country; Claude's of what we read in the greatest poets and of their perception of the country, thus raising our own towards the same level.'[22]

Landscape with Ascanius Shooting the Stag of Sylvia (1675–6) presents a scene from Virgil's *Aeneid,* in which the shooting of the stag eventually leads to the assault against the Trojans, yet the depiction of the landscape itself was of equal importance because as mentioned above it was with Claude's paintings that landscape was no longer just a background in which to set human figures. There are two aspects in landscape paintings for which Claude is particularly renowned—his ability to create an extraordinary impression of light and his approach to composition. On the latter John Barrell remarked that Claude's compositions offered 'a grammar, as it were, of landscape patterns and structures, established so thoroughly in [the connoisseur's] language and imagination that he became less and less able to separate any one landscape from any other, because he applied the same visual and linguistic procedures to them all.'[23]

In terms of composition, on the left side is the main scene, of Ascanius taking aim with his bow, with his companions and their dogs standing by and watching. Even though Ascanius is drawn as a somewhat oversized, dominant figure he is dwarfed by the building, which surmounts the hill on which they are standing.[24] The columns of the building reach out of the top of the picture, possibly a reference to reaching towards heaven. The trees are leaning inwards over the valley in a threatening attitude

---

[21] Letter to F. G. Stephens, quoted in Moore, *The Green Fuse*, p. 72.

[22] *Ibid.*

[23] Bindman, *William Blake*, quoting Barrell, *The History of British Art 1600–1870* (London: Tate Publishing, 2008), p. 130a.

[24] Whether or not this oversizing and incorrect proportion were deliberate or an example of the difficulty Claude had in drawing figures, we can only speculate.

which according to the Ashmolean picture description suggests an indication of the violence to come. The rotunda beyond the building helps to continue the dominance of landscape over the relatively small humans.

In the centre of the picture there is the deep rift of the valley through which the river runs, with the immediate foreground indicative of great depth and darkness, maybe even suggestive of the underworld. The (not particularly well-drawn) stag rests on a level piece of ground, which balances that of the ground on the other side on the river on which the hunters are standing. The buildings on the left are balanced on the right by the castle on a hill in the middle distance. In the centre of the picture the eye is drawn towards the distant mountains and far horizon by the packhorses crossing over the bridge. It is on the horizon that the characteristic light of Claude can be seen—the sky gradually lightens from the threatening clouds immediately overhead to the distant horizon, to this light which almost requires the viewer to try to glimpse what lies beyond, or at least to peer into the apparently infinite distance.

Regarding the palette which Claude has used, the overall effect is of silvery blue tones, but with the use of brighter colours on the significant characters in the story—red (now probably faded) on the huntsman's jacket and fawn the colour of the stag. Whilst probably not intended by Claude, one can perhaps discern a suggestion of transcendence in this painting—particularly light on the distant horizon, which is suggestive of straining towards something beyond, a characteristic of a later drawing which will be considered in which the viewer is encouraged almost to see beyond the canvas itself.

The next chapter will extend these analyses into the Romantic period, concluding in the twentieth century with an examination of the work of an abstract expressionist.

→ 11 ←

Romantic and Modern Art as Religious Devotion: Romanticism, Typology and the Nazarenes

In this chapter within the period of Romanticism the works of the Nazarenes, including Johann Overbeck and Ferdinand Oliver (1785–1841), as well as works by Palmer (in England) and Friedrich (in Germany) will be discussed. The last three of these artists expressed the idea of transcendence entirely through the use of landscape. A section then follows on the position of Turner, an artist of no religious persuasion but whose works could be considered as pointing towards the transcendent. The chapter concludes with an examination of the work of Mark Rothko, who in the twentieth century developed landscape to a point almost of abstraction and in so doing concentrated the energy of the viewer into a meditation on what may lie beyond the dimensions of the physical world.

Entering the period of German Romanticism, a time begins in which art was influenced by the philosophical aesthetics of Baumgarten, Kant and Schelling discussed earlier in this book. Two schools developed in Germany—that which was dominated by Caspar David Friedrich and Philippe Otto Runge, which remained confined to Germany, and the Nazarenes or Brotherhood of St Luke, formed by Johann Overbeck and Franz Pforr. The Nazarenes moved to Rome to work and were later joined by others including Peter von Cornelius and Ferdinand Oliver. The Friedrich school developed a type of landscape painting which, as demonstrated in Chapter 7, expressed the relationship between mankind and his Creator, whilst the Brotherhood of St Luke emulated the style of late medieval and early Renaissance painters, being particularly influenced by Dürer and Raphael.

Whilst most of the Nazarenes produced works that were similar to the altarpieces of the early Renaissance, they also endeavoured to include references to typology in some of their works.

In this chapter I will be examining one of *The Seven Sacraments* by Overbeck and a landscape painting by Oliver, which will lead on to an interesting comparison with a Palmer work included in the next section.

Friedrich Johann Overbeck and
The Seven Sacraments—Baptism

At the time of their production *The Seven Sacraments* (1865) were regarded as very Catholic in orientation, having been accepted by the Pope and highly esteemed by the Cardinal Archbishop of Vienna. As such, they were not so favourably viewed by those who were strongly influenced by the Reformation. The acceptance of this set of cartoons is very thoroughly described by the Nazarene scholar Cordula Grewe in her book *Painting the Sacred in the Age of Romanticism*, to which the reader is referred for more information.[1] *The Seven Sacraments* were produced as an illustrated commentary or sermon, and throughout Overbeck maintains strong Christological connections even though only two of the sacraments (baptism and the Eucharist) are regarded as major. A simple description of sacraments would describe them as visible and outward signs of God's inward and spiritual grace given to us.[2]

All of these seven cartoons were produced for the edification of the viewer. The first of them, *Baptism*, based on Acts 2, shows the descent of the Holy Spirit, or in other words the day of Pentecost. The two main features, which describe the arrival of the Holy Spirit, are that it comes with a sound like a mighty wind and the appearance of tongues as of fire, settling over the eleven

[1] C. Grewe, *Painting the Sacred in the Age of Romanticism* (Farnham: Ashgate Publishing, 2009), pp. 149–63.
[2] T. Meakin, *A Basic Church Dictionary and Compendium* (Norwich: Canterbury Press, 1992), pp. 26 and 27.

apostles (Acts 2:2–3). Obviously, Overbeck could not show the sound but he has given due prominence to the tongues of fire shown hovering above the apostles, confirming that it is indeed Pentecost that this picture is illustrating.

There are many typological links with the Old Testament, some of which have been shown in the border surrounding this picture. The festival of Pentecost has its parallel in the Feast of Weeks, which is associated with the day when the law was given at Sinai and described in Deuteronomy 16:9–12, Exodus 23:16; and Leviticus 23:15–22.[3] The use of analogy (wind—*pneuma*) for the Holy Spirit in Acts 2:2–3 indicates that it is a supernatural occurrence with which we are dealing.

Having given the biblical background, I will now examine how many of these references can be found in the painting itself. The action takes place in Jerusalem—presumably in the Temple; in the centre of the main picture foreground there is a very large and totally dominant font around which three people are being baptised—three other people are being blessed by the apostles. There is an unclothed child—possibly a symbol of purity and heaven—looking up at one of the apostles, his line of sight following along the arm of the apostle pointing upwards, emphasising the heavenly reference. One of those being baptised looks like a Moor, which highlights the idea that baptism is for all—further emphasised by the large crowd in the background. The tongues as of fire are represented by a symbolic sun at the top of the painting, with the tongues generally pointing towards the crowd waiting to be baptised (Acts 2:38).

Turning now to the borders, at the top, immediately above the sun and tongues as of fire, we see Jesus being baptised by John (Mark 1:9). This scene is set in a circle and on either side there is a collection of trees and animals representing the desert. On the left-hand side panel there is a drawing of Adam and Eve being driven from the Garden of Eden, watched by the serpent, which is slithering down the tree of knowledge. This panel represents

---

[3] For a full discussion of ritual festivals in Leviticus, the reader is referred to: P. J. Budd, *Leviticus* (London: Marshall-Pickering, 1996), pp. 314–30.

the Fall of man, after which mankind could no longer approach God directly, thus requiring God to solve the impasse by means of the incarnation and offering a route to salvation through Christ, the new Adam. The cherubim referred to in verse 24 are represented by a single cherub holding the flaming sword, which guards the tree of knowledge.

The right-hand panel shows the brass serpent located on a cross made by Moses just before the Israelites reached Sinai where they were to receive the law. Grewe writes of this panel that the cross is lifted high on an elaborate altar cross. She continues:

> Once made by Moses to save his people from the Lord's wrath (Numbers 21:5–9) the Brazen Serpent foreshadows the redemption of man's sin through the death of Christ on the cross. Overbeck's solution is remarkable for doubling and yet truncating the typological scheme. On the one hand he traces the lineage of sin and redemption within the Jewish Scriptures by pairing a negative type, the Expulsion from Paradise with a positive, the Brazen Serpent. On the other hand the true anti-type, the Crucifixion, is missing.[4]

Overbeck resolves this by showing, at the base of the brass column, a scene from the Gospel of John 3—Jesus's discourse with Nicodemus, in which Jesus emphasises the need for baptism before one could enter the Kingdom of God (verse 5 reads: 'Truly, truly, I say to you, unless one is born of water and the Spirit, he cannot enter the kingdom of God'). Thus again Overbeck focuses on the main theme of baptism.

It is in the predella that reference is made to the two Old Testament themes highlighted in the paragraphs above. In the right-hand panel is a scene in which the cloud of glory (the Shekinah) guides Moses and the Israelites through the Red (probably more correctly Reed) Sea and onward to receive the Law at Sinai. In the left-hand panel there is reference to Noah where he is shown saving people and animals by ushering them into the ark, after which there is sealed the Noachide covenant and eventually by a combination of the Law and the covenant we

---

[4] Grewe, *Painting the Sacred in the Age of Romanticism*, p. 168.

reach the Festival of the Fields as a thanksgiving. It is interesting that the painter does not explicitly link this festival with his picture of the day of Pentecost because from a typological point of view this is, I would argue, the most important connection. However, while Overbeck does not highlight this festival in any obvious way, perhaps by indicating references to Moses and the Law and to Noah he could be pointing the way to that festival as the foreshadowing of Pentecost. Perhaps this is another example of what Grewe refers to as truncated typology, but in this case it remains unresolved.

This picture, then, shows one of the Nazarenes producing a work of art that is grounded in both the Old and New Testaments and which, with so much to contemplate, obviously could be used as an altarpiece typical of the many produced in the late medieval or early Renaissance periods. This painting and those depicting the other six sacraments could all be used as aids to devotion and prayer.

The next member of the Brotherhood of St Luke to be examined has an entirely different approach and continues the theme of landscape initiated by Claude Lorrain and Rubens.

J. H. Ferdinand Oliver,
Friday, Meadow outside Aigen near Salzburg

Ferdinand Oliver often expressed the relationship between mankind and God through pictures of idyllic rural scenes. Some, such as *Friday, Meadow outside Aigen near Salzburg* (1822), show workers taking their time tending the crops and presenting a very relaxed view of working in the countryside which is actually very far from the truth. In this respect Oliver demonstrated a kinship with Samuel Palmer, who in his time at Shoreham produced similar idyllic scenes. Other paintings by Oliver such as *On the Frauensteinberg at Mödling* (1823) and *St Peter's Graveyard in Salzburg* (1818) show a similarity with the work of Friedrich but without the melancholy which is such a characteristic of the latter's work. Although he spent most of his time in Germany rather than Italy, Oliver was a member of the Brotherhood of St

Luke, and most of his works have a biblical, Catholic reference; his views are much more in accord with that Brotherhood than with the Friedrich-Carus grouping in Dresden.

Friday is part of a series of days of the week entitled *Seven Places of Salzburg and Berchtesgaden, arranged according to the Seven Days of the Week, linked by Two Allegorical Sheets.* The two allegorical plates are significant, with the first and more important, called *Dedication*, showing a tree depicting the history of art in Germany, beneath which are situated a number of figures and an inscription from the Gospel of John 11:25—'I am the resurrection and the life'. This provides an introduction to all that follows, with the inscription on the second allegorical plate (known as the *Keystone*) reading 'Blessed are those who have not seen and yet believe' (John 20:19). *Friday* shows three workers in the right-hand foreground, balanced by a tower in the left foreground. In the middle distance there are three more workers, possibly taking a crop of hay, beyond which a number of trees are dotted about as in parkland, and in the far distance lie the mountains of the Salzkammergut. The sky is shown with a very high, thin stratus cloud, indicative of fair weather.

The tower is particularly important, as it links this 'Garden of Eden' scene to Christianity. The tower emphasises the Cross, with a simple cross showing in the brick or stone work at an intermediate level, above which there is enclosed a crucifix with two people with heads bowed at its base. The space containing the crucifix is built with four columns and lintels, the whole being surmounted by a pitched roof, at the pinnacle of which there is a further simple cross. The disposition of the workers is such as to suggest with reference to Genesis 3:24 that they are tilling the ground from which they were taken. The whole scene is one of an elegiac, utopian existence where there is a simple Pietist pleasure in looking after the land which God has created.

In addition, one could add the thought that there is in this timelessness a feeling of renewal or resurrection, particularly in view of the crucifix scene enclosed at the top of the tower, and, of course, the inscription on the *Dedication*. Contemplation of this Christian metaphor would surely enhance an act of devotion in a viewer or worshipper who is susceptible to communication with Ultimate Reality through the depiction of the created world. Before leaving discussion of the Nazarenes, it is appropriate to quote from Grewe, who summarised the aspirations of the Brotherhood of St Luke as follows:

> The individual (art)work served as an expression, a vessel of the artist's own religiosity. Making art was synonymous with praying, it was a personal and private form of divine service. Moreover, the artwork was a devotional tool meant to serve the devout in their need for reminders, instruction and confirmation in the teachings of Bible and Church. Third, it was a missionary device in place to convert the unbelievers. Through these [...] stages, art helped to form the artist's identity, re-enchant society, and ultimately bring about the Kingdom of God on earth. This, at least, was the Nazarene ideal.[5]

As artists began to express themselves more through landscape, it was necessary to consider the place of landscape within the panoply of fine art because at the end of the eighteenth and beginning of the nineteenth centuries landscape painting was still rising to the level accorded to history painting. The scientist and artist, Carus, in addressing this point, endeavoured to raise the reputation of this form of art by creating a new title for this category—earth-life painting or earth-life art. Carus writes:

> When the soul is saturated with the inner meaning of all these different (organic) forms; when it has clear intimations of the mysterious, divine life of nature; when the hand has taught itself to represent securely, and the eye to see purely and acutely; and when the artist's heart is purely and entirely a consecrated, joyous vessel in which to receive the light from above: then there will infallibly be earth-life paintings [...] These works will truly deserve to be named mystic and orphic; and earth-life painting will have attained its culmination.[6]

Such a description could be applied to many of the works of

5   Grewe, *Painting the Sacred in the Age of Romanticism*, p. 301.
6   Carus, *Nine Letters on Landscape Painting*, p. 30.

Palmer, Friedrich and Oliver, including this particular scene of the Salzkammergut. But it is to the English artist Samuel Palmer that attention will now be turned.

Samuel Palmer and the bright-cloud motif

As Oliver spent most of his time in Germany, he would have been aware of the principles being espoused by Schelling and the way he was promoting the use of landscape as a means of signifying the relationship between humans and their Creator. While Palmer did not spend any great length of time in Germany, he was at times in close contact with Coleridge and with H. C. Robinson, both of whom spent time in Germany studying philosophy and aesthetics and, as has been analysed in an earlier chapter of this study, he would have been imbued with the notions of that time.

Palmer would have been close in theological outlook to Oliver, and both expressed their relationship to the Creator through the depiction of idyllic landscapes. Both chose to ignore, either through ignorance or through deliberate intention, the hardship and drudgery of farm work in the nineteenth century and expressed a benign outlook that would invoke in the viewer the encouragement to praise God and give thanks for such a wonderful creation. Oliver's and Palmer's works are too small to be used as altarpieces in a church or cathedral but both would be appropriate in a small side chapel or monk's cell and most certainly could be used for devotional purposes when the viewer contemplated the creation. The cloud motif was an important one for Palmer, emphasised in this extract from a letter to his friend John Linnell: 'Nor must be forgotten the motley clouding, the fine meshes, the aerial tissues that dapple the skies of spring; nor the rolling volumes and piled mountains of light'. He saw in the treatment of clouds in Linnell's own paintings 'how the elements of nature may be transmitted into the pure Gold of Art'.[7]

---

[7] http://www.tate.org.uk/art/artworks/palmer-the-bright-cloud-n03312

This motif is included in two paintings by Palmer produced towards the end of his time in Shoreham—*The White Cloud* (1833–4) and *The Bright Cloud* (1833–4)—as well as in the earlier sepia *Valley with a Bright Cloud* (1825); all of these have those characteristics which point towards the transcendent. While the two 'cloud' paintings are almost mirror images of each other, *The Bright Cloud* has some similarity with the *Repose on the Flight into Egypt* inasmuch as it shows what could be a biblical scene set in the countryside of Kent.

Yet both paintings show a tremendous building of cumulus cloud located so that it could almost be a representation of the Shekinah. One is reminded of the Transfiguration passage in the Gospel of Matthew 17:5: 'when lo, a bright cloud overshadowed them, and a voice from the cloud said, "This is my beloved Son with whom I am well pleased"', as well as the popular Advent hymn by Charles Wesley which Palmer would probably have known: 'Lo! He comes with clouds descending.'[8] Although Palmer did not set out to produce meteorologically accurate cloudscapes, *The White Cloud* is a good representation of a cumulus cloud building eventually to become a towering cumulo-nimbus—the thunder cloud. It is surely not taking eisegesis to an unreasonable length to suggest that the white cloud represents a theophany—the Shekinah. *The Valley with a Bright Cloud* was unusual for Palmer in not including any staffage but he may have intended the picture to show Paradise, with God being represented by the church, for he wrote:

> Landscape is of little value, but as it hints or expresses the haunts or doings of man. However gorgeous, it can be but Paradise without an Adam. Take away its churches, where for centuries the pure word of God has been read to the poor [...] and you have a frightful kind of Paradise left—a Paradise without a God.[9]

Although without people, he has shown a church in the back-

---

[8] *Hymns Ancient and Modern Revised* (London: William Clowes, c. 1950), hymn 51, p. 56.

[9] C. Harrison, *Samuel Palmer* (Oxford: Ashmolean Museum, 2010), p. 18.

ground and has annotated the picture with the comment 'This is our life, exempt from public haunt, Finds tongues in trees, books in ye running brooks, Sermons in stones, and good in everything. *As you like it.*[10] While the church symbolism is strong, once again it is the bright cloud which dominates the picture and is surely the representation of God—the Shekinah.

To summarise, these cloud works of Palmer are small but I would argue could be used in a similar manner to the icon of the Eastern Orthodox Church, and while not perhaps venerated in the same way as the traditional icon, they could certainly be used as aids to devotion.

Do the paintings of J. M. W. Turner signpost the transcendent?

While the religious and spiritual aspects of the lives of all the other artists considered in this study are readily ascertained, Turner's are difficult to determine. The usual sources of information, for example biographies, have had to be treated with care. In the early part of the twentieth century there were no reliable biographies of Turner—Sir John Rothenstein remarked 'there is to this day not even a biography of him that is both reliable and organised as a readable life'.[11]

---

[10] *Ibid.*, p. 18.

[11] J. Lindsay, *J. M. W. Turner: His Life and Work* (London: Cory, Adams and Mackay, 1966), p. 9, quoting Rothenstein. The first reliable biography seems to be that of A. J. Finberg but even here there is a lack of personal information about Turner; Lindsay's is the first accurate, detailed critical biography. More recent is the research undertaken by the late John Gage, who 'transformed Turner scholarship and greatly deepened our understanding of the role of light and colour in Western culture. His second book [...] revolutionised Turner studies with its detailed examination of many aspects of the artist's work' (*The Times*, 15 February 2012, obituary of John Gage (1938–2012)). Gage published *The Collected Correspondence of J. M. W. Turner* in 1980 and a critical biography in 1987. A detailed study of Turner's correspondence reveals nothing about his spiritual life or indeed his philosophy and the two above-mentioned biographies have very little information about his religiosity or lack thereof.

One gleans some information from Ruskin's *Lectures on Art,* but rather more from Dinah Birch's *Ruskin on Turner*—where we receive both the distilled thoughts of the famous art critic and extracts from *The Works of Ruskin.*[12] From Birch, it can be learnt that Ruskin 'sees Turner's paintings as an expression of natural truth, so faithful that they almost transcend art, and become facts of nature in themselves [...] Ruskin brooded on him as the great painter of human mortality'.[13] Furthermore, Turner had a particular affinity for the poets of the Romantic period; as Birch writes, 'Turner's deference to the spiritual grandeur of nature must be seen as a Romantic phenomenon, one which grew out of a new kind of contact between the intellectual ambitions of poets and painters'.[14]

Assessing Turner through Ruskin is fraught with difficulty because Ruskin had an almost hagiographical view of the artist, but we can perhaps assume that Turner's influence was so great that we can derive some of Turner's thought from Ruskin's *Lectures on Art.*[15] In his particular lecture on the relation of art to religion, Ruskin asserted that the great arts have 'three principal directions of purpose:—first, that of enforcing the religion of men; secondly, that of perfecting their ethical state; thirdly, that of doing them material service'.[16] He concluded that particular lecture with the hope 'That we *may* have the splendour of art again, and with that, we may truly praise and honour our Maker, and with that set forth the beauty and holiness of all that He had made'.[17] It is certainly true that Turner avidly studied the

---

[12] D. Birch, *Ruskin on Turner* (London: Cassell, 1990), including extracts from E. T. Cook and A. Wedderburn (eds), *The Works of John Ruskin,* 39 vols (London: George Allen & Unwin, 1903–12).

[13] Birch, *Ruskin on Turner,* p. 10a.

[14] *Ibid.,* p. 10b.

[15] J. Ruskin, *Lectures on Art: Delivered before the University of Oxford in Hilary Term, 1870* (London: George Allen & Sons, 1910). Birch gives some substance to this assumption when she writes 'What Ruskin wrote about art—not only Turner's art, but all art—is deeply informed by what Turner had taught him'. Birch, *Ruskin on Turner,* p. 17b.

[16] Ruskin, *Lectures on Art,* pp. 43–4.

[17] *Ibid.,* p. 77.

subject of mythology, a topic which could be said to be a means of expressing the worship of nature.[18] This is an idea which, as Birch describes, had taken a new direction in the nineteenth century, when the sun, 'as the source of all life, could be seen as the central divinity, taking various guises, of primeval religions.'[19]

To complete this investigation into Turner's spirituality or religiosity the question of whether or not it is possible to apply the concept of the anonymous Christian—a concept devised by the theologian Karl Rahner—to the artist must be considered. Essentially, Rahner postulates that spiritual self-communication is an act of God's freedom—that is, an act of giving himself in 'free and absolute love'.[20] We can see here a link with Christianity with its concept of the unmerited grace of God being available to sinful persons. In Rahner's view this free and unmerited grace is available, as an offer, to absolutely all people and is present in all people as an existential of their concrete existence, 'and is present prior to their freedom, their self-understanding and their experience'.[21] The acceptance of this grace, i.e. the acceptance of God in the living-out of human existence in the concrete world, is itself an act of God's self-communication, for, if it were not, God would be in danger of being reduced to a level of finiteness. 'God in his salvic will has offered and destined this fulfilment not only for some, but for all people, a fulfilment which consists in the fully realised acceptance of this divine self-communication.'[22]

---

[18] For a detailed study of Turner and mythology see K. Nicholson, *Turner's Classical Landscapes: Myth and Meaning* (New Jersey: Princeton University Press, 1990).

[19] Birch, *Ruskin on Turner*, p. 80b.

[20] K. Rahner, *Foundations of Christian Faith* (New York: Crossroad Publishing, 1995), p. 123.

[21] *Ibid.*, p. 127.

[22] *Ibid.* p. 129. Contemplation of the discovery of this self-communication leads us to the interpretation of transcendental experience which is offered by Christianity, salvation history and the history of revelation. A person can then legitimise their existential decision and accept the theological interpretation of the situation provided by Christianity. Thus, the holy mystery can be experienced in a hidden closeness, 'a forgiving intimacy, a real home that it is a love which shares itself,

To summarise this short investigation into the inherent spirituality of Turner, it is clear that in Ruskin's view Turner was a painter of 'the truths of nature', and in his final volume of *Modern Painters* he expresses the view that the truths of nature were 'also spiritual in a sense still wider and deeper than could be contained within Christian tradition.'[23] This does give some credence to the quoted, but possibly apocryphal, deathbed words of Turner that 'The Sun is God.'[24] So, at the very least, it could be said that Turner was a follower of heliolatry and, possibly by Rahner's criteria, an anonymous Christian.

I will now analyse the sacramental qualities of the two late paintings of Turner referred to above: *Shade and Darkness—The Evening of the Deluge* (exhibited 1843) and *Light and Colour (Goethe's Theory)—The Morning after the Deluge—Moses Writing the Book of Genesis* (exhibited 1843). For the purposes of considering their qualities as aids to religious contemplation, I will regard the two paintings (which were painted as a pair) as a diptych, and for simplicity I will refer to them as *Shade and Darkness* and *Light and Colour*. Both paintings are held in the Tate.

something familiar which he can approach and turn to from the estrangement of his own perilous and empty life'. As Rahner sees it the self-communication of God is universal and the offer to accept the grace of God is there for all. Inasmuch as it is accepted by Christians that God's self-communication reaches its acme in Jesus Christ (the objectification of that self-communication), but it is possible for someone who has had no contact with the teaching of Jesus to receive and accept the offer of God's self-communication (the justifying grace of Jesus), then that person 'has accepted what is essential in what Christianity wants to mediate to him: his salvation in that grace which objectively is the grace of Jesus Christ'. That person could then be regarded as an anonymous Christian. The question then is whether or not this applies to Turner. Whilst he obviously had knowledge of the Bible (which perhaps he treated in the same manner as he would a work by the Latin poet Ovid), and it is difficult therefore to say that he had absolutely no knowledge of the teaching of Jesus, it is possible to argue that he accepted the grace of God inasmuch as he used his God-given talent (God's self-communication) to reveal the truth of the created world.

[23] Birch, *Ruskin on Turner*, p. 81.
[24] *Ibid.*

These two pictures were painted as Turner was endeavouring to formulate a response to Goethe's theory of colour (that colours come out of the interaction between light and darkness and were a result of perception by the viewer).[25] However, my concern is how these paintings might function in a church or chapel setting. As Lindsay emphasises, one of the paintings shows Goethe's negative colours whilst the morning picture shows the positive colours, expressing, says Goethe, 'warmth and gladness'.[26] In the *Shade and Darkness* painting dark browns and reds surround a central area of white light painted in the form of a vortex. The eye is led into the vortex, perhaps emphasised by the birds, to which Turner refers in the poem (see below), at the top of the picture. The eye is led so far into the depth that one might believe that Turner is endeavouring to show the physical world dissolving into a distant metaphysical realm. As Lindsay confirms, 'the dynamic colour elements [...] merge man and nature in the concrete sphere of immediate experience'.[27] The painting is certainly an example of Turner's depiction of the sublime, where the catastrophic forces of nature, perhaps in the form of a tsunami, are shown with the utmost dramatic force.

[25] A full explanation of Goethe's colour theory is beyond the scope of this chapter, but essentially, whilst Newton in his study of optics described light in terms of the wavelength produced when light strikes an object, Goethe was much more concerned with the relationship between the object and its perception by the viewer. The following is extracted from the website referred to below: 'Goethe realises that the sensations of colour reaching our brain are also shaped by our perception—by the mechanics of human vision and by the way our brains process information. Therefore, according to Goethe, what we see of an object depends upon the object, the lighting and our perception. Goethe seeks to derive laws of colour harmony, ways of characterising physiological colours (how colours affect us) and subjective visual phenomena in general. Goethe studies after-images, coloured shadows and complementary colours.' (Taken from website, using English spelling: www.webexhibits.org/colorart/ch.html.)

[26] Lindsay, *J. W. M. Turner*, p. 212, quoting Goethe.

[27] *Ibid.*, p. 21.

In Goethe's terms the colours here 'produce a restless, susceptible, anxious impression', with the cold blue contrasting
diagonally across the painting with the dark brown, almost black,
suggestive of absence of light before, in the corner of the picture
there is just a lightening of the scene with a small area of shades
of pale yellow. The effect of the darkness is to highlight the effect
of the white vortex and add to the creation of the appearance of
a tunnel preceding the movement through into the metaphysical
world beyond.

The poem accompanying this work is:

> The morn put forth her sign of woe unheeded;
> But disobedience slept; the dark'ning Deluge closed around,
> And the last taken came: the giant framework floated,
> The roused birds forsook their nightly shelters screaming
> And the beast waded to the ark.[28]

In *Light and Colour*, Turner makes a reference to Moses writing
the book of Genesis, which to the modern eye seems strange,
but at the time when Turner was working it was probably still
the accepted view that Moses wrote parts of that book.[29] The

---

[28] J. Gage, *J. W. M. Turner A Wonderful Range of Mind* (London: Guild
Publishing by arrangement with Yale University Press, 1987), p. 222,
quoting from *Fallacies of Hope*. The Tate Britain gallery caption reads:
'Pair to "Light and Colour (Goethe's Theory), The Morning after the
Deluge—Moses writing the Book of Genesis". In these companion
pictures, Turner opposes cool and warm colours, and their contrasting
emotional associations, as described by Goethe in his "Farbenlehre"
(theory of colours). Turner has chosen the biblical Flood as the vehicle
for these ideas, returning to the historical sublime he had mastered in
some of his earliest exhibition pictures. Originally painted and framed
as octagons, this pair carries two of Turner's last and most inspired
statements of the natural vortex, while the allusion to Goethe adds a
gloss of recent science and theory to a lifetime's preoccupation with
elemental forces.' http://www.tate.org.uk/art/artworks/turner-shade-
and-darkness-the-evening-of-the-deluge-n00531

[29] Scholarship has now shown the narrative of the Flood to consist of a
combination of the P (Priestly) and J (Yahwist) traditions; it was not
written by Moses. Much of this research was undertaken between 1850
and 1880, with Wellhausen being the prominent scholar in this area.

colour scheme here is positive, with warm reds, orange and dark shades of yellow, with the only negative colour being reserved for the brazen serpent in the centre, rising towards the back of Moses, who is facing into the depths of the picture. The context of this part of the story is that after the Flood a covenant was established between God and mankind such that if mankind looks after and nurtures the world then never again will God flood mankind out of existence. The sign of this covenant was the rainbow; why Turner chose not to include this phenomenon in the painting is an unanswered question, particularly intriguing when the splitting of light through a spectrum into the colours of the rainbow was an important feature of Newton's theory of light. The nearest there is to the rainbow is the suggestion that the bubbles in the vortex surrounding the sun are themselves edged with the colours of the rainbow.

This prismatic effect is emphasised in the poem which accompanies this work:

> The ark stood firm on Ararat; th' returning Sun
> Exhaled earth's humid bubbles, and emulous of light,
> Reflected her lost forms, each in prismatic guise
> Hope's harbinger, ephemeral as the summer fly
> Which rises, flits, expands, and dies.[30]

As with *Shade and Darkness, Light and Colour* has a very large central light, almost certainly the sun, with Moses sitting at the centre and writing, suggesting a calmness that is not present in the more obvious tunnel and vortex in the former work. The importance of the sun is emphasised in Turner's poem by the use of the capital letter and is entirely consistent with Turner's supposed deathbed words 'The Sun is God', referred to earlier.

This reference to Turner as a follower of heliolatry leads on now to consideration of whether or not these works of art could be regarded as sacraments. These pictures are both small (787 × 781 mm and 787 × 787 mm) and could be placed one on each side of an altar. They both use the 'simbolising power of

---

[30] Lindsay, *J. W. M. Turner*, p. 212, quoting Turner.

colour to designate the Qualities of things' and they both tend towards the Abstract Sacred to which the radical theologian Don Cupitt refers in his book *Radicals and the Future of the Church*.[31] These two paintings are both works that seem to proceed from the physical world and point to the metaphysical. They both utilise a prominent circle or vortex—a symbol for God, according to Giotto and Pope Benedict XI. The use of the serpent symbol in *Light and Colour* suggests either the Fall and the need for redemption or the alternative interpretation of the second creation story, that on eating from the tree of knowledge mankind became sufficiently mature to leave the Garden of Eden and fend for himself. The caption to the picture in the Tate Gallery suggests that the brazen serpent symbolises the cure from the plague and eventual salvation (this is a reference to the passage in Exodus 4:3–7, when after touching the serpent Moses is cured of leprosy—whether this was intended by Turner is conjecture).[32] Moses as the agent for the establishment of the moral code, the Decalogue, symbolises the need for men and women to worship God and to live in harmony with one another. In more general terms one could see in *Shade and Darkness* (located on the left of the altar) a metaphor for the wrath of God and in *Light and Colour* a metaphor for the glory of God. Alternatively, in a typological application, placing the works in a New Testament context, one could see a metaphor for the Passion of Christ on the left, with the resurrection being suggested by *Light and Colour.*

[31] *Ibid.*, p. 212. D. Cupitt, *Radicals and the Future of the Church* (London: SCM Press, 1989), p. 26.
[32] The display caption in Tate Britain reads: 'Pair to "Shade and Darkness—The Evening of the Deluge". This triumphant explosion of light brilliantly exploits the warm side of the spectrum. It celebrates God's Covenant with Man after the Flood. The serpent in the centre represents the brazen serpent raised by Moses in the wilderness as a cure for plague. Here it symbolises Christ's redemption of Man in the New Covenant. Turner's verses rather undermine the optimism of the religious message by emphasising the transience of the natural phenomena engendered by the "returning sun".' http://www.tate.org.uk/art/artworks/turner-light-and-colour-goethes-theory-the-morning-after-the-deluge-moses-writing-the-book-n00532

So, in both pictures we have some of the most powerful themes of the three Abrahamic faiths—the Fall of man and the need for redemption; the need for adherence to the law; death and resurrection. In addition to these themes of revelation, there is also the strong suggestion of transcendence—moving through the vortex to something beyond in *Shade and Darkness* as well as being aware that there is something beyond the blinding light of the sun in *Light and Colour*. As Lindsay writes:

> The summoned carrion birds flitter in out of the upper whirl: and we feel at once the blessing of the sun that shines on good and evil alike, and the curse of light upon man who has alienated himself from nature by his violence and corruption. The sun is both creator and destroyer. The painting is Turner's final judgement on life and on death.[33]

In my view, these two paintings assist in the contemplation of our relationship with nature. If we then accept that nature is God's creation and think in terms of the natural theology that was both prevalent at the time of the Romantic period and is still current today, somewhat in the guise of green theology, then we are able to say that the contemplation of these works of art (by viewers susceptible to the visual imagery) may assist in bringing us closer to that Ultimate Reality. In other words, these two paintings of Turner fulfil the criteria required to enable them to be dedicated or consecrated for use in the worship of that ultimate reality that is called God.

Mark Rothko, Untitled and Black on Maroon

Having mentioned colour field paintings in earlier chapters, Mark Rothko's *Untitled* (1969) makes for an interesting comparison, particularly with *The Monk by the Sea*. This very large painting, produced a year before Rothko's suicide, is a study in grey and dark brown. The grey field occupies approximately 35 per cent of the picture with dark brown occupying the remaining 65 per cent. The two fields are not uniform in colour, the grey being flecked

[33] Lindsay, *J. W. M. Turner*, p. 213.

with white along the 'horizon' dividing the fields and with the field itself being filled with random 'smudges' of lighter shades of grey. The brown colour field is more uniform, with some patches of lighter brown near to the 'horizon'; to the right of the picture there is also just one patch of light brown. Perspective and aerial perspective are imagined rather than shown in any mechanistic way in the painting—it is very easy to imagine the grey foreground as very flat land looking out to a distant horizon, above which is a very dark sky—indeed it is possible that Rothko regarded his colour-field paintings as landscapes rather than as examples of abstract art, although 'It has been said that Rothko placed the darker colour at the top of the painting in order to prevent it being read as landscape, a reference which he wished to avoid.'[34]

This inconsistency suggests that while it is not unreasonable to regard this painting as a landscape it may not be what Rothko intended. To achieve an effect by comparison of light with dark is the *raison d'être* of this painting. In particular, the use of small flecks of white (presumably unpainted canvas) on the horizon encourages the viewer to strain to look, to stare at that horizon to try to see if there is anything that can be discerned beyond the wall of canvas. The effect of the dark-brown sky is to bring the eye down to that horizon. The grey is similar to the colour that Friedrich uses for the foreground in *The Monk by the Sea* (Friedrich uses a much lighter grey). The writer Pico Iyer refers to visiting an exhibition of Mark Rothko paintings, when he 'felt myself drawn beneath the surface to a stillness that seemed bottomless and rich with every colour.'[35] With some of Rothko's colour-field paintings where the colours are of the same hue but slightly different shade there is an apparent vibration that can be seen at the junction of the two shades. That does not apply in this particular Rothko work, where the effect is achieved by the white flecks. It is the sense of trying to look beyond the

---

[34] http://www.tate.org.uk/art/artworks/rothko-untitled-t04149
[35] P. Iyer, *The Sunday Times Style Supplement* 23rd November 2014 p. 72. See also Iyer, *The Art of Stillness: Adventures in Going Nowhere* (London: Simon and Schuster, 2014).

horizon in this picture which particularly gives it the quality of signposting the transcendent.

In *Black on Maroon* (1958), Rothko has created a panel with a black window frame painted over a maroon background. As Harvey writes: 'Dark colours, Rothko reasoned, were more sublime than bright ones [and] his paintings after 1949 seem to absorb rather than emit light.'[36] This produces an effect of drawing the viewer into the picture very similar to the effects identified earlier as characteristic of paintings pointing towards the transcendent. There are no overt references to the Bible in Rothko's colour-field paintings. However, in an application of eisegesis Harvey sees that

> the double and single rectangular forms that fizzle and hover like presences in the uncertain space behind the picture plane summon associations with the Shekinah and pillars of cloud and fire that went before the Israelites in the wilderness. The paintings' palette of deep reds, crimsons, maroons, and black resonate with some of the predominant colours mentioned in the Hebrew Bible and used in the design of in the Tabernacle and the Temple of Solomon, an allusion made all the more plausible in the context of the Rothko Chapel (dedicated in 1971) at Houston, Texas.[37]

While this is the interpretation of one commentator, Rothko's vision was a 'focus on the modern sensibility's need for its own authentic spiritual experience' with the image of his work being the 'symbolic expression of that idea' which suggests that this thought-provoking interpretation warrants commendation.[38] Furthermore the theologian Don Cupitt, writing in 1989 on the subject of religion as a human construct, expressed the view that 'Rothko (for example: he is by no means the only one) just invented works of art that are great religion.'[39] Cupitt then argues that the

[36] J. Harvey, *The Bible as Visual Culture* (Sheffield: Sheffield Phoenix Press, 2013), p. 121.

[37] *Ibid.*

[38] B. Clearwater, *The Rothko Book* (London: Tate Publishing, 2006), p. 190, quoting Crehan, writing in *Art Digest* in 1954.

[39] Cupitt, *Radicals and the Future of the Church*, p. 26.

major artists of the modern and post-modern periods could be viewed as 'prophets of a new religious order'.[40] Their dedication to this task and their creativity, he argued, enabled the viewers to gain the same sort of experiences that 'earlier generations once got from icons and the cult of saints'.[41] It is noteworthy that these two commentators, of very different theological persuasions, both view the contemplation of Rothko's works as likely to induce a religious experience that is either reminiscent of biblical accounts or of the religious icons of an earlier age.

In addition, it is interesting to note that Rothko was influenced by Kierkegaard and, in particular, the book *Fear and Trembling*, which deals with the preparedness of Abraham to sacrifice Isaac (Genesis 22:1–19).[42] Rothko emphasises that his paintings have intimations of sacrifice and death and could be regarded like facades of a building with just one door or maybe a window or two open.[43] The clearest evidence that Rothko considered his pictures to be works of art with a religious context can be gleaned from the fact that it is known that when he was given a commission to produce a series of paintings for a restaurant he 'immediately envisioned the refectory of the San Marco church with the wall painting by Fra Angelico'.[44]

It would appear from his various statements that his paintings were intended to provide pointers to transcendental truth and the fact that they are known to have induced religious experiences in some viewers suggests that these colour-field works could indeed point to the transcendent. It is the sense of trying to look beyond the horizon in his pictures which particularly gives them these qualities. There is no sense of the sublime, unless by the use of imagination one places oneself or a figure in the foreground, which would give the painting scale and suggest its category as 'landscape'.

[40] *Ibid.*
[41] *Ibid.*
[42] A. Borchardt-Hume (ed.), *Rothko* (London: Tate Publishing, 2008), p. 91; information given in a talk by Rothko to the Pratt Institute in 1958.
[43] *Ibid.*, p. 91.
[44] *Ibid.*, p. 95.

Untitled and *Black on Maroon* are two of a number of paintings, any one of which could be used as an altarpiece. At an exhibition at the Tate Britain gallery (26 September 2008 to 1 February 2009) the Rothko colour fields were set in a room devoted to his paintings alone and the atmosphere created in that room by the lighting and the paintings rendered it such that it could easily have been considered to be a chapel, and hence most appropriate for spiritual or religious contemplation.

Summary

To summarise these last two chapters, the early Renaissance pictures, whether or not used as altarpieces, were illustrations of biblical scenes involving different levels of interpretation. It should be remembered that at this time the church services were not held in the vernacular and only a few of those attending would have understood the Latin used for all Roman Catholic services, and hence biblical illustration was necessary as an aid to understanding. Even so, as I have demonstrated above, in the examples of Raphael and Dürer multiple layers of interpretation can be applied to these paintings, giving them characteristics both illustrative as well as suggestive of transcendence.

Rubens, with his late works including the *Landscape with a Rainbow*, foreshadows the view of Schelling, who wrote in 1859: 'The inclination unique to Christianity is that from the finite to the infinite [...] inclination suspends all symbolic intuition and comprehends the finite only as the allegory of the infinite.'[45] So, in the Rubens, we have both a symbolism derived from the Bible (the rainbow and the covenant with Noah) and a transcendent symbolism, with the rainbow pointing from the physical world to the Kingdom of Heaven.

With the Nazarenes we see a clear attempt to root their work firmly in the Bible, requiring us in many cases to apply a typological understanding in order to appreciate fully the

---

[45] F. W. J. Schelling, *The Philosophy of Art* (Minneapolis: University of Minnesota, 1989), p. 75.

depth of meaning contained within their works. In other words, one could approach most Nazarene art on two levels—there is the superficial appreciation of a biblical scene and then as one contemplates and analyses the paintings in more depth other possibilities of theological understanding begin to be discerned. There is the danger, of course, as with all eisegesis, of trying to read too much into a single painting, almost to the point of creating a far-fetched interpretation, but as I hope the above analyses have demonstrated, the application of logic helps to determine when the interpretative destination has been reached.

The symbolism of the paintings of Oliver and Palmer allows us to view the whole of nature as a Christian metaphor—the scenes are so idyllic so as to suggest strongly the Kingdom of Heaven. A more realistic, less naïve, view of nature is taken by Friedrich, whose works symbolise the insignificance of mankind compared with the awesome power of the Creator; they symbolise both the uncertainty and longing within the mind of those contemplating taking the leap of faith necessary to attain what St Paul described as living 'by the power of the Holy Spirit [and] abound[ing] in hope' (Romans 15:13). In Rothko's colour-field paintings one can see a development from Friedrich's *Monk by the Sea*; here, by the removal of people from the picture, the artist leaves more scope for the viewer's imagination and interpretation to develop to a greater depth, with the contrast between alienation and union with a life in Christ, and the need to overcome the leap of faith necessary to achieve this.

It is my contention that many other artists and groups of artists achieve the Nazarenes' aim, and realise that objective through their own very different styles of artistic endeavour. Whilst I hesitate to differ from the Very Revd John Drury, who received his doctorate of divinity from the Archbishop of Canterbury for his work on religious art, I cannot wholly agree with his statement that painters 'have to go a good way further than theologians down the ethical road of incarnation with the [...] obedient humility and love for the world of mortal appearances which it demands, if they are to make the mystery of things visible.'[46] My disagreement is that it is an unattainable goal to make the mystery of the spiritual realm visible—the greatest that artists can achieve is to point the way to the transcendent Truth. However close they may get to that Truth, they can never achieve that end. Expressed in mathematical terms, the best that can be achieved by the artist (poet or painter) is to produce a poem or painting which could be considered asymptotic to that Truth.[47] While this is the best that can be achieved I would argue that it has been attained by a much wider range of artists than merely the Brothers of St Luke. If we accept that this 'best' has been achieved by some artists, can the thought be developed to another stage, where perhaps we should regard these paintings—hieroglyphs, to use Schlegel's expansion of the term—as sacraments in themselves? In other words, can a modern theory of the hieroglyph be developed?

I have argued throughout that these paintings and, no doubt, many others not considered, could be used as altarpieces or aids to devotion or contemplation. As Cupitt has suggested, these paintings can give the viewer 'the sort of charge that earlier generations once got from icons and the cult of saints.'[48] In other words all the works considered in these two chapters could certainly be used, by the predisposed viewer, as aids to religious contemplation. Furthermore, I would contend that it would be entirely appropriate for art—be it sculpture or painting—to be used in a similar way to the anointing oils or to the bread and wine in the Eucharist. There are three types of oil used: to anoint the sick, to prepare for baptism and for extreme unction, all of which become holy when they are blessed by a bishop on Maundy Thursday. Similarly, the unleavened bread and wine become holy when blessed by the priest in the service of Holy Communion. The uses of these artefacts, which take on a special

---

[46] J. Drury, *Painting the Word: Christian Pictures and their Meanings* (London and New Haven: Yale University Press, 2000), p. 181.
[47] An asymptote is a line or curve that approaches ever nearer to another line or curve but never actually reaches it.
[48] Cupitt, *Radicals and the Future of the Church*, p. 26.

symbolic significance after they have been blessed, are an aid to affirming faith, and I would argue that appropriate works of art could take their place alongside these consecrated elements as contributors to and additional to sacramental liturgy.[49]

There is a further parallel. Although the gift of the sacraments through justification is available to all who choose to accept the grace of God, not all choose to do so. In the same way, whilst many would accept the suggestion of the transcendent Truth that is evoked by these hieroglyphs not everyone is affected in the same way or even affected at all. Furthermore, another parallel that can be drawn is that of religious experience itself—some may have an experience that is initiated by a particular activity or by nature or by a particular piece of music or by celebration of the Eucharist. Just as these experiences (including out-of-body and near-death experiences) have been shown by the many records of such experiences collected by the Alister Hardy Trust to be very personal, so I would suggest that the experience of the transcendent or mystical brought about by a particular work of art is a personal one, dependent not only on the characteristics of

---

[49] As J. D. Crichton makes clear in ch. 1 (a theology of worship) of *The Study of Liturgy*, ed. Jones, Wainwright *et al.*, p. 23: 'The ultimate subject of liturgical celebration is [...] Christ who acts in and through his Church. Obviously, his action is invisible, but the people of God, his body, is a visible and structured community and over the whole range of its liturgical action, which, to repeat, consists of both word and sacrament, manifests Christ's presence, shows forth the nature of his activity, which is redemptive, and by his power makes his redeeming work effectual and available to men and women of today. The liturgy then is essentially and by its nature sacramental [...] It addresses a word to us but it *embodies* this word in actions, gestures and symbols; and if "the supernatural saving reality, veiled in historical events and surrounded by the darkness of mystery, is present to us only in earthly form (*sacramentum*), and demands the revealing word" [Schillebeeckx, The Sacraments: an Encounter with God, in *Christianity Divided* (London: Sheed and Ward,1961), p. 246] the gesture or thing (water, bread, wine) forces us to attend to the word, enables us to grasp its import and to appropriate its content [...] To say that the liturgy is sacramental is to say that it is symbolic, though its symbols are not merely decorative but purposeful.'

the work of art but also on the perceptibility of the viewer.[50] With all these parallels between works of art and the artefacts used in church services, between the acceptance of the sacraments or oils by penitent communicants and the experience of viewing a hieroglyph by those who are open to receiving such experiences, I suggest that the argument for regarding blessed hieroglyphs in the same category as the consecrated elements is strong indeed.

[50] The Alister Hardy Trust is responsible for a collection of over 6000 accounts of religious experiences, which are currently held in the Religious Experience Research Centre at the University of Wales, Trinity Saint David, Lampeter, Ceredigion (see Chapter 4).

Reflection and Summarising Thoughts

This book has been concerned with the ways in which artists have endeavoured to express the numinous or point towards the transcendent through landscape painting. The transcendent is described as that recognition in mankind of the capacity of knowing truth intuitively. Alternatively, it can be regarded as attaining a knowledge of an order of existence *transcending* the reach of the senses, and of which we can have no sensible experience. My starting point was Michael Podro's theory of art, which may be summarised as: 1. Art reveals through the skill of the artist some aspect of a subject that would not be immediately apparent. 2. The artist's depiction of an object makes a reference to the perceptual process of the viewer which enables an understanding to be achieved through, for example, the use of analogy. 3. The artist engages with the state of mind of the viewer to achieve an elevated or heightened emotional response to the work of art which may suggest a transcendence that lies behind the objects depicted.

The first chapter continued with a description of the reawakening of the study of aesthetics, which was begun by Baumgarten and continued by Kant, who established the precise criteria necessary to define the beautiful and the sublime. Kant set out in detail a formal treatise on aesthetic judgement and established the subject as one worthy of consideration as a separate discipline. The major discrepancy identified in Kant's argument was that he argued on the one hand that the appreciation of beauty and the sublime was ontologically subjective, whilst on the other that beauty and the sublime have a quality of universality that ought to be recognised by everyone. This discrepancy was recognised by Schiller, who developed the concept of *Spieltrieb*—play-drive operating within the mind as a description of the interplay between the two natures of the rational and sensual parts of the mind, which could lead to greater integration of the personality. This, in turn, led to his suggestion that contemplation could be said to have a moral influence. This reading of Schiller suggested that despite the creation of the play-drive there was still too great a separation between art and reality, sensuality and reason, to enable art to describe truth fully; for a further development it was necessary to turn to Hegel and Schelling. Consideration of the work of Hegel suggested to me that he concluded this paradigm with his development of the concept of the Ideal. Hegel's comment that truth no longer found its expression in the visual arts determined this paradigm, leaving Schelling, Runge and Carus to begin a new paradigm.

Building on the work of his predecessors, Schelling developed further the concept of intellectual intuition, which refers to direct, unmediated knowledge rather than the achievement of knowledge by rational thought alone. He concluded that painting was very well suited to express this transcendental knowledge, the infinite within the finite, but was dependent on the skill (genius) of the artist and receptivity of the observer. Schelling was a major influence on Runge, who summarised the theory of transcendental knowledge for students of art, combining an existential approach to the transcendent with some practical suggestions for its achievement. Chapter 3 continued by highlighting the work of Carus, who particularly stressed the thought that the divine could and should be expressed through landscape painting, which he preferred to call 'earth-life painting'. The chapter concluded by stating that while a concept of the Absolute will always involve an element of faith, it could be said that an artist who achieves the goals set by Schelling, Runge and Carus will enable the receptive viewer to glimpse a revelation of that Ultimate Reality.

Chapter 4 dealt with the characteristics of religious experience and possible trigger factors, highlighting the theology of Schleiermacher, his influence on Otto and the definition of the numinous. The factors which Otto ascribed to the expression of the numinous in art—great spatial distance, emptiness and darkness—were identified. The trigger factors involved in invoking religious experience were discussed and those occasioned by the exposure to sublime or beautiful examples of the natural world were described in some detail. From this it was argued that it was a short step from the natural world inducing a state of mystical feeling to such a response being induced by the representation of that world through the medium of visual art. This was followed by an analysis of a number of case histories from the archive of spiritual experiences held by the Alister Hardy Religious Experience Research Centre. These all featured the evoking of a religious experience by an encounter with a work of art.

Then began a detailed analysis of the iconography of the two main artists under consideration—Palmer and Friedrich. Works of Palmer which could be considered as pointing towards the transcendent were analysed, with the common characteristics of far-distant horizons, a strong contrast between light and dark and an effect which leads the viewer into staring at the horizon looking for something beyond the veil of the canvas, being identified. Other specific qualities were identified in individual pictures, which were suggestive of pointing towards the transcendent. In addition, the biblical symbolism in Palmer was recognised in his evocations of an Edenic spiritual paradise, emphasised by the juxtaposition of biblical quotations, for example from a Psalm, with specific paintings.

Friedrich was placed in the context of German Romanticism, with an analysis of a number of his works which portrayed the numinous and hence signposted the transcendent. Friedrich's characteristic *leitmotif* of depicting the back view of a visitor to a scene was examined in detail; it was argued that this use of the *Rückenfigur* invited the viewer to share the experience of the traveller. Many of his paintings use this technique, which when combined with a misty scene encourage the viewer to stare into the picture, endeavouring to discern what may be located deep within the painting, to the extent of trying to see what may lie beyond the veil created by the canvas itself. As in the case of Palmer, all the Friedrich paintings analysed met the two Otto criteria of the contrast between light and dark, and the suggestion of a tremendous distance or huge empty space. In addition, the use of the lonely visitor icon in some paintings emphasised the insignificance of the human in the face of the forces of the natural world unleashed by the Creator.

Chapter 9 was concerned with practical theology and argued that in certain circumstances a work of art could be regarded as a sacrament akin to the bread and wine of the Eucharist, or as 'an outward and visible sign of an inward and spiritual grace'. I suggested that the criteria or conducive properties required for a work of art to be viewed as a sacrament are the intention of the artist, the content of the picture and the experiential effect on the viewer. This claim was then examined through an analysis of two works of Turner and one painting by Friedrich.

The final chapters were more discursive and wide-ranging, describing works of art that, whether used as an altarpiece or as a small painting in a private chapel, could help the viewer towards an appreciation of that higher power or Ultimate Reality. Covering a wider period than the rest of the book, the analyses began in the Renaissance with Dürer and Raphael and concluded in the twentieth century with a discussion of the colour-field paintings of the abstract expressionist Rothko.

As Schlegel wrote, 'Every *true* painting ought to be a hiero-glyph, a *divine symbol*'.[1]

As a divine symbol the painting must take its place alongside the other consecrated artefacts utilised by Christians in their day-to-day worship.

---

[1] Grewe, *Painting the Sacred in the Age of Romanticism*, p. 305, quoting Schlegel.

BIBLIOGRAPHY

Alexander, D., *Rebuilding the Matrix: Science and Faith in the 21st Century.* Grand Rapids: Zondervan, 2001.

Armstrong, K., *The Case for God: What Religion Really Means.* London: Bodley Head, 2009.

Ashton, R., *The German Idea.* Cambridge: Cambridge University Press, 1980.

Astley, J., and L. Francis (eds), *Christian Perspectives on Faith Development.* Leominster: Gracewing, 1992.

Barraclough, G. (ed.), *The Times Atlas of World History.* London: Times Books (3rd edn, ed. Norman Stone), 1989.

Barrell, J., *The History of British Art 1600–1870.* London: Tate Publishing, 2008.

Beckett, W., *The Mystical Now: Art and the Sacred.* New York: Universe, 1993.

Bell, J., *Mirror of the World: A New History of Art.* London: Thames and Hudson, 2007.

Belting, H., *Likeness and Presence: A History of the Image before the Era of Art.* Chicago: University of Chicago Press, 1996.

Bergmann, S., *In the Beginning is the Icon: A Liberative Theology of Images, Visual Arts and Culture.* London: Equinox Publishing, 2009.

Bernstein, J. M. (ed.), *Classic and Romantic German Aesthetics.* Cambridge: Cambridge University Press, 2003.

Birch, D., *Ruskin on Turner.* London: Cassell, 1990.

Bisanz, R. M., *German Romanticism and Philipp Otto Runge.* DeKalb: Northern Illinois University Press, 1970.

Blake, W., *Seen in my Visions. A Descriptive Catalogue of Pictures,* ed. M. Myrone. London: Tate Publishing, 2009.

Borchardt-Hume, A. (ed.), *Rothko.* London: Tate Publishing, 2008.

Bowden, J., *Who's Who in Theology*. New York: Crossroad Publishing, 1990.

Bowker, J., *The Sacred Neuron: Extraordinary New Discoveries Linking Science and Religion*. London: I. B. Tauris, 2005.

Burke, E., *A Philosophical Enquiry into the Origin of our Ideas of the Sublime and Beautiful*, edited with an introduction and notes by James R. Boulton. London: Routledge and Kegan Paul, 1958.

Butlin, B., *Samuel Palmer: The Sketchbook of 1824*. London: Thames and Hudson, 2005.

Campbell-Johnson, R., *Mysterious Wisdom: The Life and Work of Samuel Palmer*. London: Bloomsbury, 2011.

Carlyle, T., *History of Friedrich II of Prussia called Frederick the Great*, abridged version edited and with introduction by John Clive. Chicago: University of Chicago Press, 1969.

Carus, C. G., *Nine Letters on Landscape Painting* (with intr. by Oskar Bätschmann). Los Angeles: The Getty Research Institute, 2002.

Church in Wales, *The Book of Common Prayer for Use in the Church in Wales*. Cardiff: Church in Wales Publications, 1984.

Clark, K., *The Nude: A Study of Ideal Art*. London: The Reprint Society, 1958.

Clearwater, B., *The Rothko Book*. Tate Publishing, 2006.

Crim. K. (ed.), *The Perennial Dictionary of World Religions*. San Francisco: Harper and Row, 1981.

Cupitt, D., *Radicals and the Future of the Church*. London: SCM Press, 1989.

Davies, B., *An Introduction to the Philosophy of Religion*. 2nd edn. Oxford: Oxford University Press, 1993.

De Borchgrave, H., *A Journey into Christian Art*. Oxford: Lion Publishing, 2001.

Dissanayake, E., *What is Art For?* Seattle: University of Washington Press, 2002.

Donald, J., *Chambers' Etymological Dictionary of the English Language*. London: W. and R. Chambers, 1872.

Drury, J., *Painting the Word: Christian Pictures and their*

Meanings. New Haven and London: Yale University Press, 2000.

Dykes-Bower, J. *et al.* (eds), *Hymns Ancient and Modern Revised*. London: William Clowes, 1950.

Eaves, M., *The Counter Arts Conspiracy: Art and Industry in the Age of Blake*. Ithaca, New York: Cornell University Press, 1992.

Eaves, M., *William Blake's Theory of Art*. Princeton: Princeton University Press, 1982.

Eaves, M. (ed.), *Cambridge Companion to Blake*. Cambridge: Cambridge University Press, 2003.

Eitner, L., *Neoclassicism and Romanticism 1750–1850*. London: Prentice-Hall International, 1971.

Farmer, D. H., *The Oxford Dictionary of Saints*. Oxford: Oxford University Press, 1997.

Forsyth, P. T., *Christ on Parnassus: Lectures on Art, Ethic and Theology*. London: Hodder and Stoughton, 1911.

Fowler, J. W., *Stages of Faith: The Psychology of Human Development and the Quest for Meaning*. New York: Harper Collins, 1981 (paperback edition 1995).

Fuller, P., *Theoria: Art and the Absence of Grace*. London: Chatto and Windus, 1988.

Gage, J., *J. M. W. Turner: A Wonderful Range of Mind*. London: Guild Publishing by arrangement with Yale University Press, 1987.

Gombrich, E., *Symbolic Images: Studies in the Art of the Renaissance*. London: Phaidon Press, 1972.

Gray, H. D., *Emerson: A Statement of New England Transcendentalism*. Stanford: Stanford University Press, 1917.

Grayson, K., *Dying, We Live: A New Enquiry into the Death of Christ in the New Testament*. London: Darton, Longman and Todd, 1990.

Grewe, C., *Painting the Sacred in the Age of Romanticism*. Farnham: Ashgate Publishing Limited, 2009.

Hammermeister, K., *The German Aesthetic Tradition*. Cambridge: Cambridge University Press, 2002.

Happold, F. C., *Mysticism: A Study and an Anthology*. London: Penguin Books, 1964.

Harries, R., *The Image of Christ in Modern Art.* Farnham: Ashgate, 2013.

Harrison, C., *Samuel Palmer.* Oxford: Ashmolean Museum, 2010.

Harvey, J., *The Bible as Visual Culture.* Sheffield: Sheffield Phoenix Press, 2013.

Hay, D., *Young Romantics.* London: Bloomsbury, 2010.

Hegel, G. W. F., *Introductory Lectures on Aesthetics.* London: Penguin, 2004.

Hemenway, P., *The Secret Code.* Cologne: Evergreen, 2008.

Hick, J., *The Fifth Dimension: An Exploration of the Spiritual Realm.* Oxford: Oneworld Publications, 1999.

Hick, J., *The Second Christianity:* London: Xpress Reprints (SCM Press), 1994.

Hinz, S., *Caspar David Friedrich in Briefen und Bekenntnissen.* Munich: Rogner & Bernhard, 1968.

Hofmann, W., *Caspar David Friedrich.* London: Thames and Hudson, 2000 (first English edition, reprinted 2007).

Honderich, T. (ed.), *Oxford Companion to Philosophy.* Oxford: Oxford University Press, 1995 (second ed. 2005).

Hutter, I., *Early Christian and Byzantine Art.* London: Weidenfield and Nicolson, 1971.

Irwin. D., *Winckelmann Writings on Art.* London: Phaidon Press, 1972.

James, W., *The Varieties of Religious Experience.* London: Fontana Library of Theology and Philosophy, 1971.

Jansen, H. W., *A History of Art.* London: Thames and Hudson, 1982.

Johnson, P., *Art: A New History.* London: Wiedenfeld and Nicholson, 2003.

Jones, C., G. Wainwright *et al.* (eds), *The Study of Liturgy.* London: SPCK, and New York: Oxford University Press, 1992.

Kaiser, K., *Carl Gustav Carus und die Zeitgenossische Dresdner Landschaftsmaierei.* Schweinfurt, 1970.

Keay, C., *Henry Fuseli.* London: Academy Editions, 1974.

Koerner, J., *Caspar David Friedrich and the Subject of Landscape.* London: Reaktion Books, 1990.

Küng, H., *Christianity: Its Essence and History.* London: SCM Press, 1995.

Küng, H., *Great Christian Thinkers*. London: SCM Press, 1994.
Leighton, J., *Technical Bulletin Volume 13, 1989: A 'Winter Landscape' by Caspar David Friedrich*. London: National Gallery, 1989.
Leighton, J., and C. J. Bailey, *Caspar David Friedrich: Winter Landscape*. London: National Gallery Publications, 1990.
Lindsay, J., *J. M. W. Turner: His Life and Work*. London: Cory, Adams and Mackay, 1966.
Macquarrie, J., *Existentialism*. Harmondsworth: Penguin Books, 1978.
Macquarrie, J., *A Guide to the Sacraments*. London: SCM Press, 1997.
Macquarrie, J., *Principles of Christian Theology*. London: SCM Press, 1966.
Macquarrie, J., *Two Worlds are Ours*. London: SCM Press, 2004.
Makkreel, R., *Imagination and Interpretation in Kant*. Chicago: University of Chicago Press, 1994.
Marina, J. (ed.), *The Cambridge Companion to Friedrich Schleiermacher*. Cambridge: Cambridge University Press, 2005.
Marrett, R. R., *Sacrament of Simple Folk*. London: Clarendon Press, 1933.
Marshall, I. H., *The Acts of the Apostles: An Introduction and Commentary*. Leicester: Inter-Varsity Press, 1989.
Mattick, P. (ed.), *Eighteenth-Century Aesthetics and the Reconstruction of Art*. Cambridge: Cambridge University Press, 2008.
McGrath, A., *The Intellectual World of C. S. Lewis*. Chichester: Wiley-Blackwell, 2014.
Mautner, T., *Dictionary of Philosophy*. London: Penguin Books, 2000.
Meakin, T., *A Basic Church Dictionary and Compendium*. Norwich: Canterbury Press, 1992.
Meredith, J. C., *The Critique of Judgement by Immanuel Kant*. Oxford: Oxford University Press, 1952.
Miles, G., *Science and Religious Experience*. Eastbourne: Sussex Academic Press, 2007.

Moore, J. N., *The Green Fuse: Pastoral Vision in English Art 1820–2000*. Woodbridge: Antique Collectors Club, 2007.

Moorman, J. H. R., *A History of the Church in England*. London: A. & C. Black, 1986.

Myrone, M. (ed.), *Seen in My Visions: A Descriptive Catalogue of Pictures by William Blake*. London: Tate Publishing, 2009.

Nicholson, K., *Turner's Classical Landscapes: Myth and Meaning*. Princeton: Princeton University Press, 1990.

Nicolson, H., *The Age of Reason (1700–1789)*. London: Constable and Co. Readers Union edition, 1962.

Onions, C. T., *et al.* (eds), *Shorter Oxford English Dictionary*. Oxford: Oxford University Press, 1983.

Osborne, H. (ed.), *Oxford Companion to Art*. Oxford: Oxford University Press, 1970.

Otto, R., *The Idea of the Holy*. Oxford: Oxford University Press, 1958 (reprint of 1923 edition, translated by John Harvey).

Peters, T., and G. Bennett (eds.), *Bridging Science and Religion*. London: SCM Press, 2002.

Podro, M., *The Critical Historians of Art*. New Haven: Yale University Press, 1991.

Podro, M., *The Manifold in Perception*. Oxford: Clarendon Press, 1972.

Potts, A., *Flesh and the Ideal: Winckelmann and the Origin of Art History*, New Haven and London: Yale University Press, 1994.

Prettejohn, E., *Beauty and Art (1750–2000)*. Oxford: Oxford University Press, 2005.

Purdie, E., *Von Deutscher Art und Kunst*. Oxford: Clarendon Press, 1964.

Rahner, K., *Foundations of Christian Faith*. New York: Crossroad Publishing, 1995.

Rankin, M., *An Introduction to Religious and Spiritual Experience*. London: Continuum, 2008.

Reardon, B. M. G., *Religion in the Age of Romanticism*. Cambridge: Cambridge University Press, 1985.

Robbins, K. (ed.), *Protestant Evangelicalism: Britain, Ireland, Germany and America, c. 1750–1950*. Oxford: Blackwell, 1990.

Rollins, C., *Correlations between Non-German and German Art in the 19th Century.* New Haven: Yale University Art Gallery, 1972.

Rosenblum, R., *Modern Painting and the Northern Romantic Tradition: Friedrich to Rothko.* New York: Harper and Row, 1975.

Ruskin, J., *Lectures on Art: Delivered before the University of Oxford in Hilary Term, 1870.* London: George Allen & Sons, 1910.

Sallis, J., *Spacings of Reason and Imagination in Texts of Kant, Fichte, Hegel.* Chicago: University of Chicago Press, 1987.

Schelling, F. W. J., *The Philosophy of Art,* trans. D. W. Scott. Minneapolis: University of Minnesota Press, 1989.

Schleiermacher, F., *On Religion: Speeches to its Cultured Despisers,* trans. R. Crouter. Cambridge: Cambridge University Press, 1996.

Schleiermacher, F., *The Christian Faith* (trans. and ed. by H. R. Mackintosh and J. S. Stewart). Edinburgh: T. & T. Clark, 1928.

Schwarz, C. (ed.), *The Chambers Dictionary.* Edinburgh: Chambers, 1994.

Scruton, R., *Our Church: A Personal History of the Church of England.* London: Atlantic Books, 2012.

Seymour, M., *Noble Endeavours: The Life of Two Countries, England and Germany, in Many Stories.* London: Simon and Schuster, 2013.

Smart, N., *The Religious Experience of Mankind.* New York: Scribner's Sons, 1984.

Stokoe, F. W., *German Influence in the English Romantic Period.* Cambridge: Cambridge University Press, 1926.

Stone, N. (ed.), *The Times Atlas of World History,* 3rd edn. London: Times Books, 1989.

Temple, W., *Nature, Man and God.* London: Macmillan, 1940.

Thorne, J. O., and T. C. Collocott (eds.), *Chambers Biographical Dictionary.* Edinburgh: W. and R. Chambers, 1982.

Tillich, P., *On Art and Architecture,* ed. J. and J. Dillenberger. New York: Crossroad, 1989.

Tillich, P., *The Eternal Now.* London: SCM Press, 2002 [1963].

Tillich, P., *Systematic Theology Volume I.* London: SCM Press, 1978.

Underhill, E., *Worship.* London: Nisbet, 1936.

Vallins, D., *Coleridge's Writings volume 5: On the Sublime.* Basingstoke: Palgrave Macmillan, 2003.

Vaughan, W., *Friedrich.* London: Phaidon Press, 2004.

Vaughan, W., *German Romanticism and English Art.* London: Yale University Press, 1979.

Vaughan, W., *German Romantic Painting.* New Haven and London: Yale University Press, 1982.

Vaughan, W., *Romanticism in Art.* London: Thames and Hudson, 1995.

Vaughan, W., *Samuel Palmer: Vision and Landscape.* London: British Museum Press, 2006.

Vesey, G. (ed.), *Royal Institute of Philosophy Lectures, Volume 2: Talk of God.* London: Macmillan, 1969.

Vigus, J., *Essays on Kant, Schelling and German Aesthetics by Henry Crabb Robinson.* London: Modern Humanities Research Association, 2010.

Watkin, C., *From Plato to Postmodernism: The Story of Western Culture through Philosophy, Literature and Art.* London: Bristol Classical Press, 2011.

Watson, J. S., *The Reign of George III 1760–1815.* Oxford History of England 12. Oxford: Clarendon Press, 1992.

Watson, P., *The German Genius: Europe's Third Renaissance.* London: Simon and Schuster, 2010.

Wedderburn, A. (ed.), *The Works of John Ruskin.* 39 vols. London: George Allen, 1903–12.

Wellek, R., *Confrontations.* Princeton: Princeton University Press, 1965.

Wellek, R., *History of Modern Criticism: 1750–1950: The Romantic Age* (vol. 2). London: Jonathan Cape, 1955.

Williams, H. A., *The Joy of God.* London: Mitchell Beazley, 1979.

Williams, N. M., *William Blake Studies.* Basingstoke: Palgrave Macmillan, 2006.

Williams, R., *Grace and Necessity: Reflections on Art and Love.* London: Morehouse, 2005.

INDEX

Index

Index

www.ingramcontent.com/pod-product-compliance
Lightning Source LLC
Chambersburg PA
CBHW020737180526
45163CB00001B/269